Ask a Cat

CHARLES BRUBAKER

SMALLBUG
PRESS

To Max, Biscuit, Belle, and Gizmo

ASK A CAT is published online at
www.gocomics.com/ask-a-cat/

Support ASK A CAT at
www.patreon.com/smallbug

www.bakertoons.com
cbrubaker@gmail.com

Printed in USA
First Printing, 2017

ISBN: 978-0-9989482-0-1

INTRODUCTION

One of the things I learned when reading about how a series got started, whether it's a comic strip or a TV series, is that it can originate as a minor part of a bigger thing before the said "minor" thing eventually overshadow the supposed bigger thing. One of the more famous examples is *The Simpsons*, which started off as a minor part of *The Tracey Ullman Show* before getting their own half-hour. Comics-wise, George Herriman's *Krazy Kat* first appeared as a filler for another strip he was doing called *The Dingbat Family*.

I bring this up because this is essentially what happened with *Ask a Cat*. In 2014, I was doing a comic about a witch, because I thought witches were going to be a big thing. Having a (probably hopeless) entrepreneurial spirit, I made attempts to market the webcomic in an effort to get readers. I knew that one of the things many comic creators do on the internet is to have an "ask a character" thing, where readers can send in questions and the character will respond, usually in a humorous way. I was thinking of doing the same with the witch comic. However, for reasons unknown even to me, I decided that, rather than have a character from the comic answer it, I should just draw a random cat for this instead. On a message board I went to, I started a thread and solicited questions for the cat to answer.

I managed to get a few questions, and so on December 11, 2014, *Ask a Cat* made its debut on my tumblr. It was about the *League of Legends*, something I know very little about due to my lack of interest in video games, but I managed to get something out of it anyhow; you can see that comic on page 5. I started getting more questions, maybe about a dozen, and drew responses to most of them. At the time, I didn't think I'd do more than a handful of strips, but before I knew it I ended up drawing about 20 or so in only a short time.

By then, I was starting to get serious freelance work, having sold comics to *SpongeBob Comics* and *MAD Magazine*. I decided to submit the *Ask a Cat* strips around, figuring it could help me get work. In addition, I was about to go to my first comic convention as a seller in the early part of 2015. Wanting to have more items to sell, I compiled all the *Cat* strips drawn at that point as a mini-comic.

I took about 20 copies of the mini to the convention. Within a few hours, I sold every single one. That was my first realization that this comic had a future. I got another positive indication not long after, when I received an email from Shena Wolf, the acquisitions editor for Universal Uclick (now Andrews McMeel Syndication). They wanted to run *Ask a Cat* on the GoComics website, the official online home for such strips as *Phoebe and Her Unicorn*, *FoxTrot*, *Calvin and Hobbes*, and many others. That event changed my life.

Ask a Cat made its GoComics debut on June 22, 2015, and as I write this it's still there, with a new strip appearing every Sunday.

Few things have changed since then; I finally dropped the witch webcomic when *Cat* ultimately took over as my main item (I eventually started a new ongoing comic called *The Fuzzy Princess*, but that's for another time). I also changed my approach to drawing in general, giving a more polished look compared to slapdash art in early strips. But aside from that, the core of the strip hasn't changed. It's still about a cartoon cat answering humans' emails.

If the internet is any indication, cats are eventually going to take over the world. Might as well prepare yourself by reading this strip.

It's the least you can do...

- Charles Brubaker, March 2017

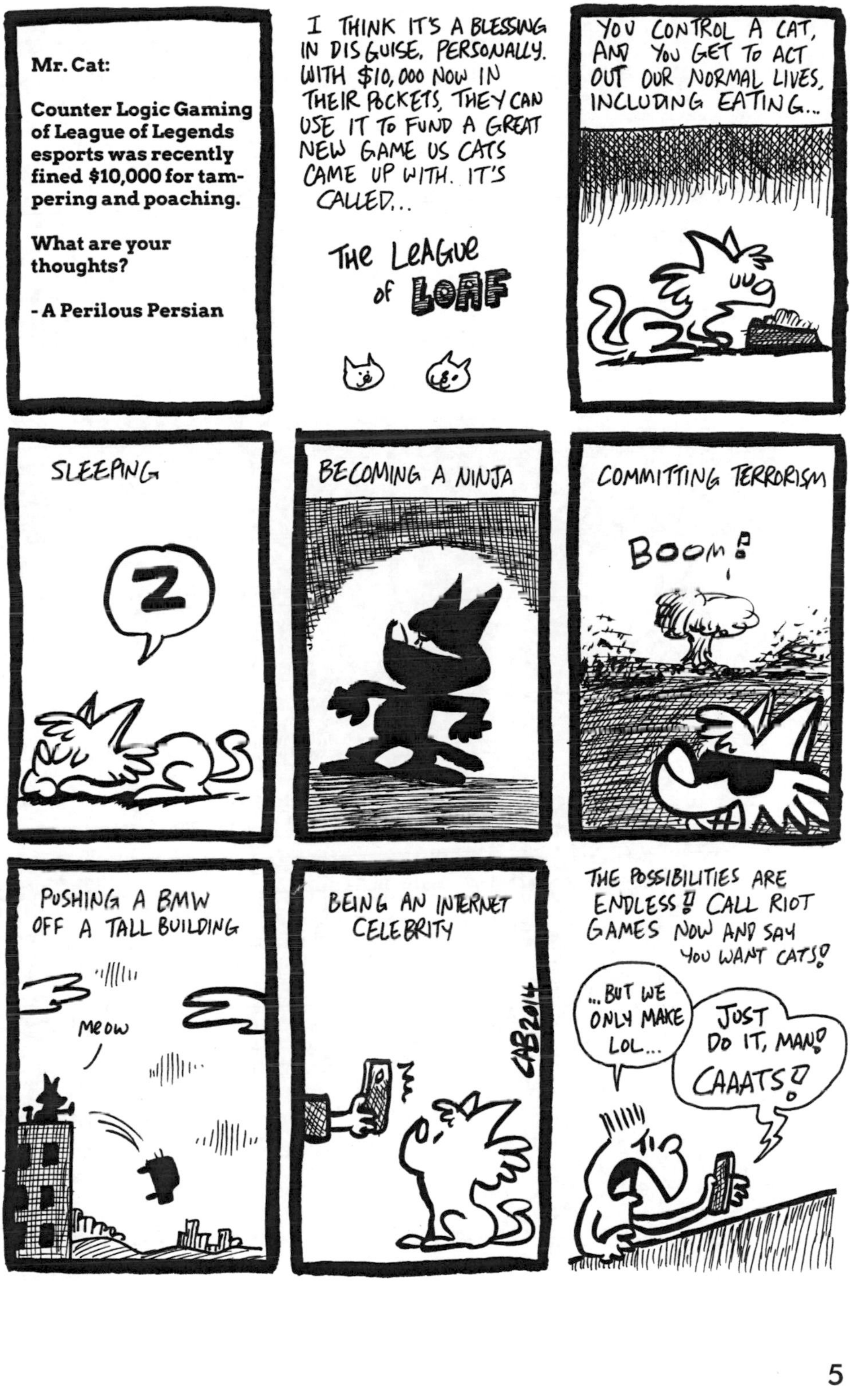
Mr. Cat:
Counter Logic Gaming of League of Legends esports was recently fined $10,000 for tampering and poaching.
What are your thoughts?
- A Perilous Persian
I THINK IT'S A BLESSING IN DISGUISE, PERSONALLY. WITH $10,000 NOW IN THEIR POCKETS, THEY CAN USE IT TO FUND A GREAT NEW GAME US CATS CAME UP WITH. IT'S CALLED...
THE LEAGUE OF LOAF
YOU CONTROL A CAT, AND YOU GET TO ACT OUT OUR NORMAL LIVES, INCLUDING EATING...
SLEEPING
Z
BECOMING A NINJA
COMMITTING TERRORISM
BOOM!
PUSHING A BMW OFF A TALL BUILDING
MEOW
BEING AN INTERNET CELEBRITY
CAB2014
THE POSSIBILITIES ARE ENDLESS! CALL RIOT GAMES NOW AND SAY YOU WANT CATS!
...BUT WE ONLY MAKE LOL...
JUST DO IT, MAN!
CAAATS!

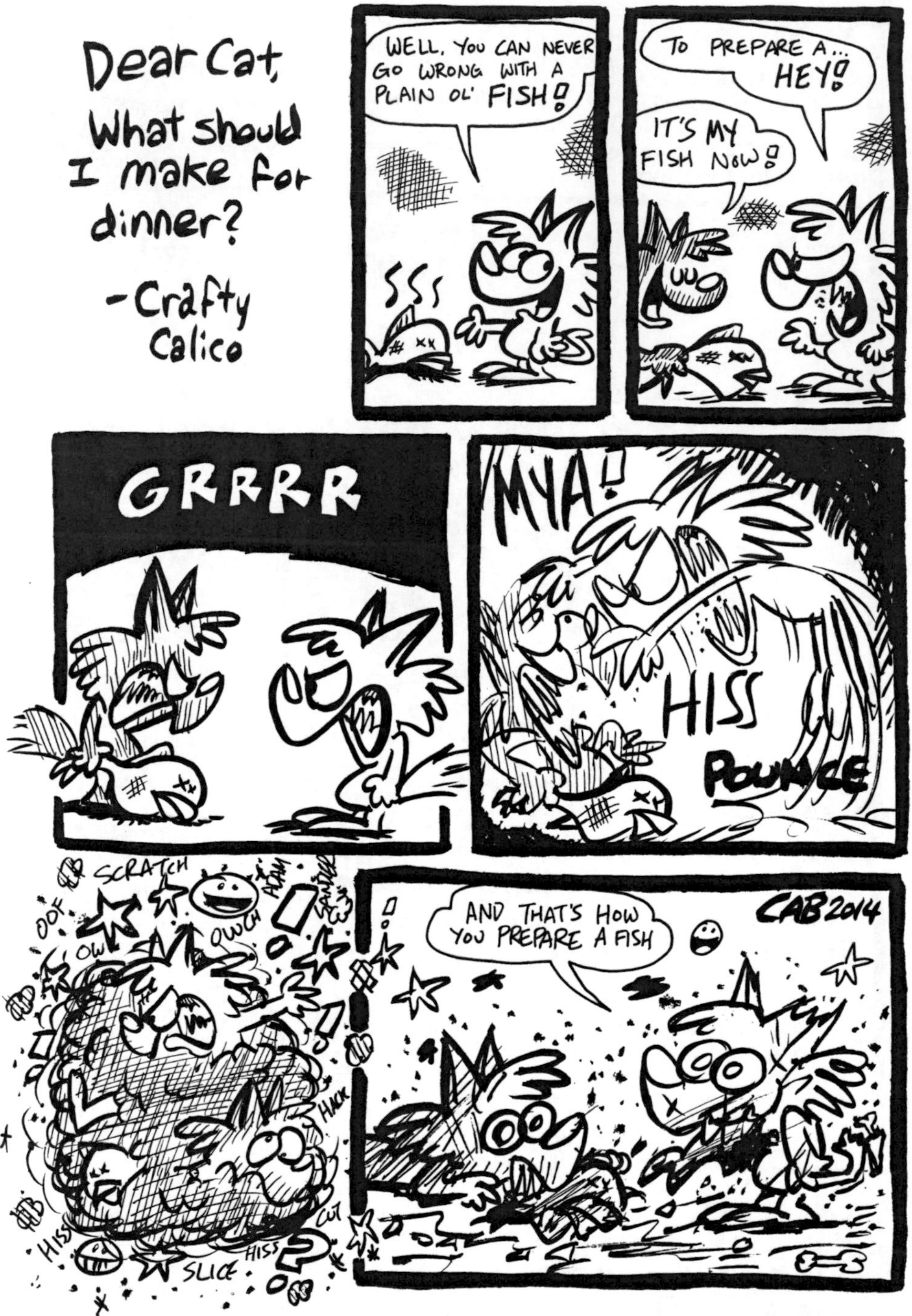
Dear Cat,
What should I make for dinner?
-Crafty Calico
WELL, YOU CAN NEVER GO WRONG WITH A PLAIN OL' FISH!
TO PREPARE A... HEY!
IT'S MY FISH NOW!
GRRRR
MYA!
HISS
POUNCE
SCRATCH
OOF
OW
OUCH
HACK
HISS
SLICE
HISS
CUT
AND THAT'S HOW YOU PREPARE A FISH
CAB 2014

Dear Cat,
Did humans really land on the moon?

-Tabby with a Treat

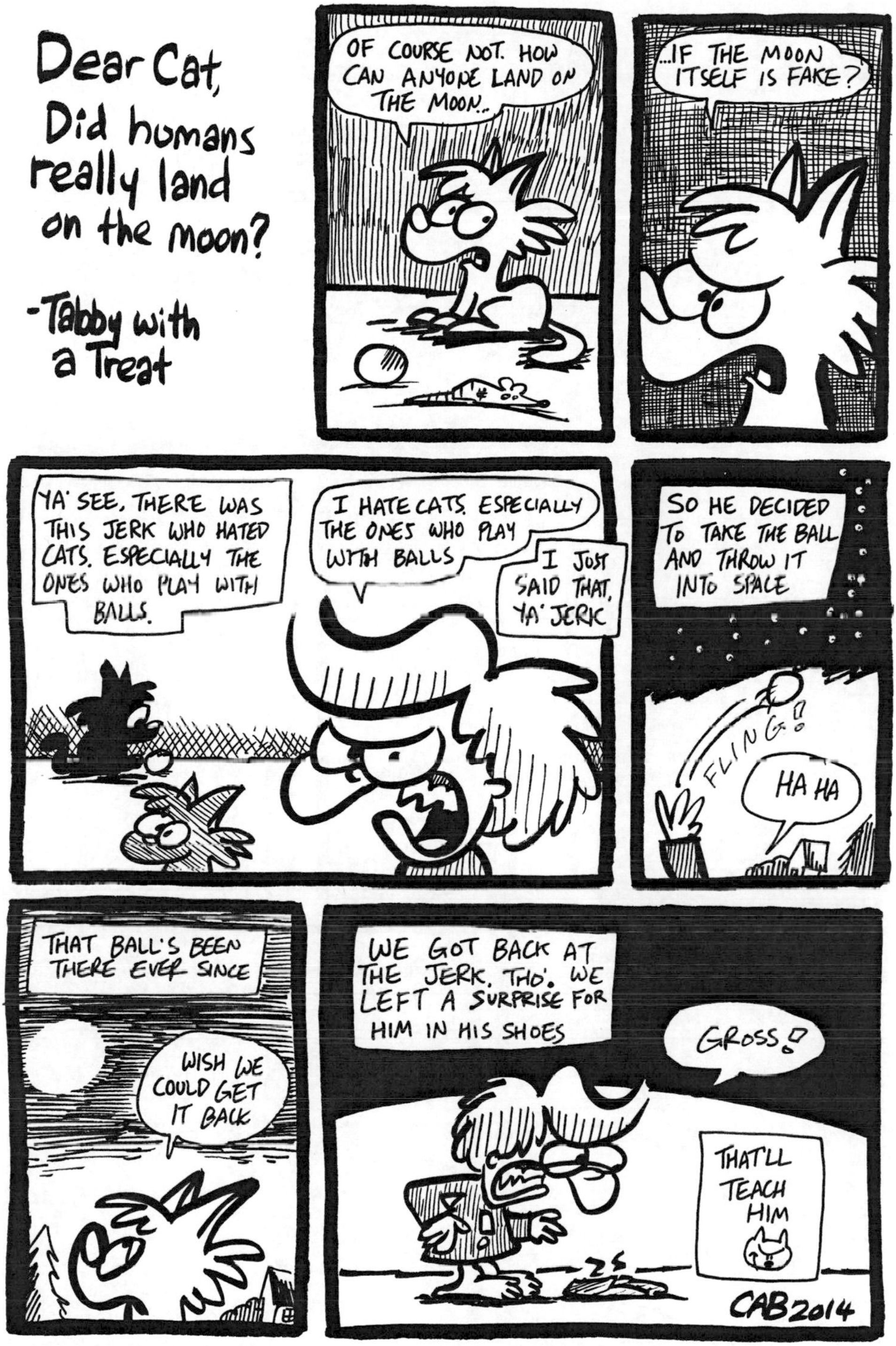
OF COURSE NOT. HOW CAN ANYONE LAND ON THE MOON..
...IF THE MOON ITSELF IS FAKE?
YA' SEE, THERE WAS THIS JERK WHO HATED CATS. ESPECIALLY THE ONES WHO PLAY WITH BALLS.
I HATE CATS. ESPECIALLY THE ONES WHO PLAY WITH BALLS
I JUST SAID THAT, YA' JERK
SO HE DECIDED TO TAKE THE BALL AND THROW IT INTO SPACE
FLING!!
HA HA
THAT BALL'S BEEN THERE EVER SINCE
WISH WE COULD GET IT BACK
WE GOT BACK AT THE JERK, THO'. WE LEFT A SURPRISE FOR HIM IN HIS SHOES
GROSS!!
THAT'LL TEACH HIM
CAB 2014

Dear Cat, what should we do with a drunken sailor?

-A Still Living Curious Cat

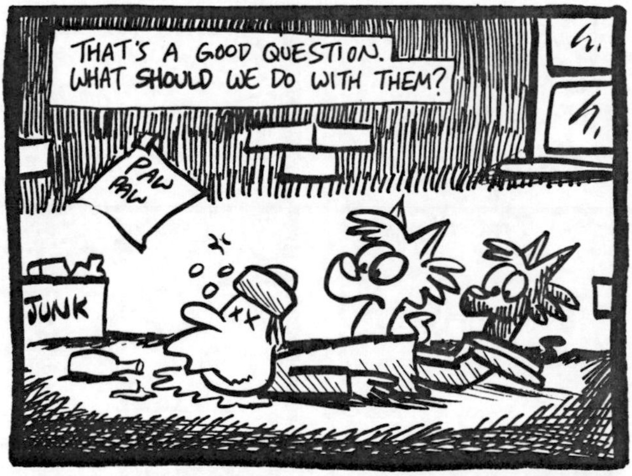

THAT'S A GOOD QUESTION. WHAT SHOULD WE DO WITH THEM?
PAW PAW
JUNK

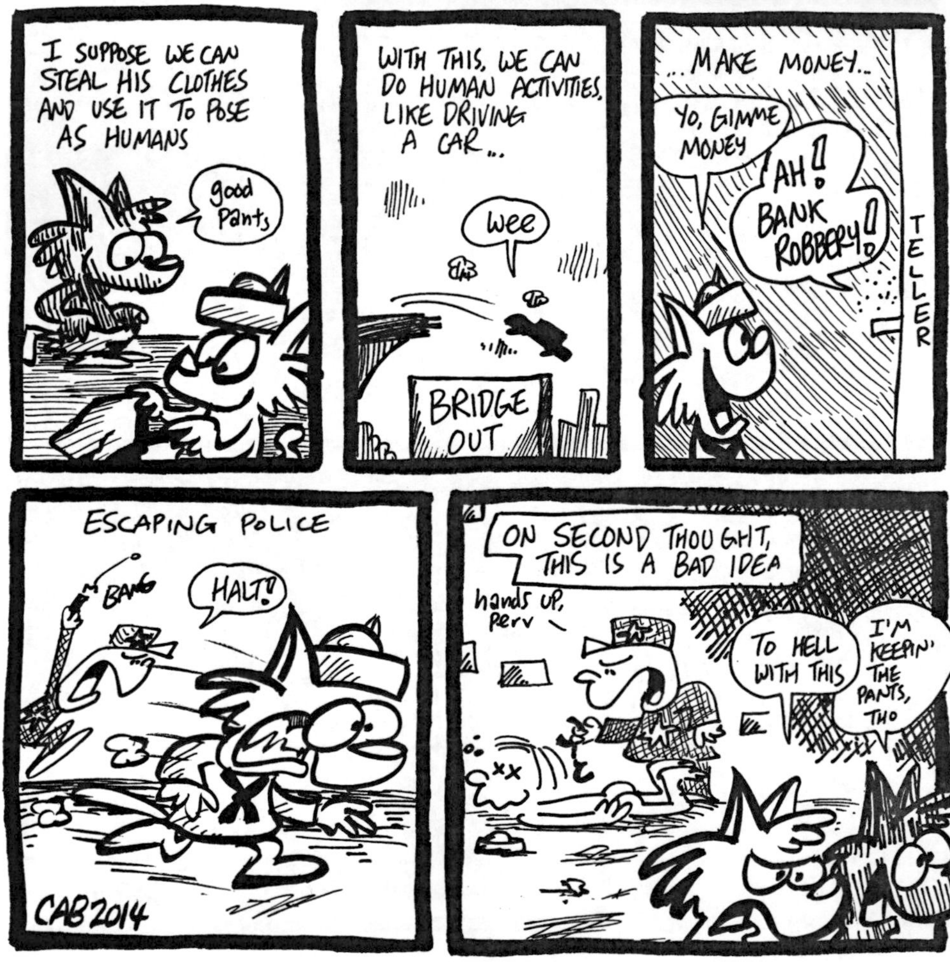

I SUPPOSE WE CAN STEAL HIS CLOTHES AND USE IT TO POSE AS HUMANS
good Pants
WITH THIS, WE CAN DO HUMAN ACTIVITIES, LIKE DRIVING A CAR...
Wee
BRIDGE OUT
...MAKE MONEY...
Yo, GIMME MONEY
AH! BANK ROBBERY!
TELLER
ESCAPING POLICE
BANG
HALT!
CAB 2014
ON SECOND THOUGHT, THIS IS A BAD IDEA
hands up, perv
TO HELL WITH THIS
I'M KEEPIN' THE PANTS, THO

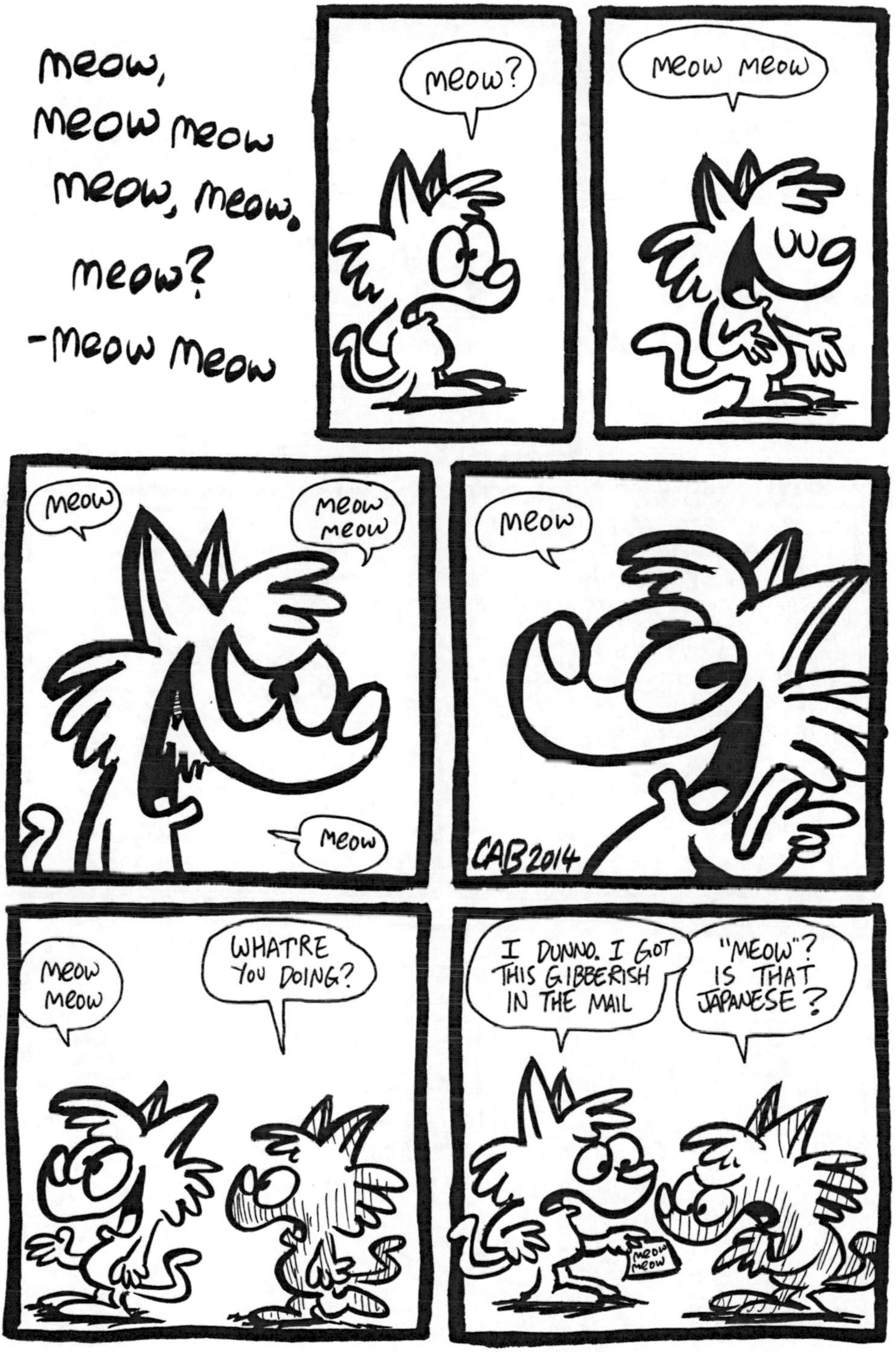
meow,
meow meow
meow, meow,
meow?
-Meow Meow
meow?
Meow Meow
meow
meow meow
meow
meow
meow meow
WHAT'RE YOU DOING?
I DUNNO. I GOT THIS GIBBERISH IN THE MAIL
"MEOW"? IS THAT JAPANESE?
CAB 2014

Dear Cat,
How accurate is the 1978 movie "The Cat from Outer Space"?
-Saucy Siamese

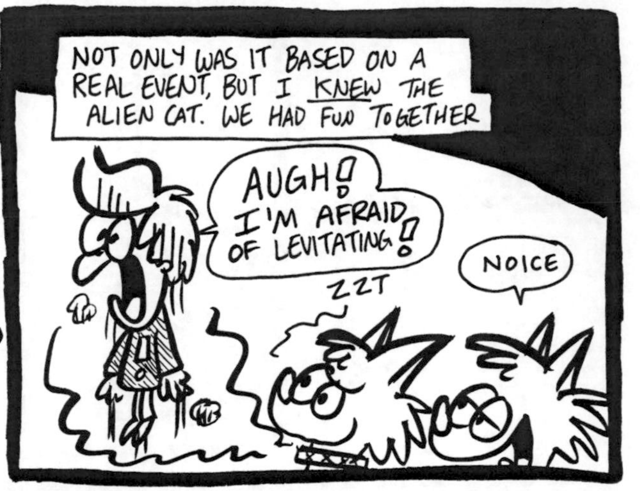
NOT ONLY WAS IT BASED ON A REAL EVENT, BUT I KNEW THE ALIEN CAT. WE HAD FUN TOGETHER
AUGH! I'M AFRAID OF LEVITATING!
NOICE
ZZT

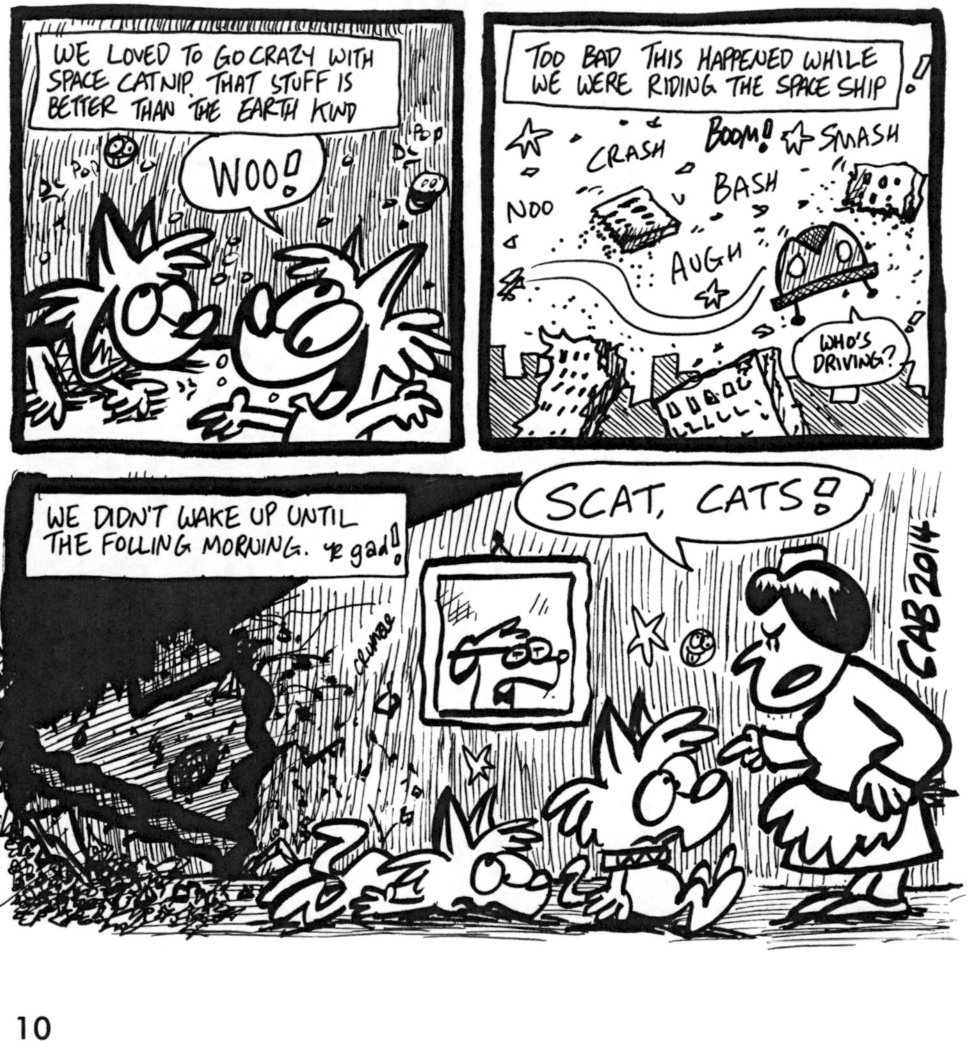
WE LOVED TO GO CRAZY WITH SPACE CATNIP. THAT STUFF IS BETTER THAN THE EARTH KIND
WOO!
POP
POP
TOO BAD THIS HAPPENED WHILE WE WERE RIDING THE SPACE SHIP!
CRASH
BOOM!
SMASH
BASH
NOO
AUGH
WHO'S DRIVING?
WE DIDN'T WAKE UP UNTIL THE FOLLING MORNING. ye gad!
SCAT, CATS!
CRUMBLE
CAB 2014

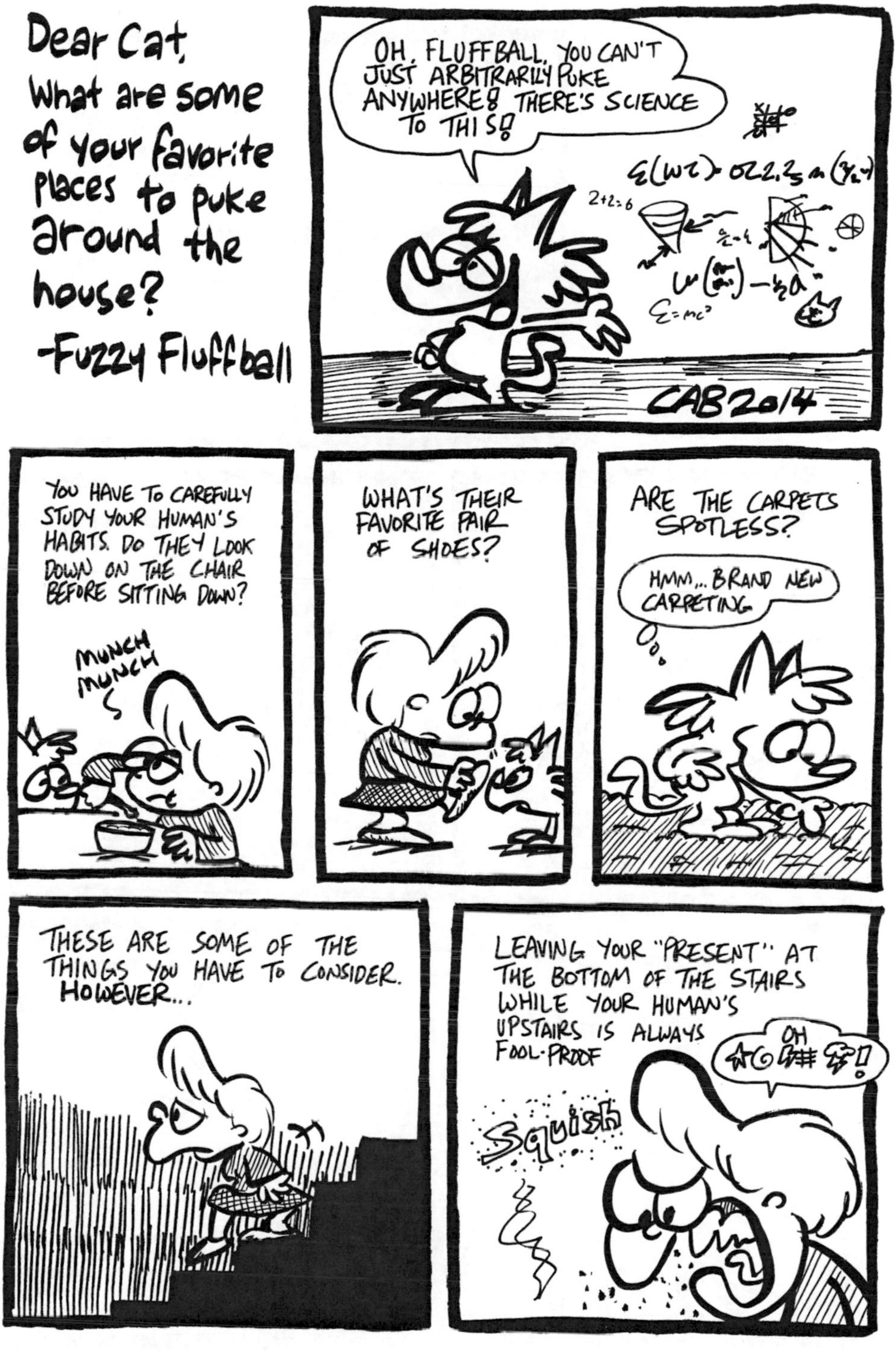
Dear Cat,
What are some of your favorite places to puke around the house?
-Fuzzy Fluffball
OH, FLUFFBALL, YOU CAN'T JUST ARBITRARILY PUKE ANYWHERE! THERE'S SCIENCE TO THIS!
CAB 2014
YOU HAVE TO CAREFULLY STUDY YOUR HUMAN'S HABITS. DO THEY LOOK DOWN ON THE CHAIR BEFORE SITTING DOWN?
MUNCH MUNCH
WHAT'S THEIR FAVORITE PAIR OF SHOES?
ARE THE CARPETS SPOTLESS?
HMM... BRAND NEW CARPETING
THESE ARE SOME OF THE THINGS YOU HAVE TO CONSIDER. HOWEVER...
LEAVING YOUR "PRESENT" AT THE BOTTOM OF THE STAIRS WHILE YOUR HUMAN'S UPSTAIRS IS ALWAYS FOOL-PROOF
OH
Squish

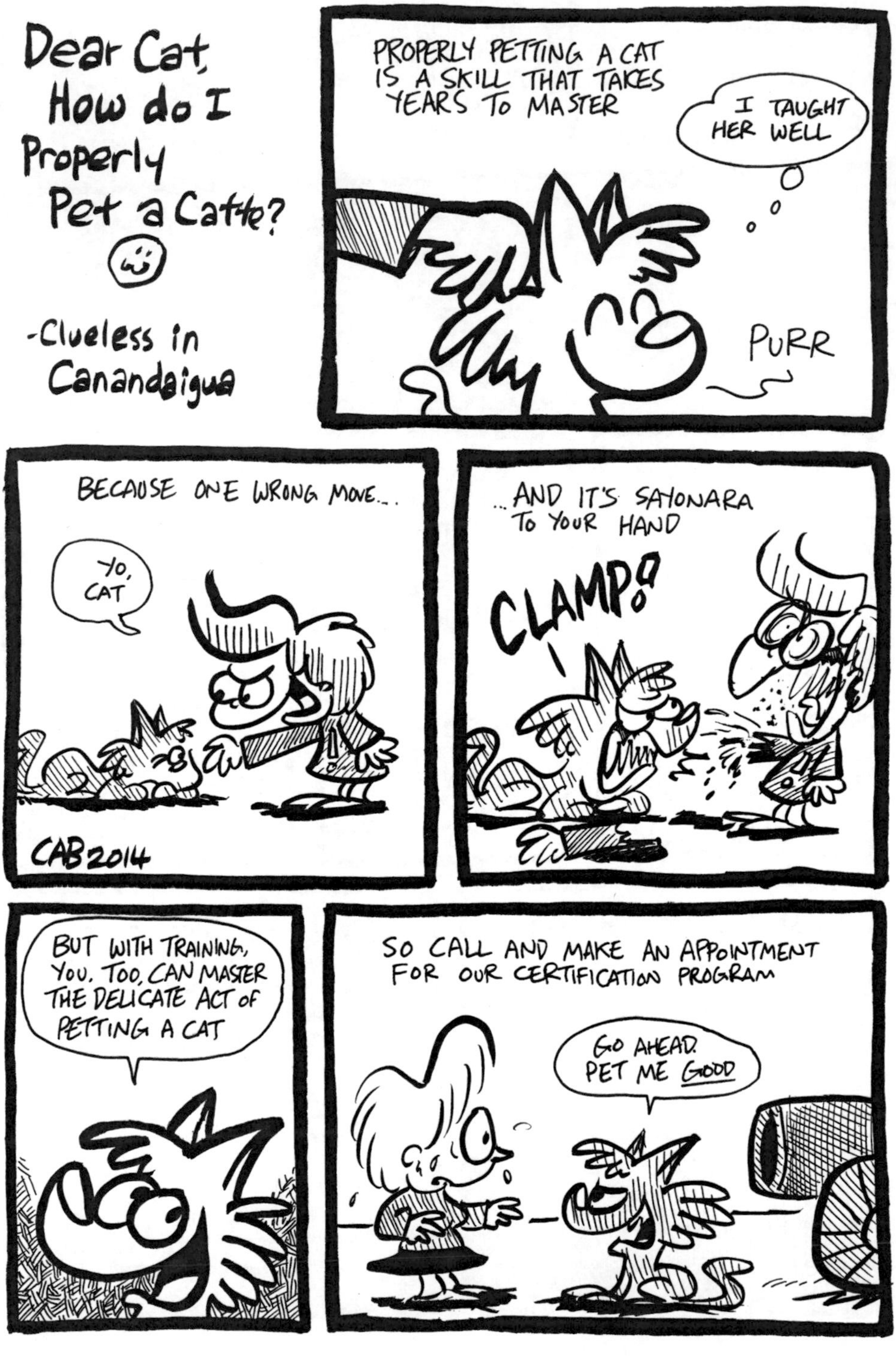

Dear Cat, How do I Properly Pet a Cattle?
-Clueless in Canandaigua
PROPERLY PETTING A CAT IS A SKILL THAT TAKES YEARS TO MASTER
I TAUGHT HER WELL
PURR
BECAUSE ONE WRONG MOVE...
YO, CAT
CAB 2014
...AND IT'S SAYONARA TO YOUR HAND
CLAMP!
BUT WITH TRAINING, YOU, TOO, CAN MASTER THE DELICATE ACT OF PETTING A CAT
SO CALL AND MAKE AN APPOINTMENT FOR OUR CERTIFICATION PROGRAM
GO AHEAD. PET ME GOOD

Dear Cat,
Is it true that humans only love you because there's a certain kind of PARASITE inside you that makes people believe you are cute and cuddly and worth Protection? - a TALKATIVE AXOLOTL

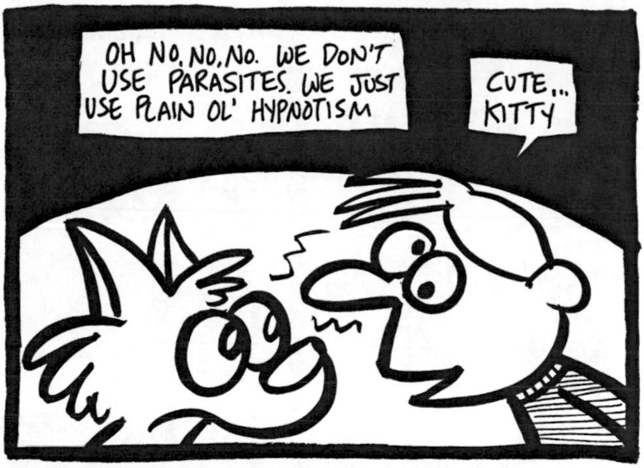
OH NO, NO, NO. WE DON'T USE PARASITES. WE JUST USE PLAIN OL' HYPNOTISM
CUTE... KITTY

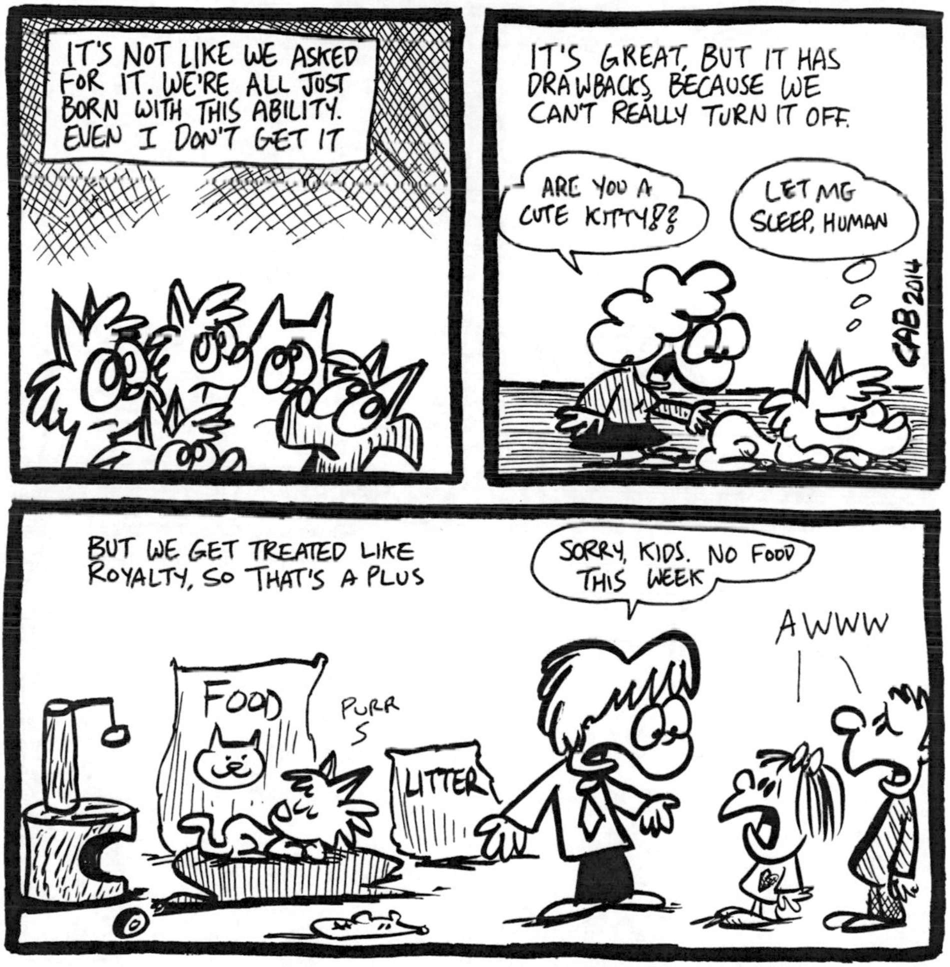
IT'S NOT LIKE WE ASKED FOR IT. WE'RE ALL JUST BORN WITH THIS ABILITY. EVEN I DON'T GET IT
IT'S GREAT, BUT IT HAS DRAWBACKS, BECAUSE WE CAN'T REALLY TURN IT OFF.
ARE YOU A CUTE KITTY?!?
LET ME SLEEP, HUMAN
CAB 2014
BUT WE GET TREATED LIKE ROYALTY, SO THAT'S A PLUS
SORRY, KIDS. NO FOOD THIS WEEK
AWWW
FOOD
PURR
LITTER

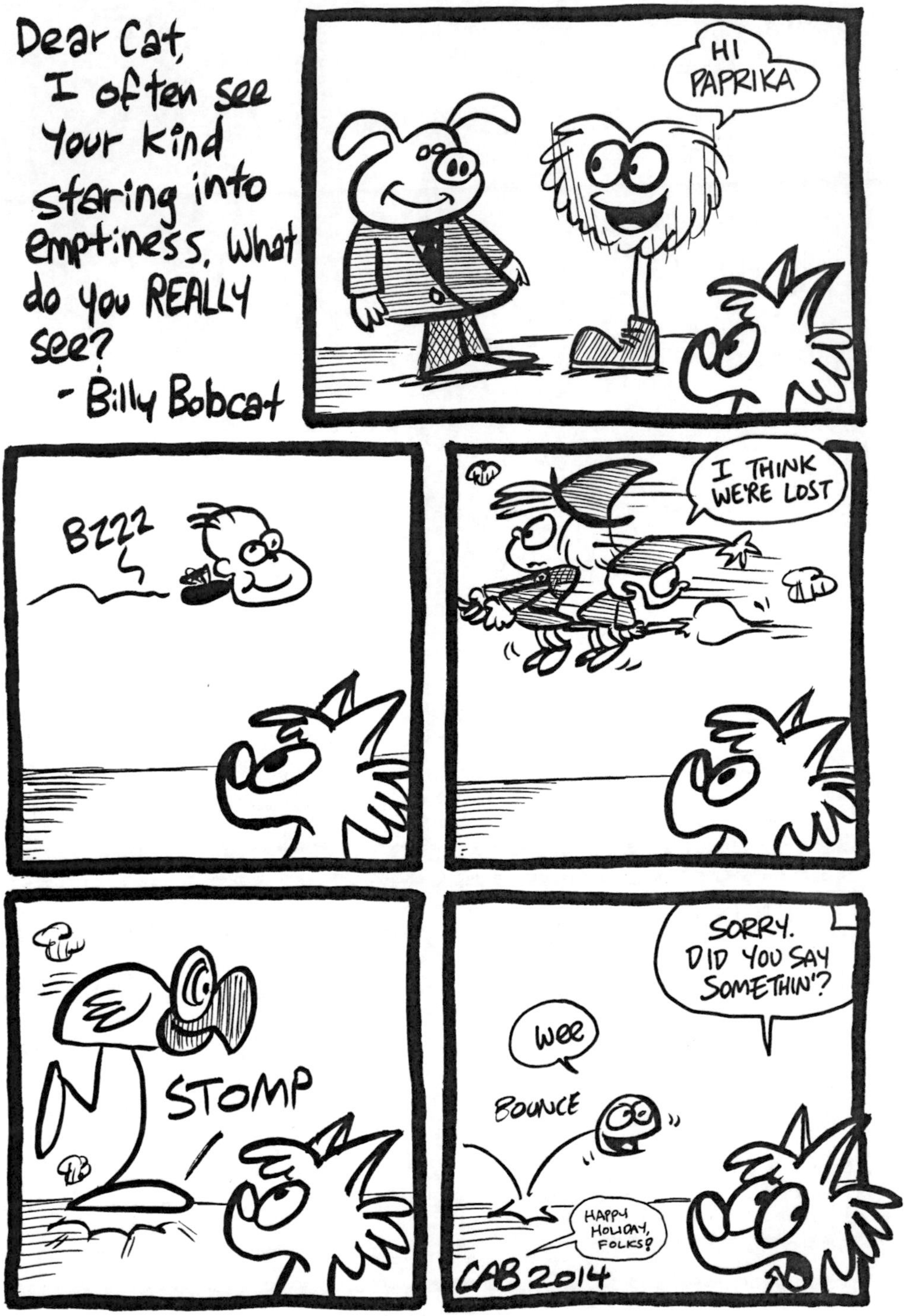
Dear Cat,
I often see your kind staring into emptiness. What do you REALLY see?
- Billy Bobcat
HI PAPRIKA
BZZZ
I THINK WE'RE LOST
STOMP
SORRY. DID YOU SAY SOMETHIN'?
Wee
BOUNCE
HAPPY HOLIDAY, FOLKS!
CAB 2014

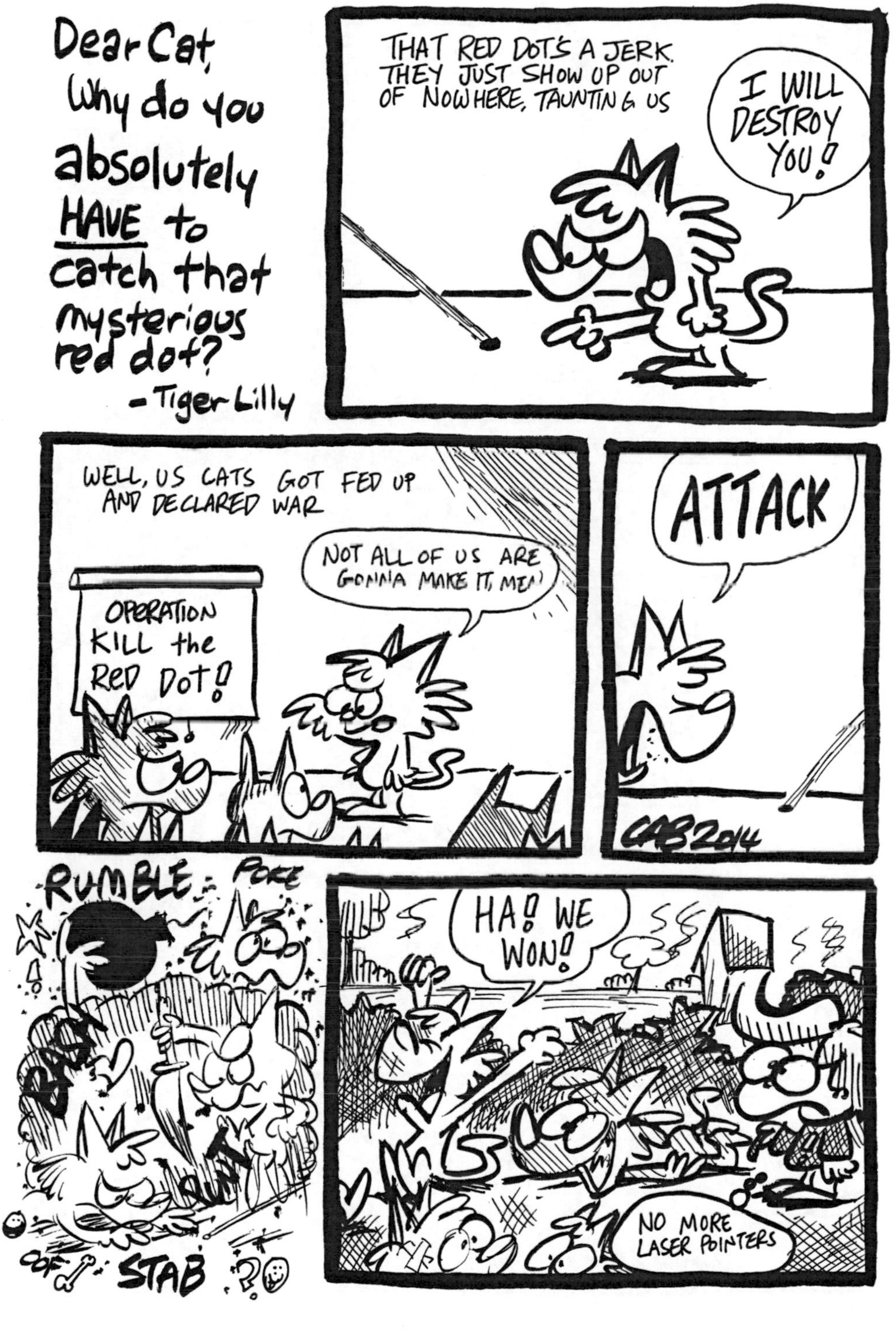
Dear Cat,
Why do you absolutely HAVE to catch that mysterious red dot?
-Tiger Lilly
THAT RED DOT'S A JERK. THEY JUST SHOW UP OUT OF NOWHERE, TAUNTING US
I WILL DESTROY YOU!
WELL, US CATS GOT FED UP AND DECLARED WAR
NOT ALL OF US ARE GONNA MAKE IT, MAN
OPERATION KILL the RED DOT!
ATTACK
CAB 2014
RUMBLE
POKE
OOF
STAB
HA! WE WON!
NO MORE LASER POINTERS

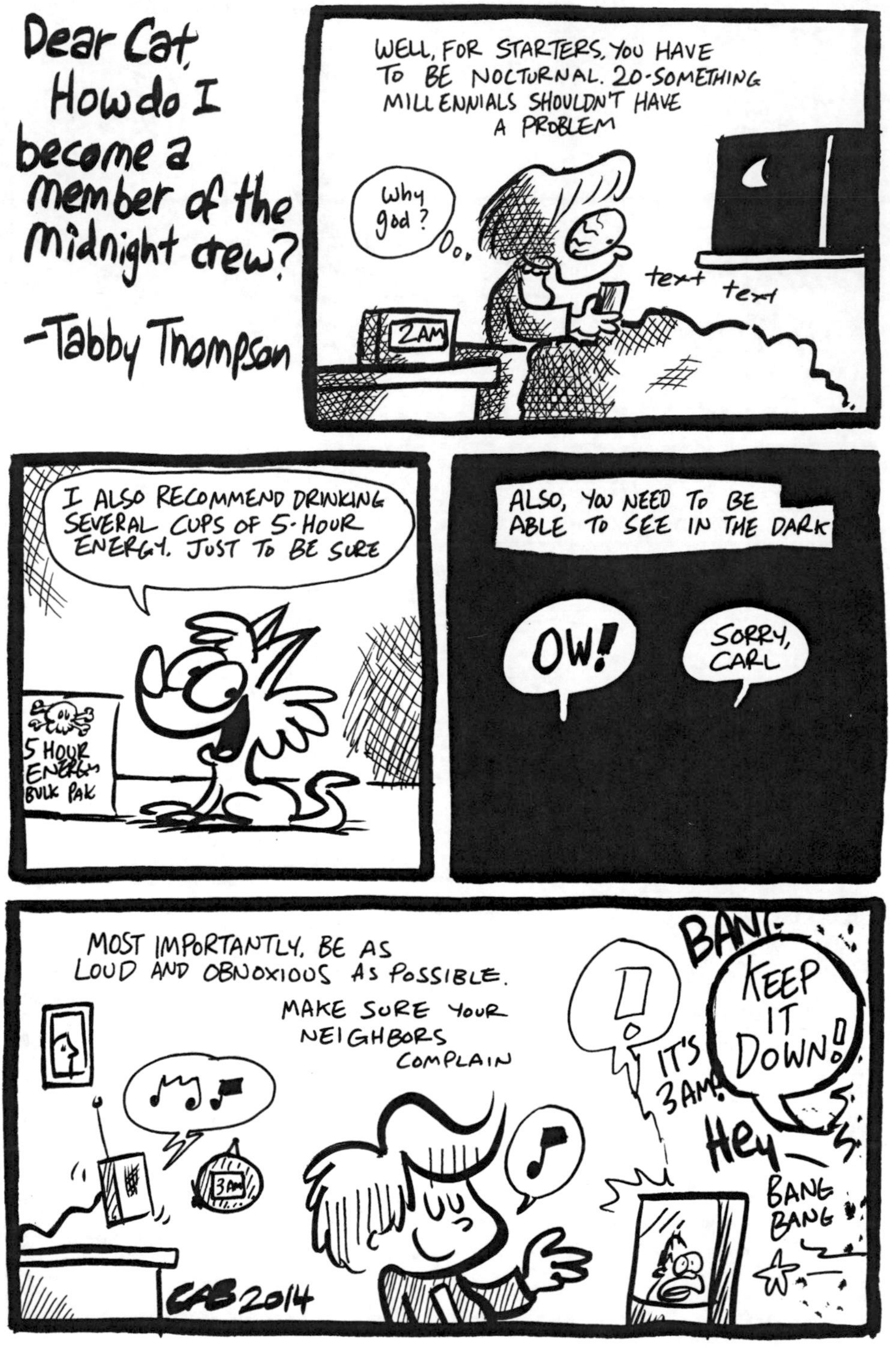
Dear Cat,
How do I become a member of the midnight crew?
-Tabby Thompson
WELL, FOR STARTERS, YOU HAVE TO BE NOCTURNAL. 20-SOMETHING MILLENNIALS SHOULDN'T HAVE A PROBLEM
Why god?
2AM
text text
I ALSO RECOMMEND DRINKING SEVERAL CUPS OF 5-HOUR ENERGY. JUST TO BE SURE
5 HOUR ENERGY BULK PAK
ALSO, YOU NEED TO BE ABLE TO SEE IN THE DARK
OW!
SORRY, CARL
MOST IMPORTANTLY, BE AS LOUD AND OBNOXIOUS AS POSSIBLE.
MAKE SURE YOUR NEIGHBORS COMPLAIN
3AM
BANG
KEEP IT DOWN!
IT'S 3AM!
Hey
BANG BANG
GAB 2014

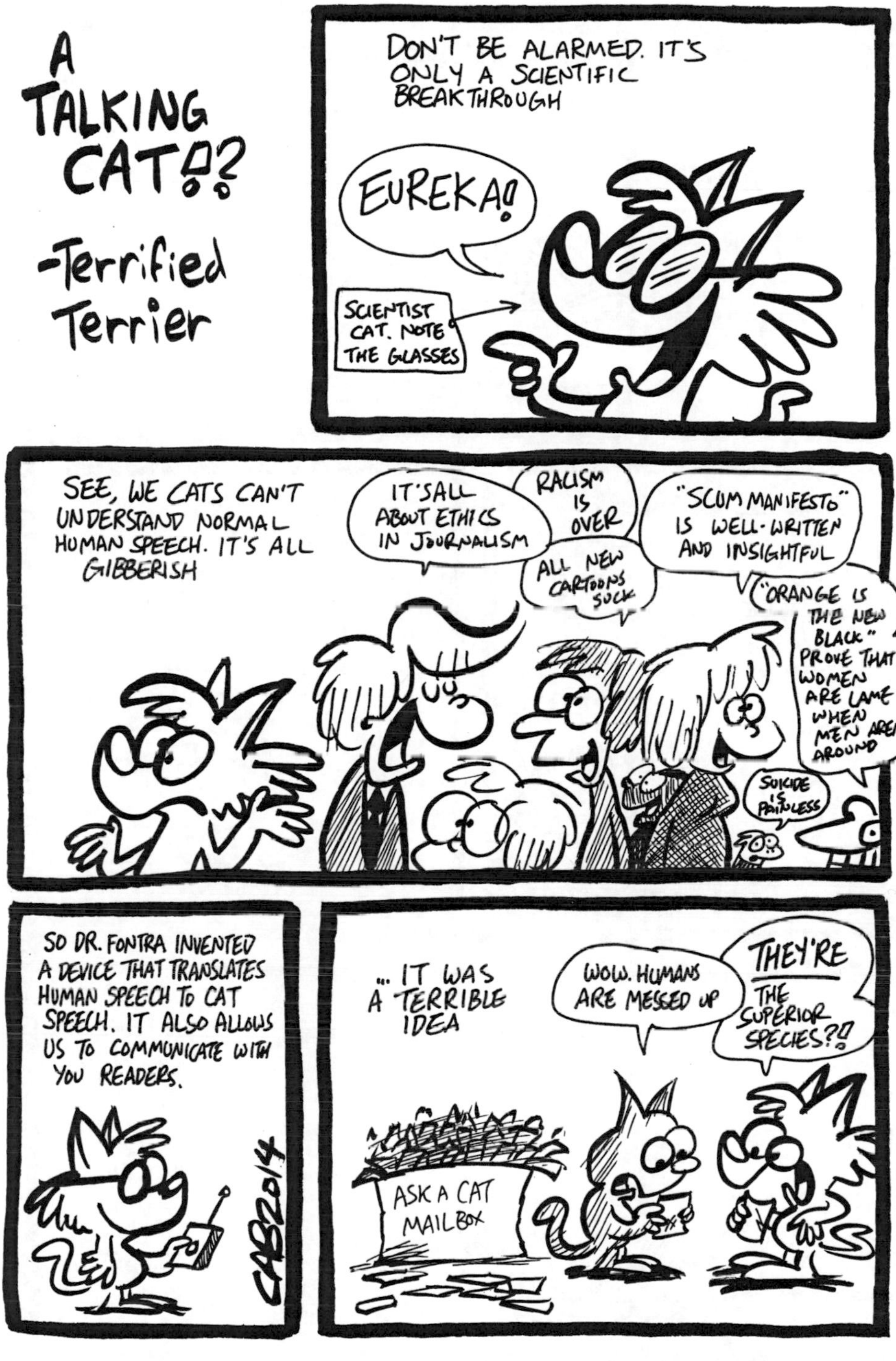
A TALKING CAT!?
-Terrified Terrier
DON'T BE ALARMED. IT'S ONLY A SCIENTIFIC BREAKTHROUGH
EUREKA!
SCIENTIST CAT. NOTE THE GLASSES
SEE, WE CATS CAN'T UNDERSTAND NORMAL HUMAN SPEECH. IT'S ALL GIBBERISH
IT'S ALL ABOUT ETHICS IN JOURNALISM
RACISM IS OVER
ALL NEW CARTOONS SUCK
"SCUM MANIFESTO" IS WELL-WRITTEN AND INSIGHTFUL
"ORANGE IS THE NEW BLACK" PROVE THAT WOMEN ARE LAME WHEN MEN AREN'T AROUND
SUICIDE IS PAINLESS
SO DR. FONTRA INVENTED A DEVICE THAT TRANSLATES HUMAN SPEECH TO CAT SPEECH. IT ALSO ALLOWS US TO COMMUNICATE WITH YOU READERS.
CABR2014
... IT WAS A TERRIBLE IDEA
WOW. HUMANS ARE MESSED UP
THEY'RE THE SUPERIOR SPECIES?!
ASK A CAT MAILBOX

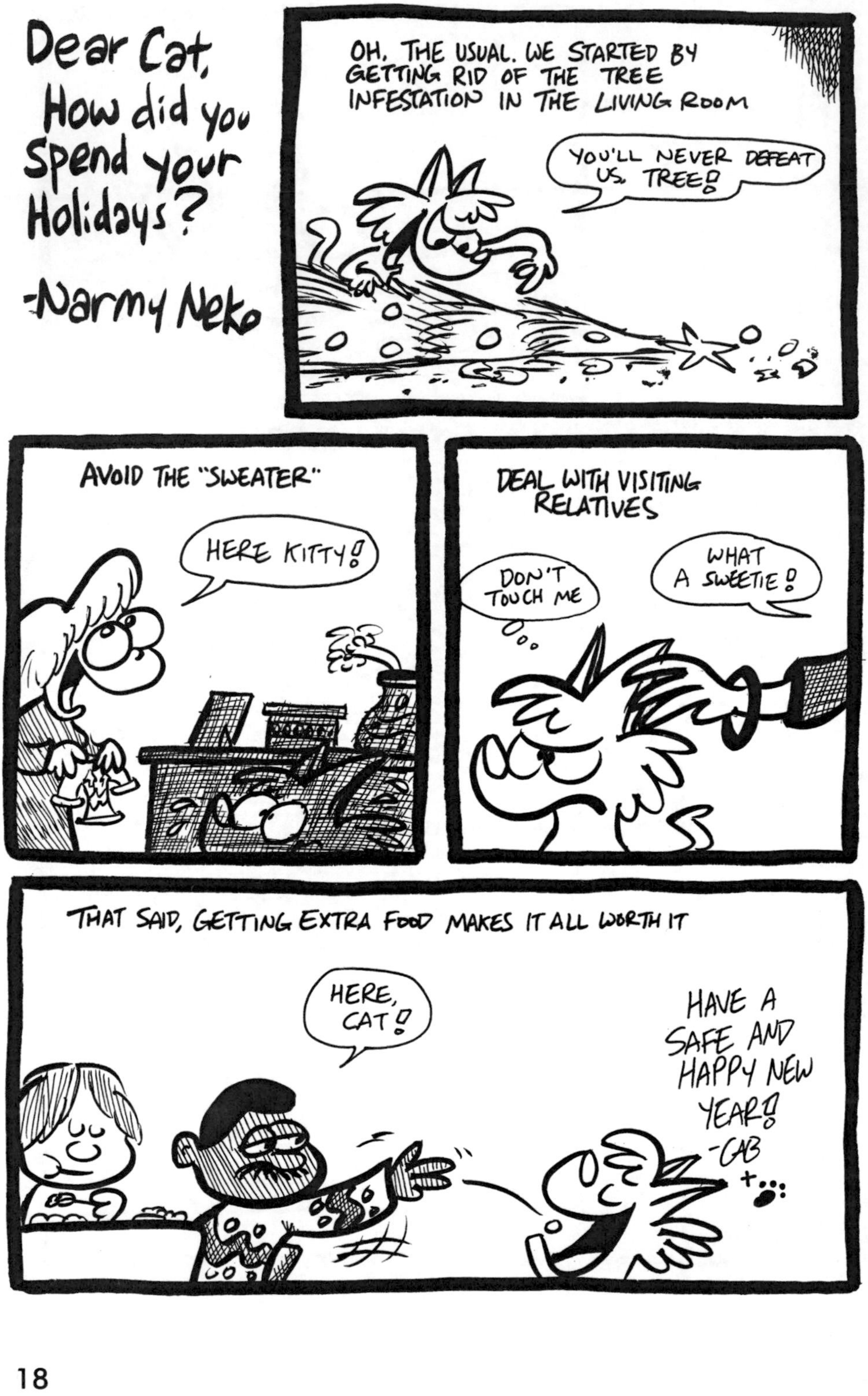
Dear Cat,
How did you spend your Holidays?
-Narmy Neko
OH, THE USUAL. WE STARTED BY GETTING RID OF THE TREE INFESTATION IN THE LIVING ROOM
YOU'LL NEVER DEFEAT US, TREE!
AVOID THE "SWEATER"
HERE KITTY!
DEAL WITH VISITING RELATIVES
DON'T TOUCH ME
WHAT A SWEETIE!
THAT SAID, GETTING EXTRA FOOD MAKES IT ALL WORTH IT
HERE, CAT!
HAVE A SAFE AND HAPPY NEW YEAR!
-CAB

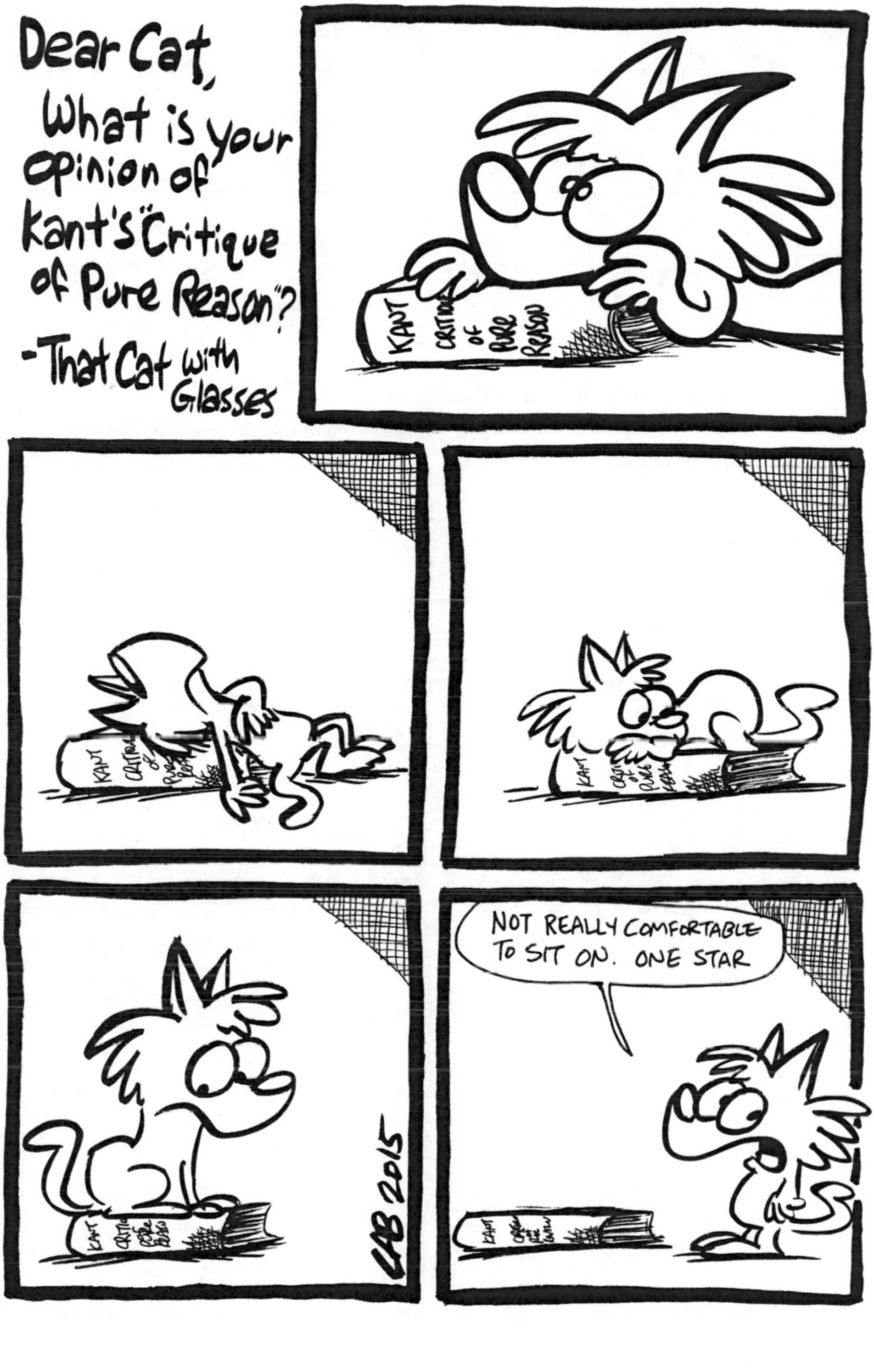

Dear Cat,
What is your opinion of Kant's "Critique of Pure Reason"?
-That Cat with Glasses
NOT REALLY COMFORTABLE TO SIT ON. ONE STAR
CAB 2015

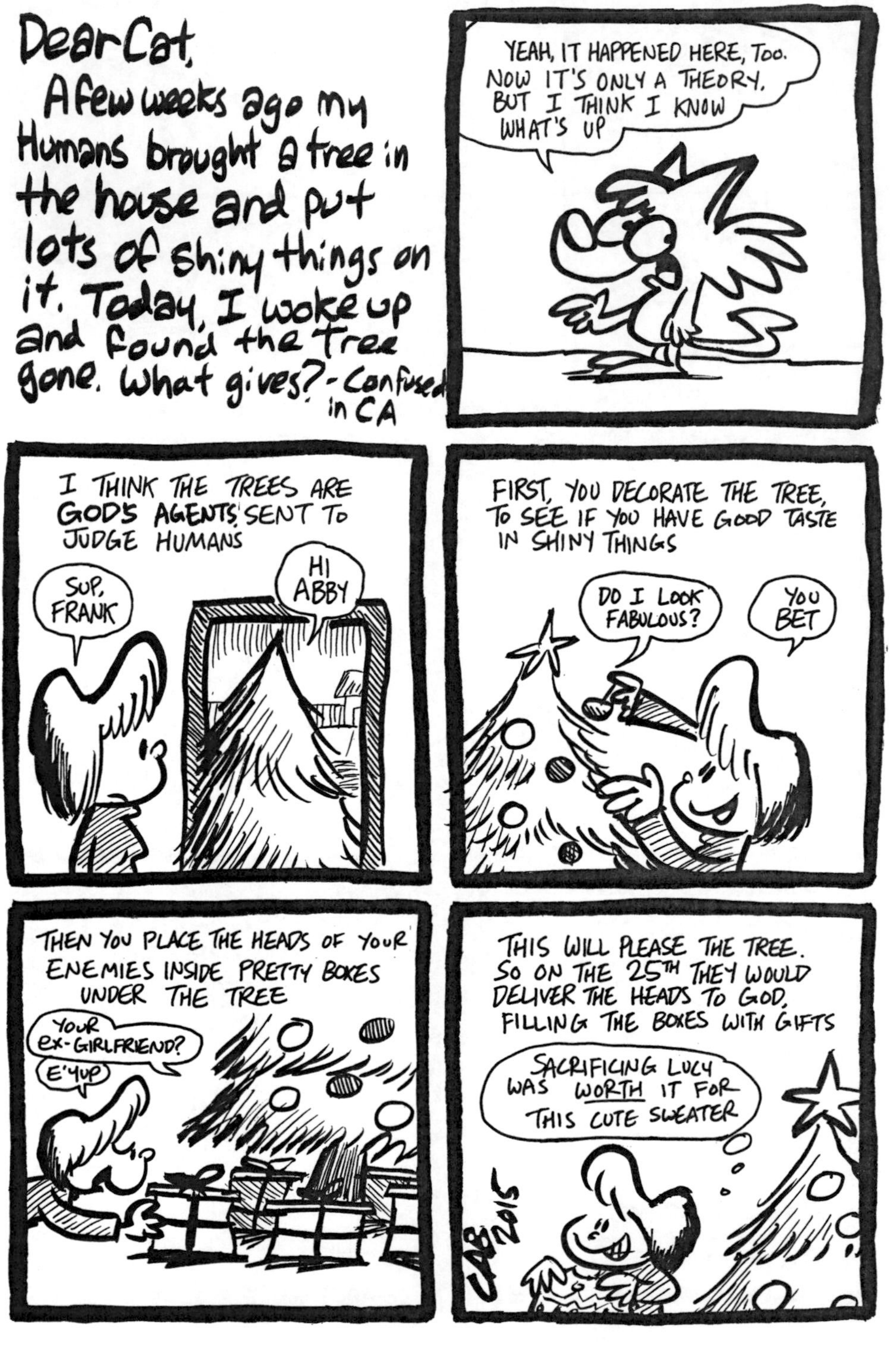
Dear Cat,
A few weeks ago my Humans brought a tree in the house and put lots of shiny things on it. Today, I woke up and found the tree gone. What gives? - Confused in CA
YEAH, IT HAPPENED HERE, TOO. NOW IT'S ONLY A THEORY, BUT I THINK I KNOW WHAT'S UP
I THINK THE TREES ARE GOD'S AGENTS SENT TO JUDGE HUMANS
SUP, FRANK
HI ABBY
FIRST, YOU DECORATE THE TREE, TO SEE IF YOU HAVE GOOD TASTE IN SHINY THINGS
DO I LOOK FABULOUS?
YOU BET
THEN YOU PLACE THE HEADS OF YOUR ENEMIES INSIDE PRETTY BOXES UNDER THE TREE
YOUR ex-GIRLFRIEND?
E'YUP
THIS WILL PLEASE THE TREE. SO ON THE 25TH THEY WOULD DELIVER THE HEADS TO GOD, FILLING THE BOXES WITH GIFTS
SACRIFICING LUCY WAS WORTH IT FOR THIS CUTE SWEATER
CAB 2015

Dear Cat,
If all dogs go to heaven, where do cats go?

-Righteous Ragdoll

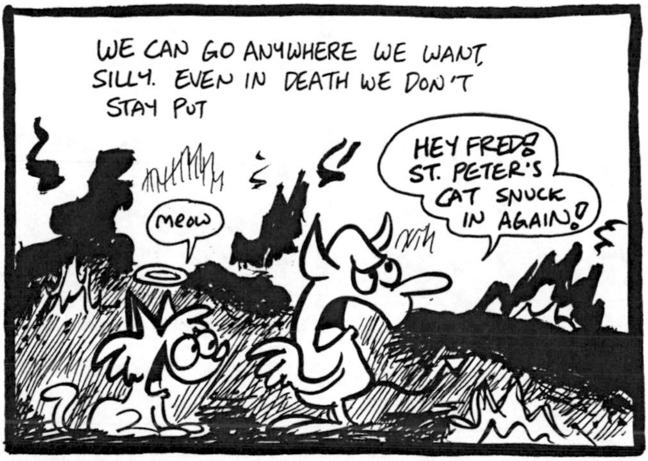
WE CAN GO ANYWHERE WE WANT, SILLY. EVEN IN DEATH WE DON'T STAY PUT
MEOW
HEY FRED! ST. PETER'S CAT SNUCK IN AGAIN!

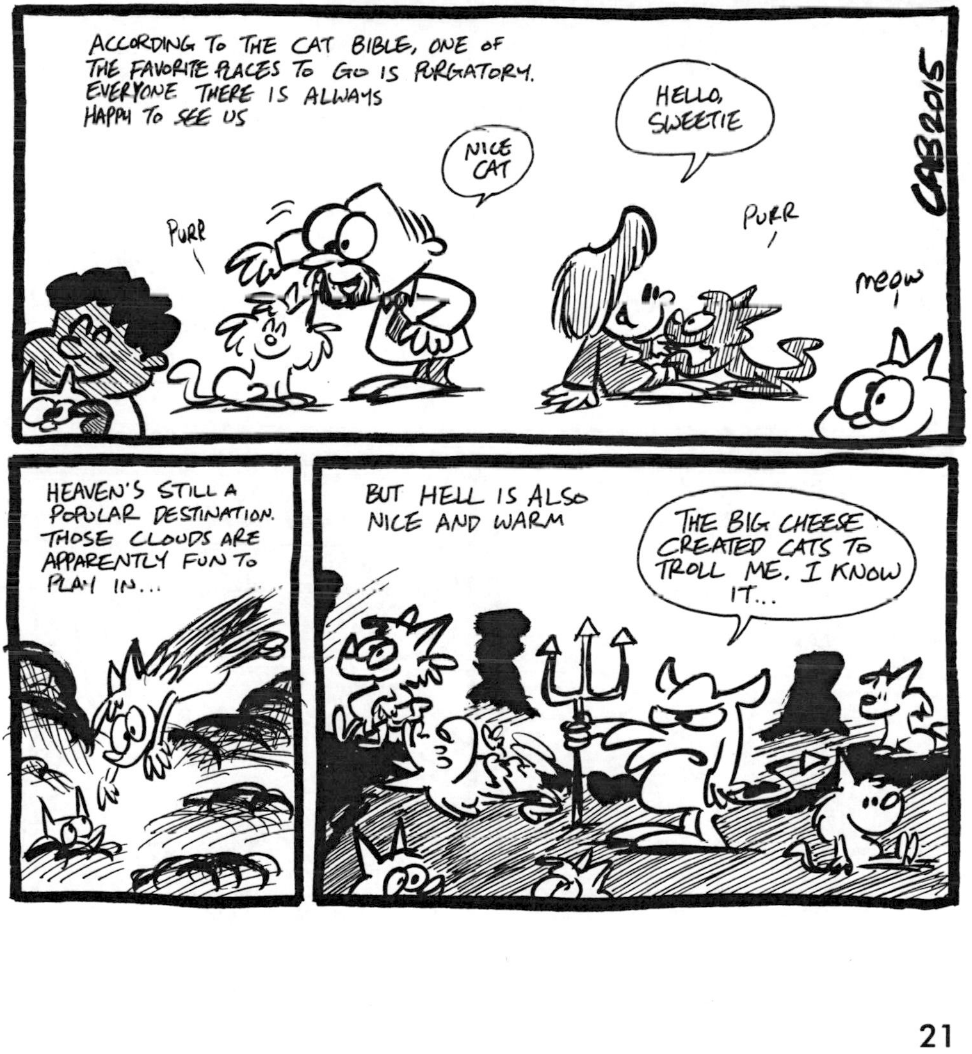
ACCORDING TO THE CAT BIBLE, ONE OF THE FAVORITE PLACES TO GO IS PURGATORY. EVERYONE THERE IS ALWAYS HAPPY TO SEE US
CAB2015
HELLO, SWEETIE
NICE CAT
PURR
PURR
MEOW
HEAVEN'S STILL A POPULAR DESTINATION. THOSE CLOUDS ARE APPARENTLY FUN TO PLAY IN...
BUT HELL IS ALSO NICE AND WARM
THE BIG CHEESE CREATED CATS TO TROLL ME. I KNOW IT...

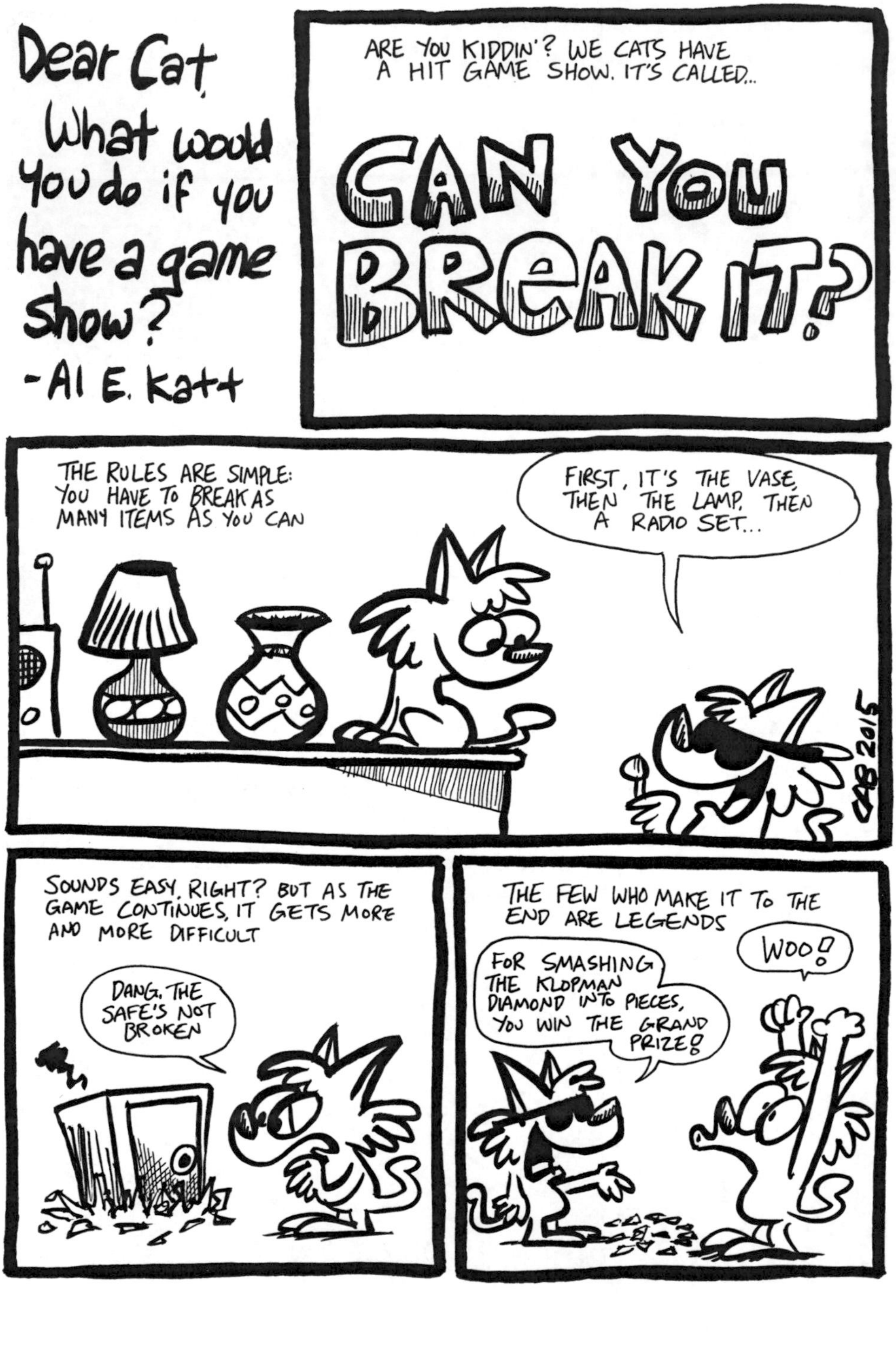

Dear Cat,
What would you do if you have a game show?
-Al E. Katt
ARE YOU KIDDIN'? WE CATS HAVE A HIT GAME SHOW. IT'S CALLED...
CAN YOU BREAK IT?
THE RULES ARE SIMPLE: YOU HAVE TO BREAK AS MANY ITEMS AS YOU CAN
FIRST, IT'S THE VASE, THEN THE LAMP, THEN A RADIO SET...
CAB 2015
SOUNDS EASY, RIGHT? BUT AS THE GAME CONTINUES, IT GETS MORE AND MORE DIFFICULT
DANG, THE SAFE'S NOT BROKEN
THE FEW WHO MAKE IT TO THE END ARE LEGENDS
FOR SMASHING THE KLOPMAN DIAMOND INTO PIECES, YOU WIN THE GRAND PRIZE!!
WOO!!

Dear Cat,

So... dogs?

-Wanderin' Kitty

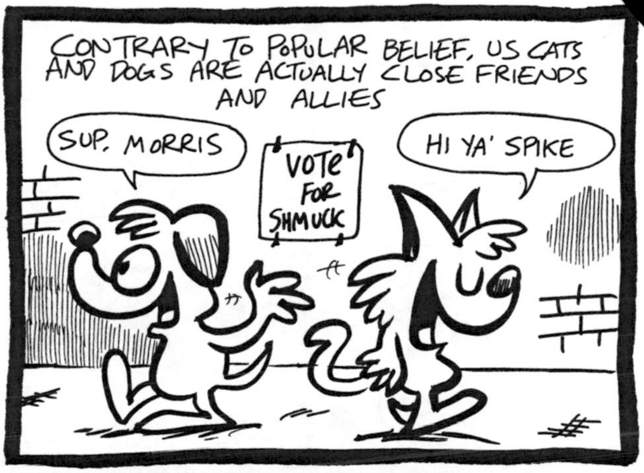

CONTRARY TO POPULAR BELIEF, US CATS AND DOGS ARE ACTUALLY CLOSE FRIENDS AND ALLIES
SUP, MORRIS
VOTE FOR SHMUCK
HI YA' SPIKE

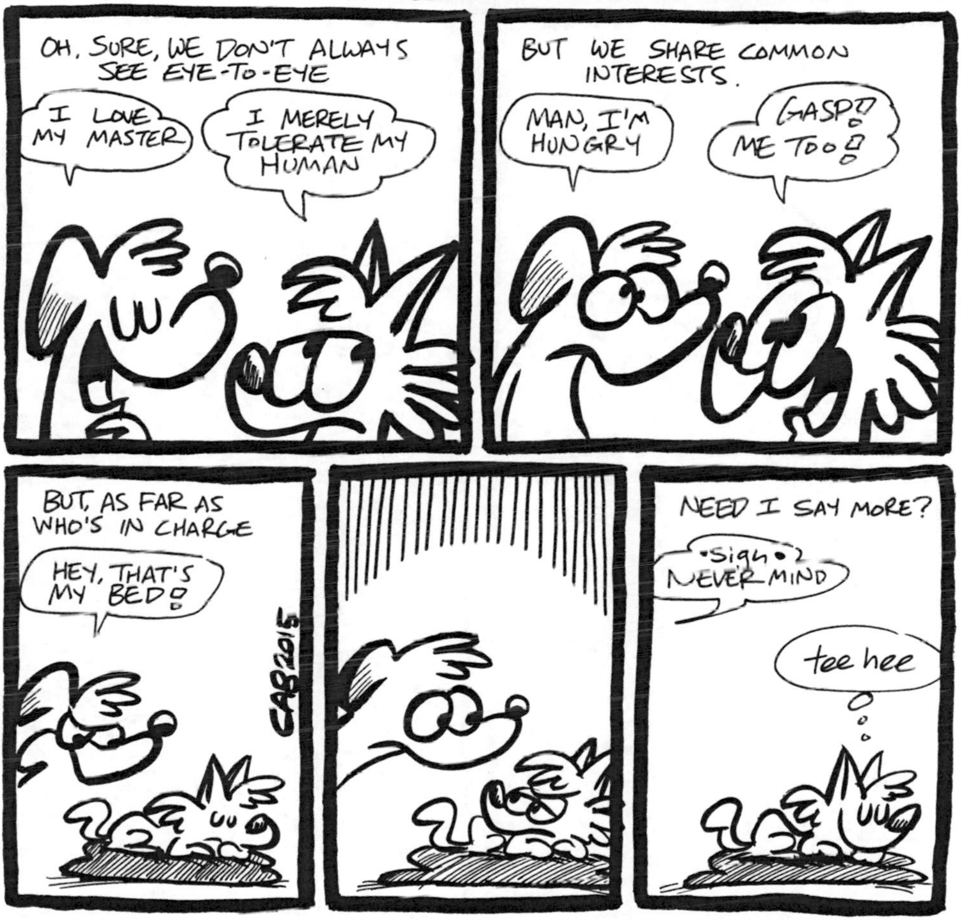

OH, SURE, WE DON'T ALWAYS SEE EYE-TO-EYE
I LOVE MY MASTER
I MERELY TOLERATE MY HUMAN
BUT WE SHARE COMMON INTERESTS.
MAN, I'M HUNGRY
GASP!? ME TOO!!
BUT, AS FAR AS WHO'S IN CHARGE
HEY, THAT'S MY BED!!
CAB 2015
NEED I SAY MORE?
•Sigh• NEVER MIND
tee hee

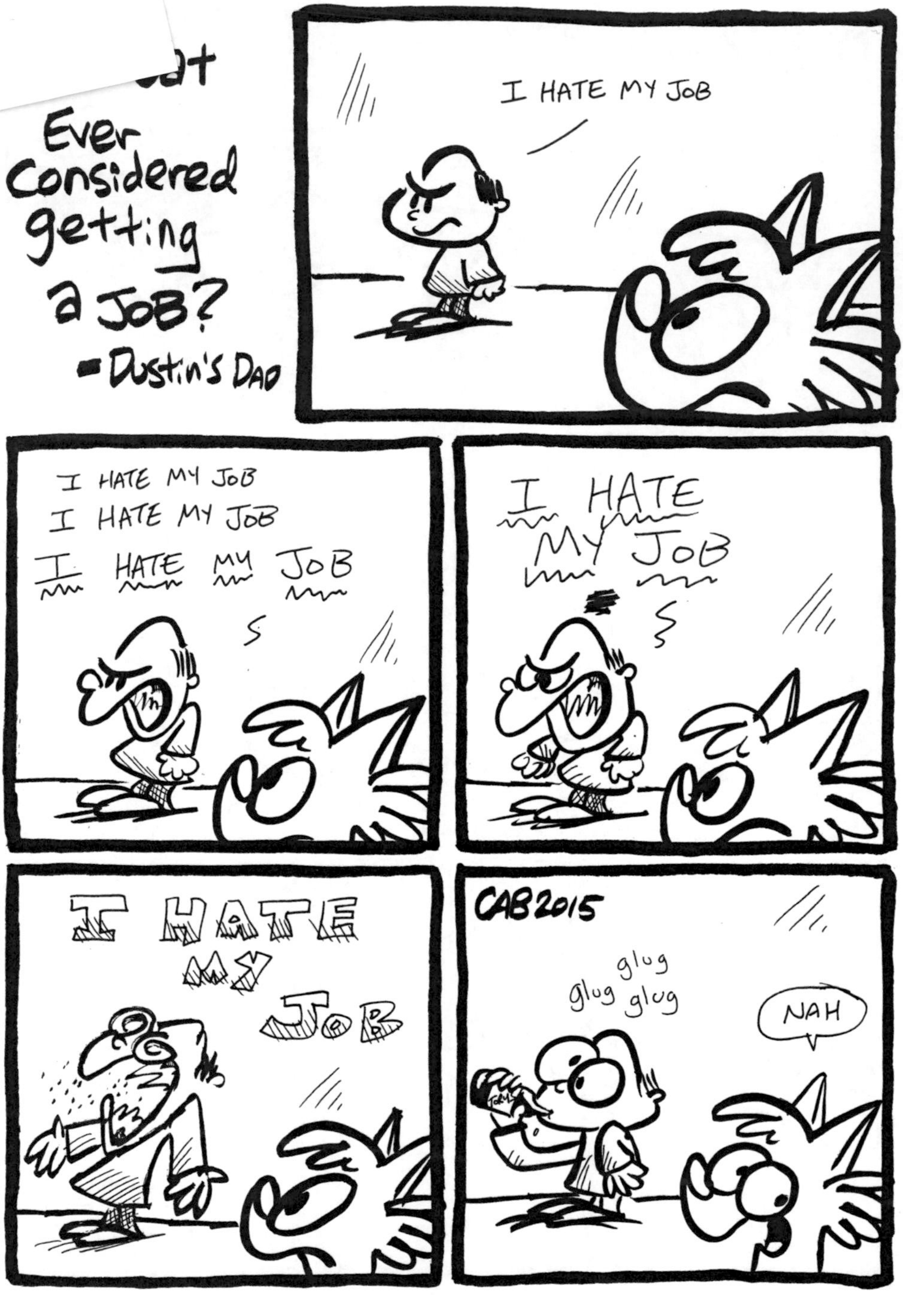
Ever considered getting a JOB?
— Dustin's Dad
I HATE MY JOB
I HATE MY JOB
I HATE MY JOB
I HATE MY JOB
I HATE MY JOB
I HATE MY JOB
CAB 2015
glug glug glug
NAH

Dear Cat,
Why do you want a door to be opened, only to return shortly after?

It's kinda annoying

- Disgruntled David

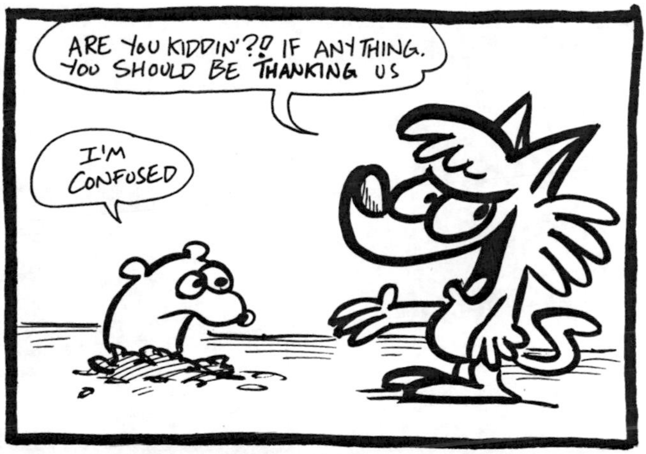
ARE YOU KIDDIN'?! IF ANYTHING. YOU SHOULD BE THANKING US
I'M CONFUSED

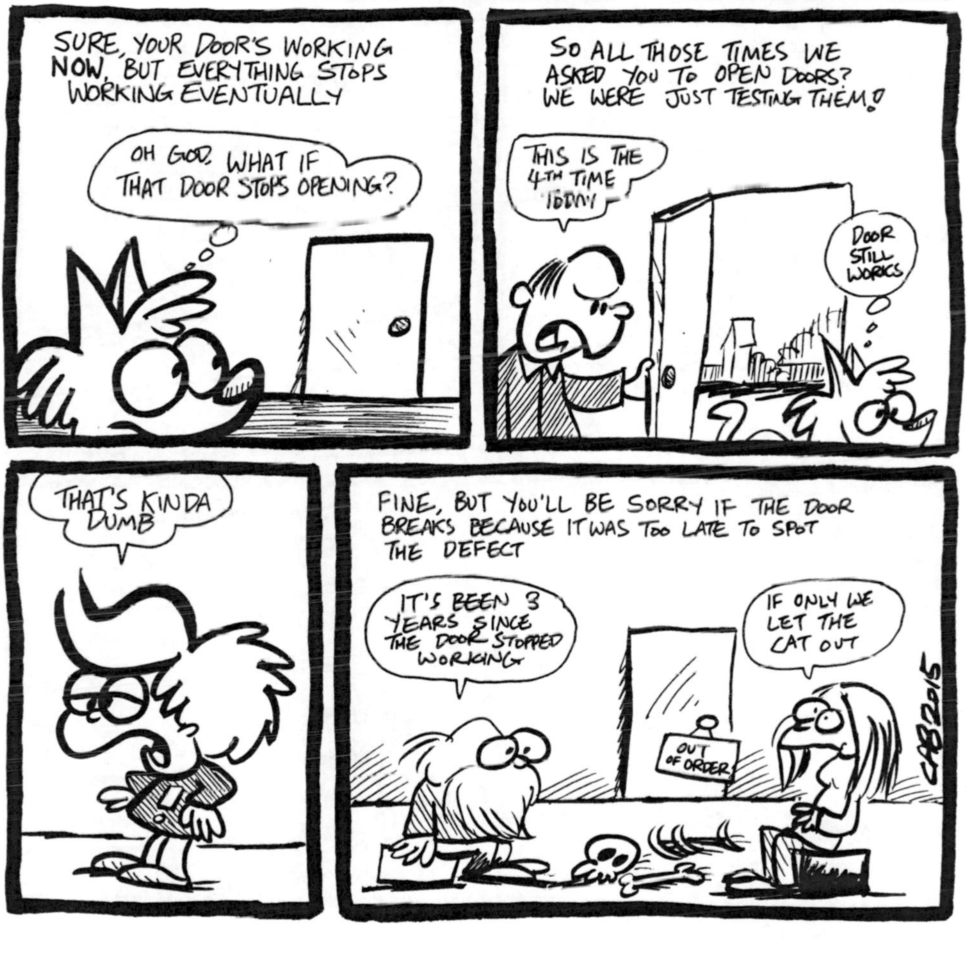
SURE, YOUR DOOR'S WORKING NOW, BUT EVERYTHING STOPS WORKING EVENTUALLY
OH GOD. WHAT IF THAT DOOR STOPS OPENING?
SO ALL THOSE TIMES WE ASKED YOU TO OPEN DOORS? WE WERE JUST TESTING THEM!
THIS IS THE 4TH TIME TODAY
DOOR STILL WORKS
THAT'S KINDA DUMB
FINE, BUT YOU'LL BE SORRY IF THE DOOR BREAKS BECAUSE IT WAS TOO LATE TO SPOT THE DEFECT
IT'S BEEN 3 YEARS SINCE THE DOOR STOPPED WORKING
IF ONLY WE LET THE CAT OUT
OUT OF ORDER
CAB 2015

Dear Cat,
Why do you knead on people?
-Wanderin' Kitten

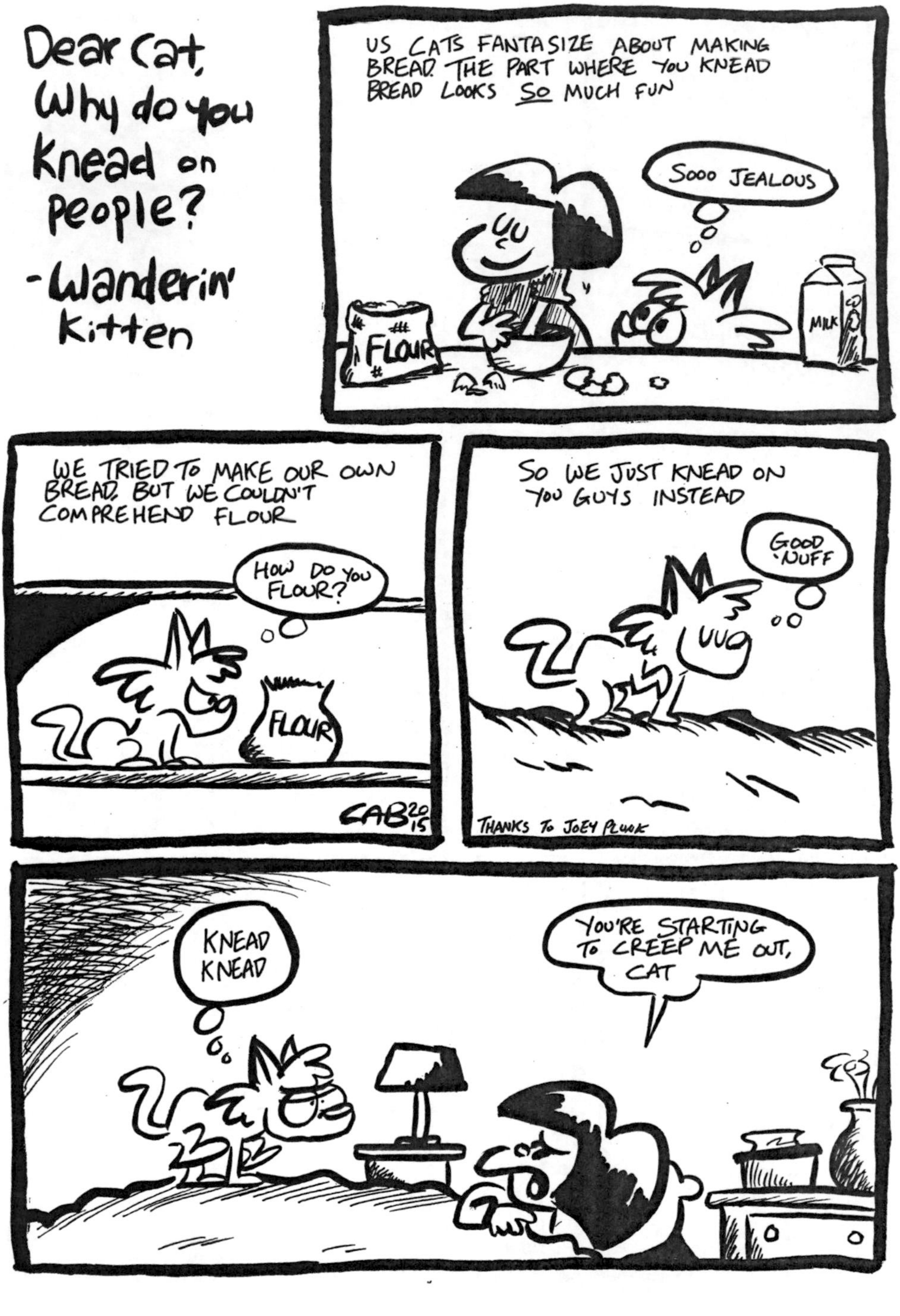
US CATS FANTASIZE ABOUT MAKING BREAD. THE PART WHERE YOU KNEAD BREAD LOOKS SO MUCH FUN
SOOO JEALOUS
FLOUR
MILK
WE TRIED TO MAKE OUR OWN BREAD, BUT WE COULDN'T COMPREHEND FLOUR
HOW DO YOU FLOUR?
FLOUR
CAB 2015
SO WE JUST KNEAD ON YOU GUYS INSTEAD
GOOD 'NUFF
THANKS TO JOEY PLUOK
KNEAD KNEAD
YOU'RE STARTING TO CREEP ME OUT, CAT

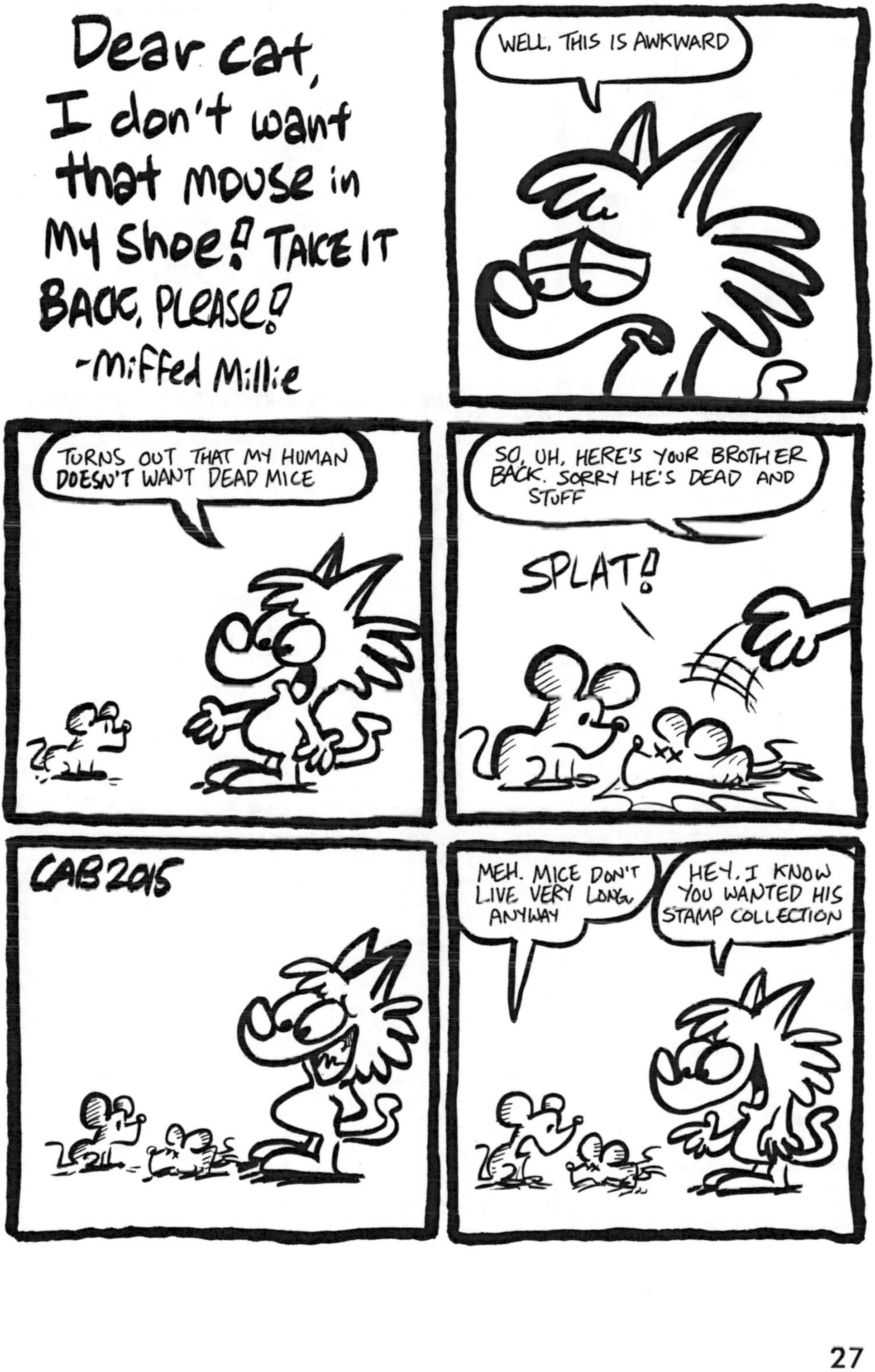
Dear cat, I don't want that mouse in my shoe!! TAKE IT BACK, PLEASE!!
-Miffed Millie
WELL, THIS IS AWKWARD
TURNS OUT THAT MY HUMAN DOESN'T WANT DEAD MICE
SO, UH, HERE'S YOUR BROTHER BACK. SORRY HE'S DEAD AND STUFF
SPLAT!!
CAB 2015
MEH. MICE DON'T LIVE VERY LONG ANYWAY
HEY. I KNOW YOU WANTED HIS STAMP COLLECTION

Dear Cat, What's in the Box?!!

-Boxcutter Junkie

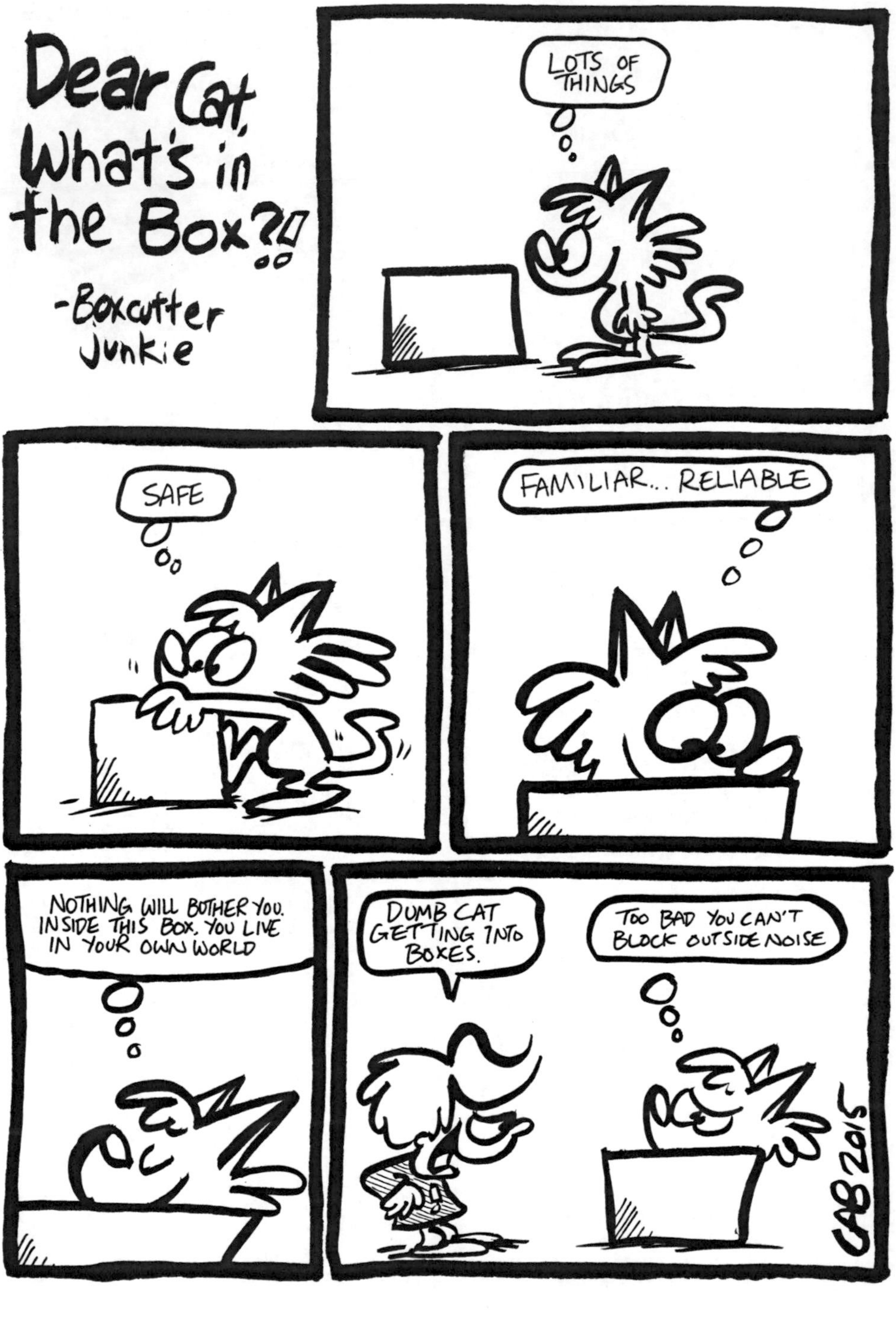

LOTS OF THINGS
SAFE
FAMILIAR... RELIABLE
NOTHING WILL BOTHER YOU. INSIDE THIS BOX, YOU LIVE IN YOUR OWN WORLD
DUMB CAT GETTING INTO BOXES.
TOO BAD YOU CAN'T BLOCK OUTSIDE NOISE
GAB 2015

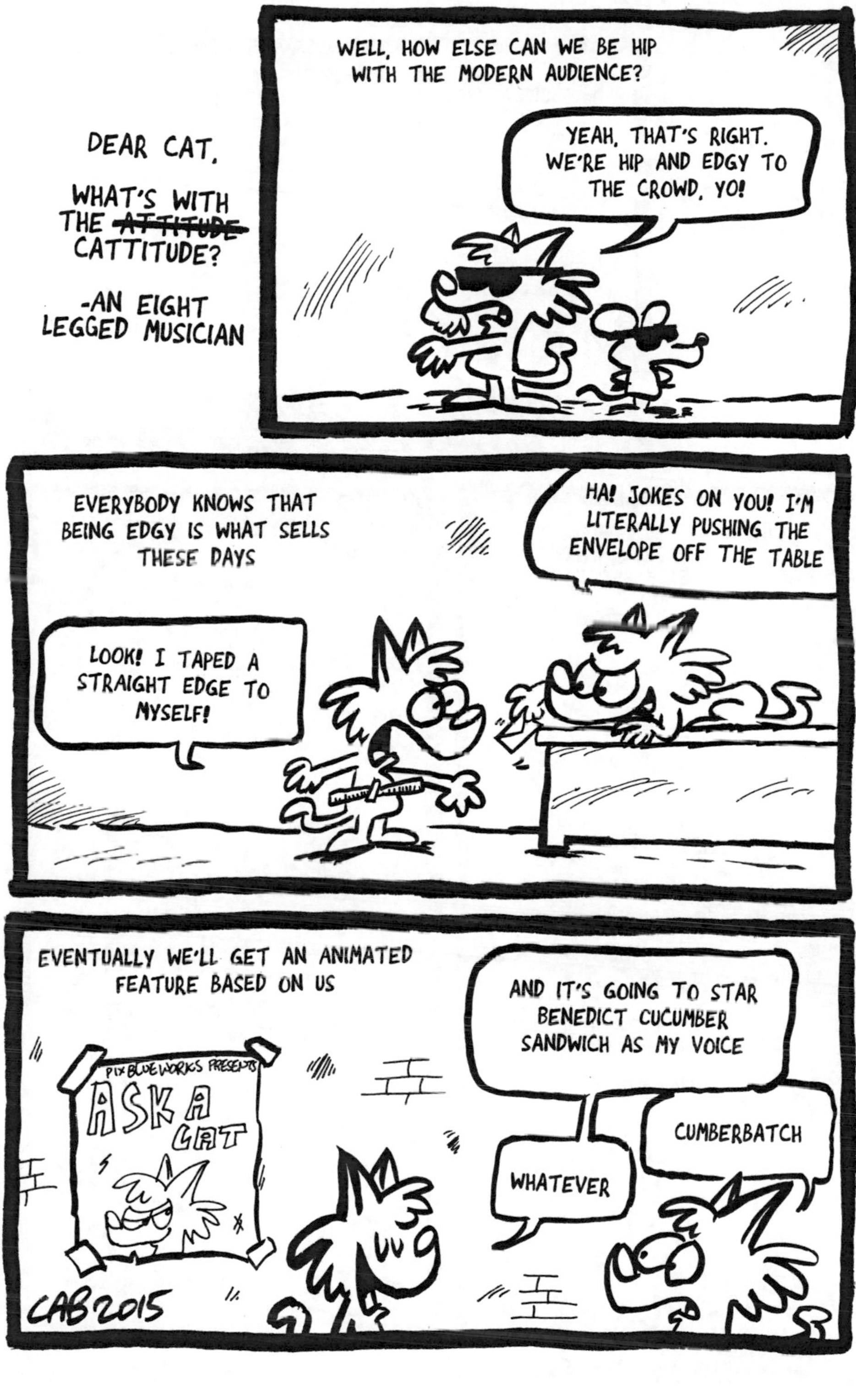
DEAR CAT,
WHAT'S WITH THE ~~ATTITUDE~~ CATTITUDE?
-AN EIGHT LEGGED MUSICIAN
WELL, HOW ELSE CAN WE BE HIP WITH THE MODERN AUDIENCE?
YEAH, THAT'S RIGHT. WE'RE HIP AND EDGY TO THE CROWD, YO!
EVERYBODY KNOWS THAT BEING EDGY IS WHAT SELLS THESE DAYS
HA! JOKES ON YOU! I'M LITERALLY PUSHING THE ENVELOPE OFF THE TABLE
LOOK! I TAPED A STRAIGHT EDGE TO MYSELF!
EVENTUALLY WE'LL GET AN ANIMATED FEATURE BASED ON US
AND IT'S GOING TO STAR BENEDICT CUCUMBER SANDWICH AS MY VOICE
PIXBLUEWORKS PRESENTS
ASK A CAT
CUMBERBATCH
WHATEVER
CAB 2015

DEAR CAT,

WHY DO YOU HATE WATER SO MUCH?

-MAGICAL DOLPHIN

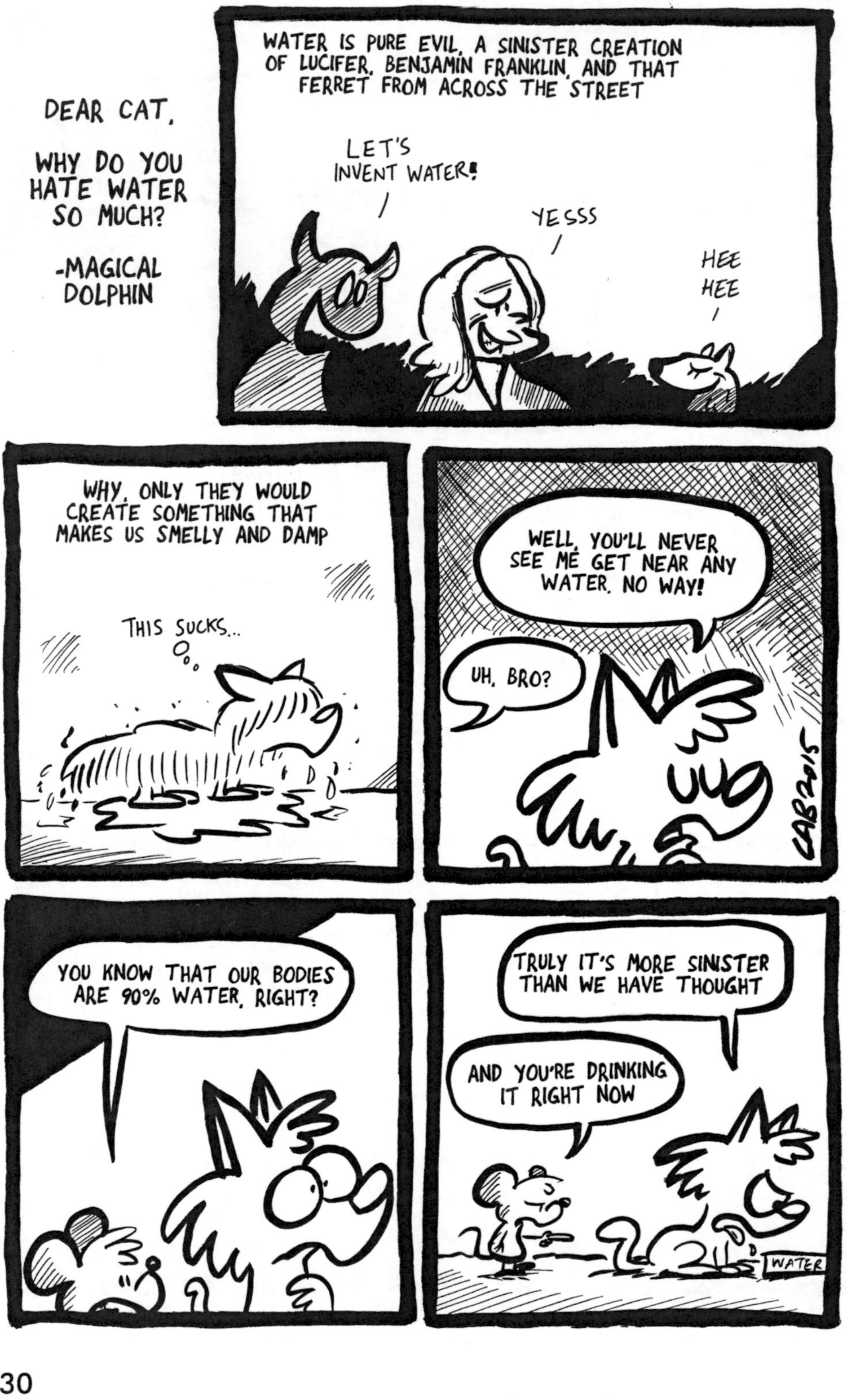
WATER IS PURE EVIL, A SINISTER CREATION OF LUCIFER, BENJAMIN FRANKLIN, AND THAT FERRET FROM ACROSS THE STREET
LET'S INVENT WATER!
YESSS
HEE HEE
WHY, ONLY THEY WOULD CREATE SOMETHING THAT MAKES US SMELLY AND DAMP
THIS SUCKS...
WELL, YOU'LL NEVER SEE ME GET NEAR ANY WATER. NO WAY!
UH, BRO?
CAB2015
YOU KNOW THAT OUR BODIES ARE 90% WATER, RIGHT?
TRULY IT'S MORE SINISTER THAN WE HAVE THOUGHT
AND YOU'RE DRINKING IT RIGHT NOW
WATER

DEAR CAT,

WHY DID YOU INCLUDE BEN FRANKLIN IN YOUR LIST OF EVIL IN THE LAST STRIP?

-BOBBY KITTY

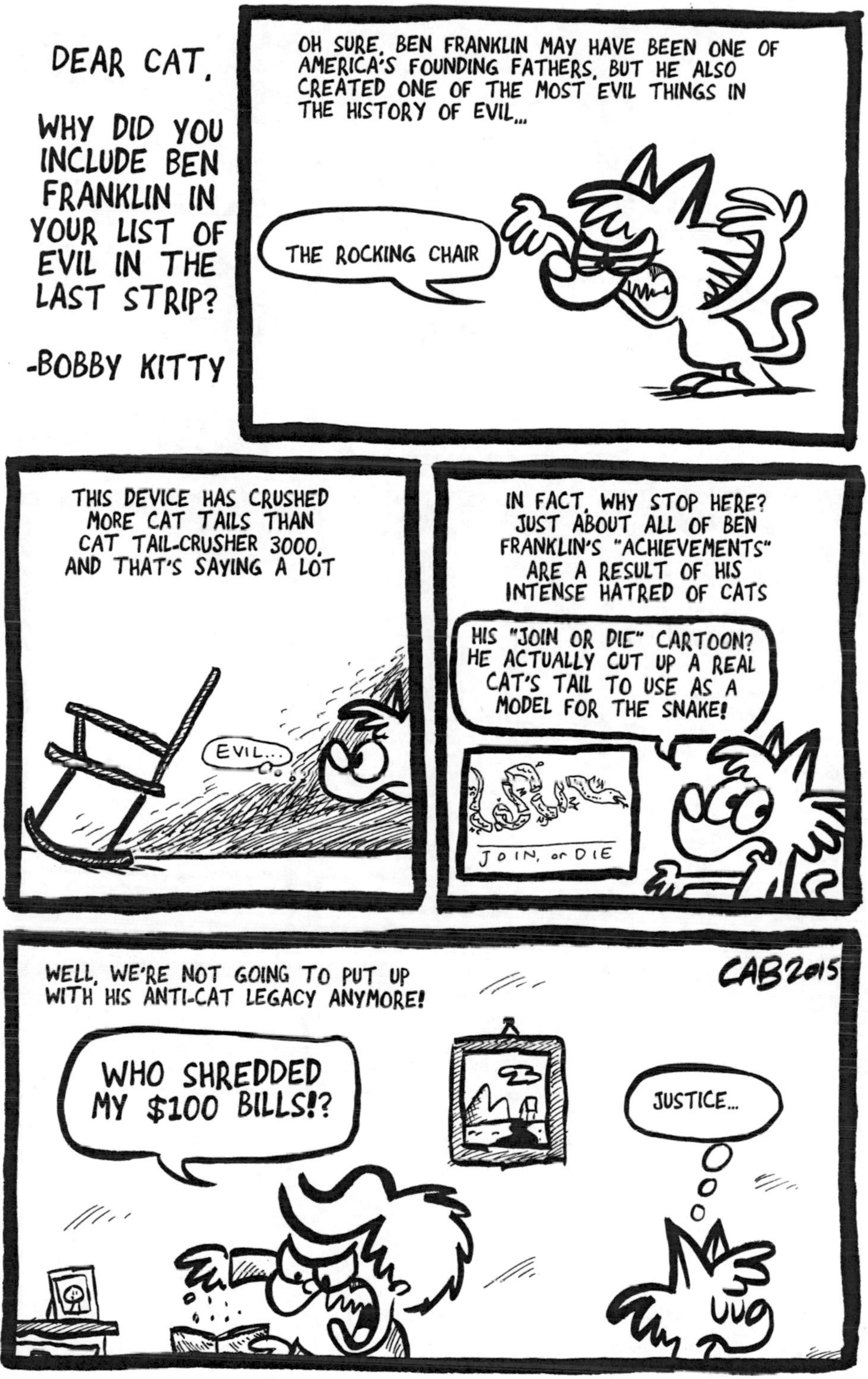

OH SURE, BEN FRANKLIN MAY HAVE BEEN ONE OF AMERICA'S FOUNDING FATHERS, BUT HE ALSO CREATED ONE OF THE MOST EVIL THINGS IN THE HISTORY OF EVIL...
THE ROCKING CHAIR
THIS DEVICE HAS CRUSHED MORE CAT TAILS THAN CAT TAIL-CRUSHER 3000, AND THAT'S SAYING A LOT
EVIL...
IN FACT, WHY STOP HERE? JUST ABOUT ALL OF BEN FRANKLIN'S "ACHIEVEMENTS" ARE A RESULT OF HIS INTENSE HATRED OF CATS
HIS "JOIN OR DIE" CARTOON? HE ACTUALLY CUT UP A REAL CAT'S TAIL TO USE AS A MODEL FOR THE SNAKE!
JOIN, or DIE
WELL, WE'RE NOT GOING TO PUT UP WITH HIS ANTI-CAT LEGACY ANYMORE!
CAB 2015
WHO SHREDDED MY $100 BILLS!?
JUSTICE...

DEAR CAT,

WHY DO YOU ASK FOR BELLY RUBS WHEN YOU CLEARLY DON'T WANT THEM?

- MR. RUB OUT

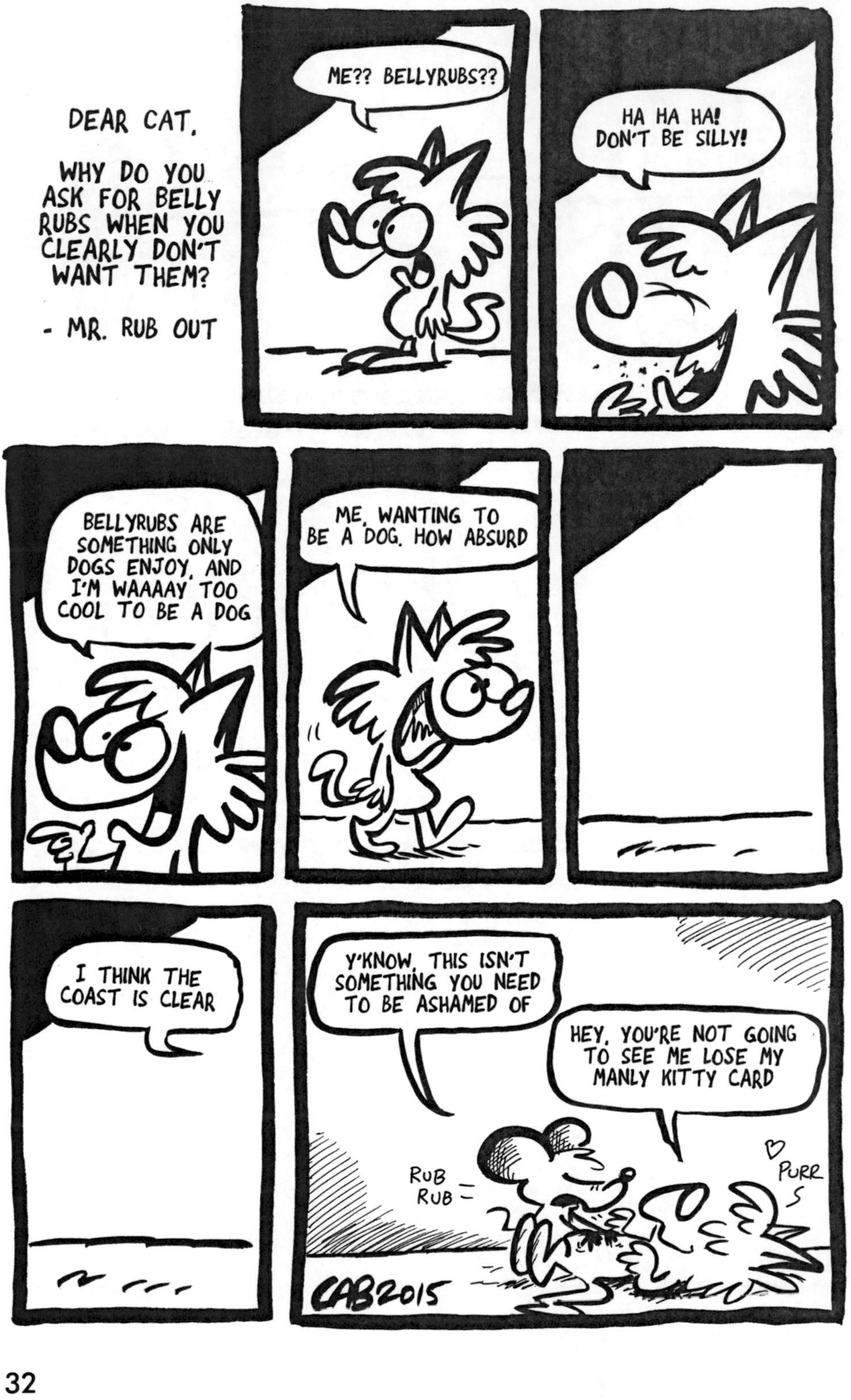

ME?? BELLYRUBS??
HA HA HA! DON'T BE SILLY!
BELLYRUBS ARE SOMETHING ONLY DOGS ENJOY, AND I'M WAAAAY TOO COOL TO BE A DOG
ME, WANTING TO BE A DOG. HOW ABSURD
I THINK THE COAST IS CLEAR
Y'KNOW, THIS ISN'T SOMETHING YOU NEED TO BE ASHAMED OF
HEY, YOU'RE NOT GOING TO SEE ME LOSE MY MANLY KITTY CARD
RUB RUB
PURR
CAB 2015

DEAR CAT,

DID YOU FILE YOUR TAXES THIS YEAR?

-MR. L. SHARK

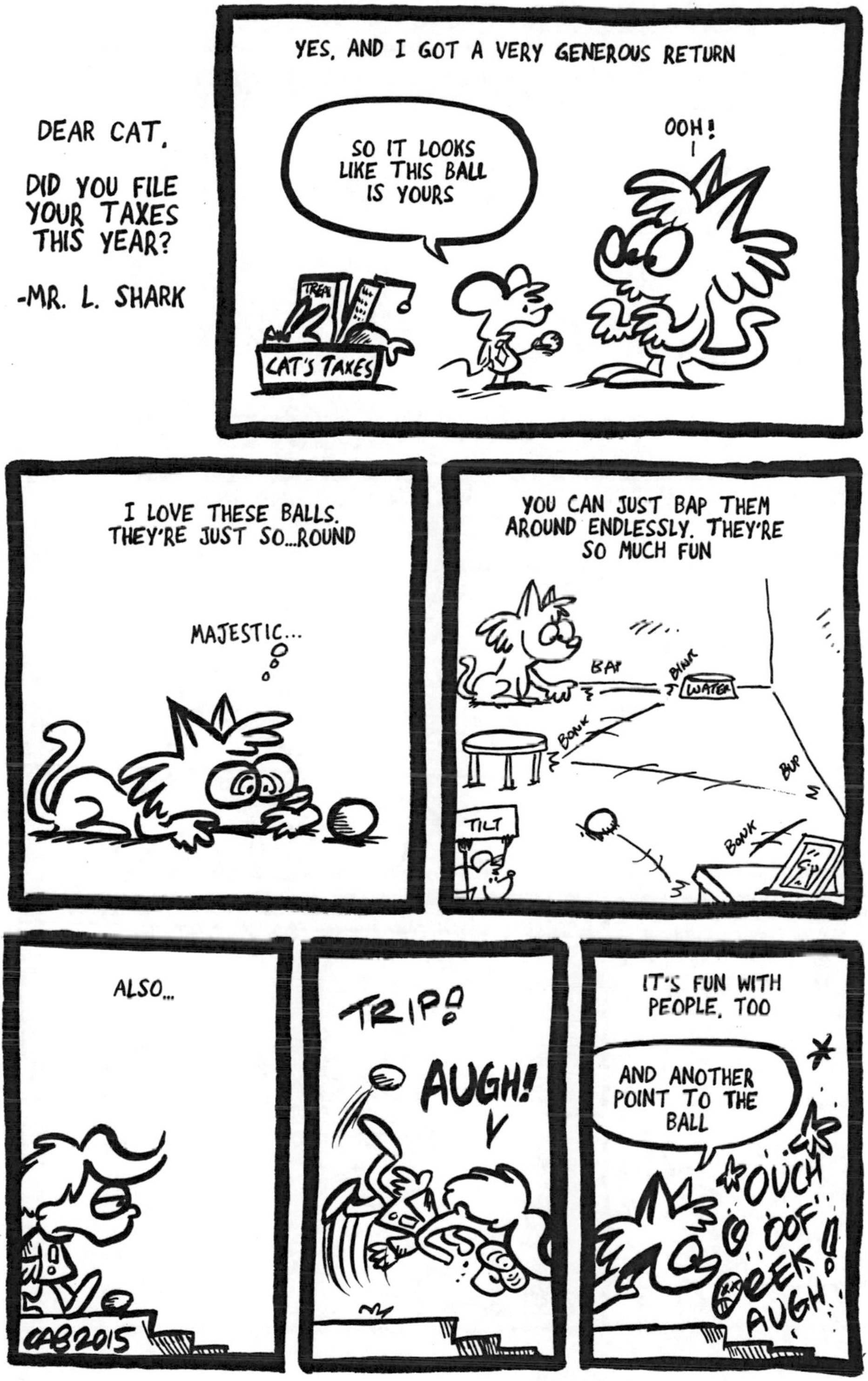
YES, AND I GOT A VERY GENEROUS RETURN
SO IT LOOKS LIKE THIS BALL IS YOURS
OOH!
CAT'S TAXES
I LOVE THESE BALLS. THEY'RE JUST SO...ROUND
MAJESTIC...
YOU CAN JUST BAP THEM AROUND ENDLESSLY. THEY'RE SO MUCH FUN
BAP
BINK
WATER
BONK
BUP
TILT
BONK
ALSO...
CAB2015
TRIP!
AUGH!
IT'S FUN WITH PEOPLE, TOO
AND ANOTHER POINT TO THE BALL
OUCH
OOF
EEK!
AUGH!

DEAR CAT,

YOU GET SO MANY QUESTIONS, HOW DO YOU FIND TIME TO ANSWER THEM ALL?

-MR. SOMECAT

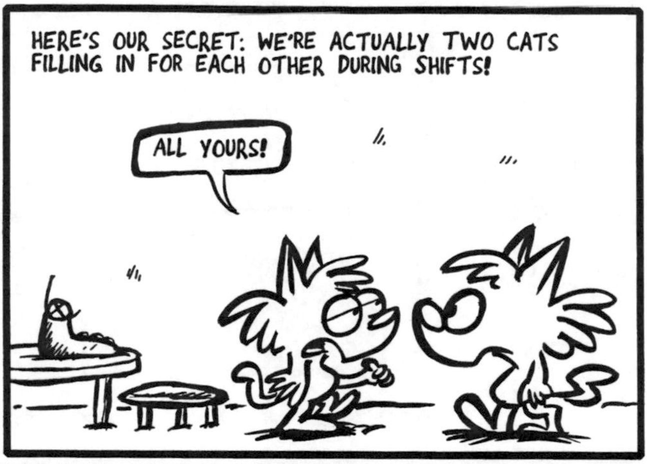
HERE'S OUR SECRET: WE'RE ACTUALLY TWO CATS FILLING IN FOR EACH OTHER DURING SHIFTS!
ALL YOURS!

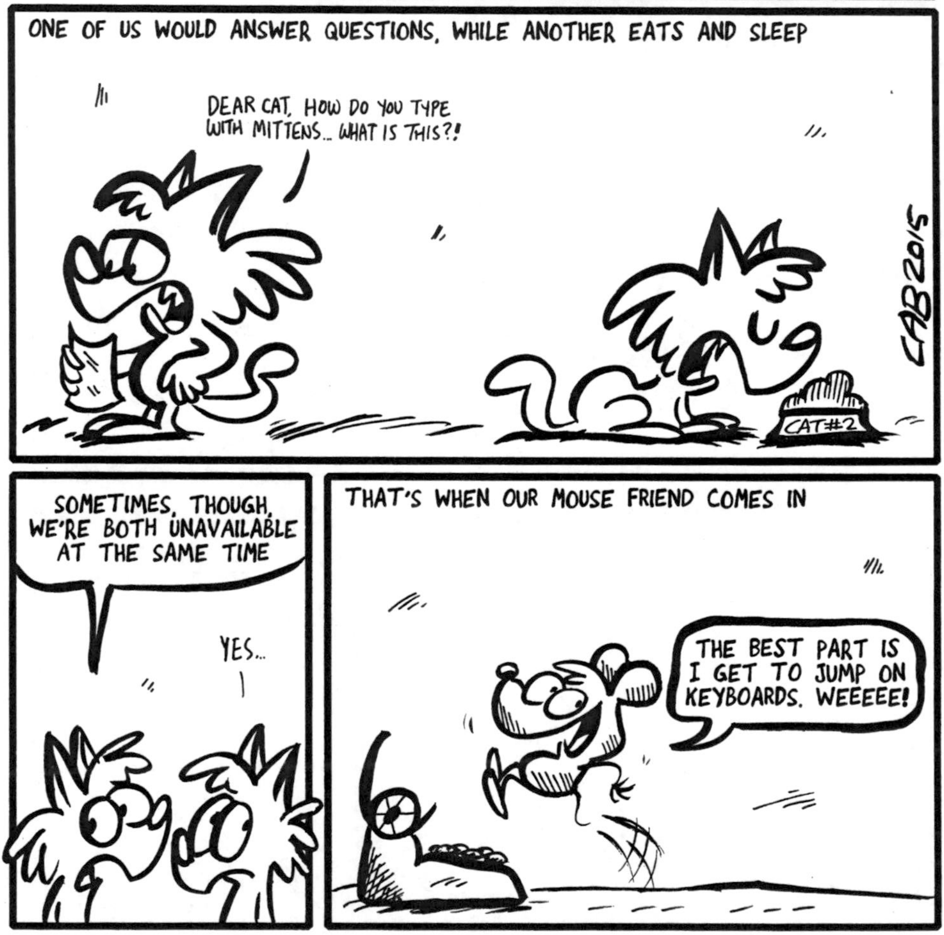
ONE OF US WOULD ANSWER QUESTIONS, WHILE ANOTHER EATS AND SLEEP
DEAR CAT, HOW DO YOU TYPE WITH MITTENS... WHAT IS THIS?!
CAB 2015
CAT#2
SOMETIMES, THOUGH, WE'RE BOTH UNAVAILABLE AT THE SAME TIME
YES...
THAT'S WHEN OUR MOUSE FRIEND COMES IN
THE BEST PART IS I GET TO JUMP ON KEYBOARDS. WEEEEE!

DEAR CAT,

DO YOU THINK YOU'D BE A GOOD SUPERHERO?

-MR. CALVED

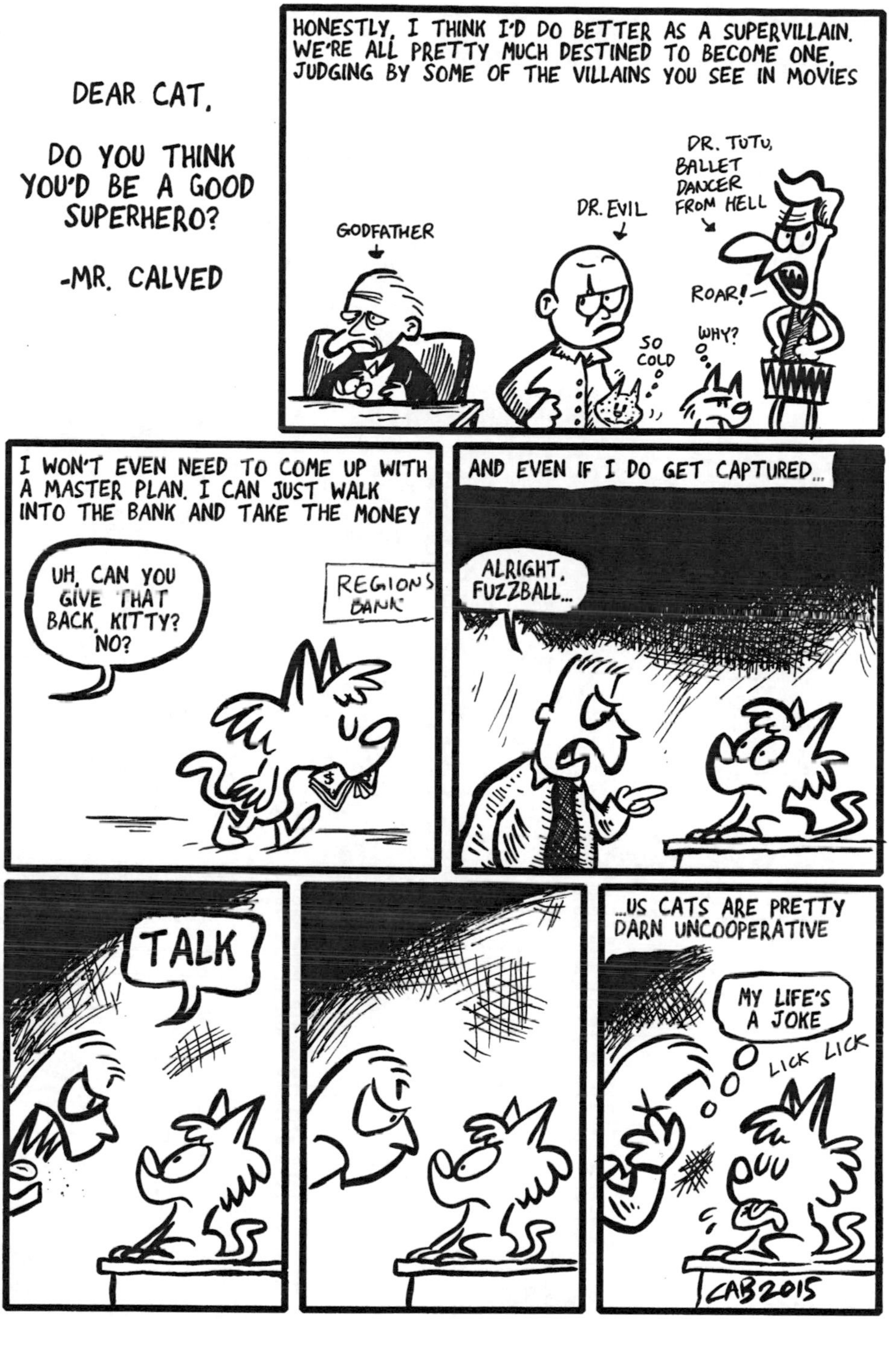

HONESTLY, I THINK I'D DO BETTER AS A SUPERVILLAIN. WE'RE ALL PRETTY MUCH DESTINED TO BECOME ONE, JUDGING BY SOME OF THE VILLAINS YOU SEE IN MOVIES
GODFATHER
DR. EVIL
DR. TUTU, BALLET DANCER FROM HELL
ROAR!
SO COLD
WHY?
I WON'T EVEN NEED TO COME UP WITH A MASTER PLAN. I CAN JUST WALK INTO THE BANK AND TAKE THE MONEY
UH, CAN YOU GIVE THAT BACK, KITTY? NO?
REGIONS BANK
AND EVEN IF I DO GET CAPTURED...
ALRIGHT, FUZZBALL...
TALK
...US CATS ARE PRETTY DARN UNCOOPERATIVE
MY LIFE'S A JOKE
LICK LICK
CAB 2015

DEAR CAT,

IF YOU HAD WINGS, WHAT WOULD YOU DO?

-WAITING FOR JETPACKS

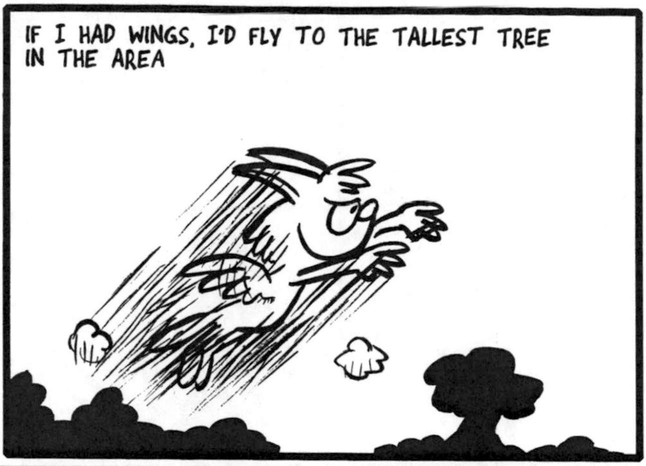

IF I HAD WINGS, I'D FLY TO THE TALLEST TREE IN THE AREA

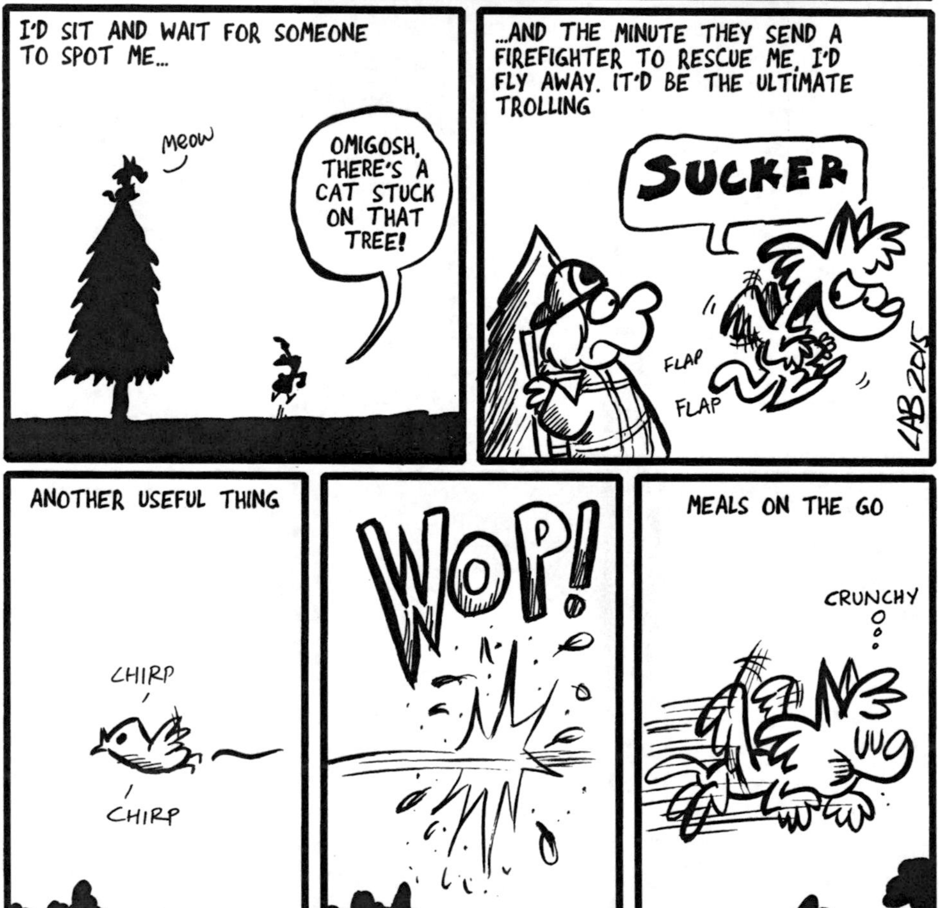

I'D SIT AND WAIT FOR SOMEONE TO SPOT ME...
MEOW
OMIGOSH, THERE'S A CAT STUCK ON THAT TREE!
...AND THE MINUTE THEY SEND A FIREFIGHTER TO RESCUE ME, I'D FLY AWAY. IT'D BE THE ULTIMATE TROLLING
SUCKER
FLAP
FLAP
LAB 2015
ANOTHER USEFUL THING
CHIRP
CHIRP
WOP!
MEALS ON THE GO
CRUNCHY

DEAR CAT,

WHY DO YOU INSIST ON TAPPING MY FACE AT MIDNIGHT?

-PLEASE STOP TAPPING

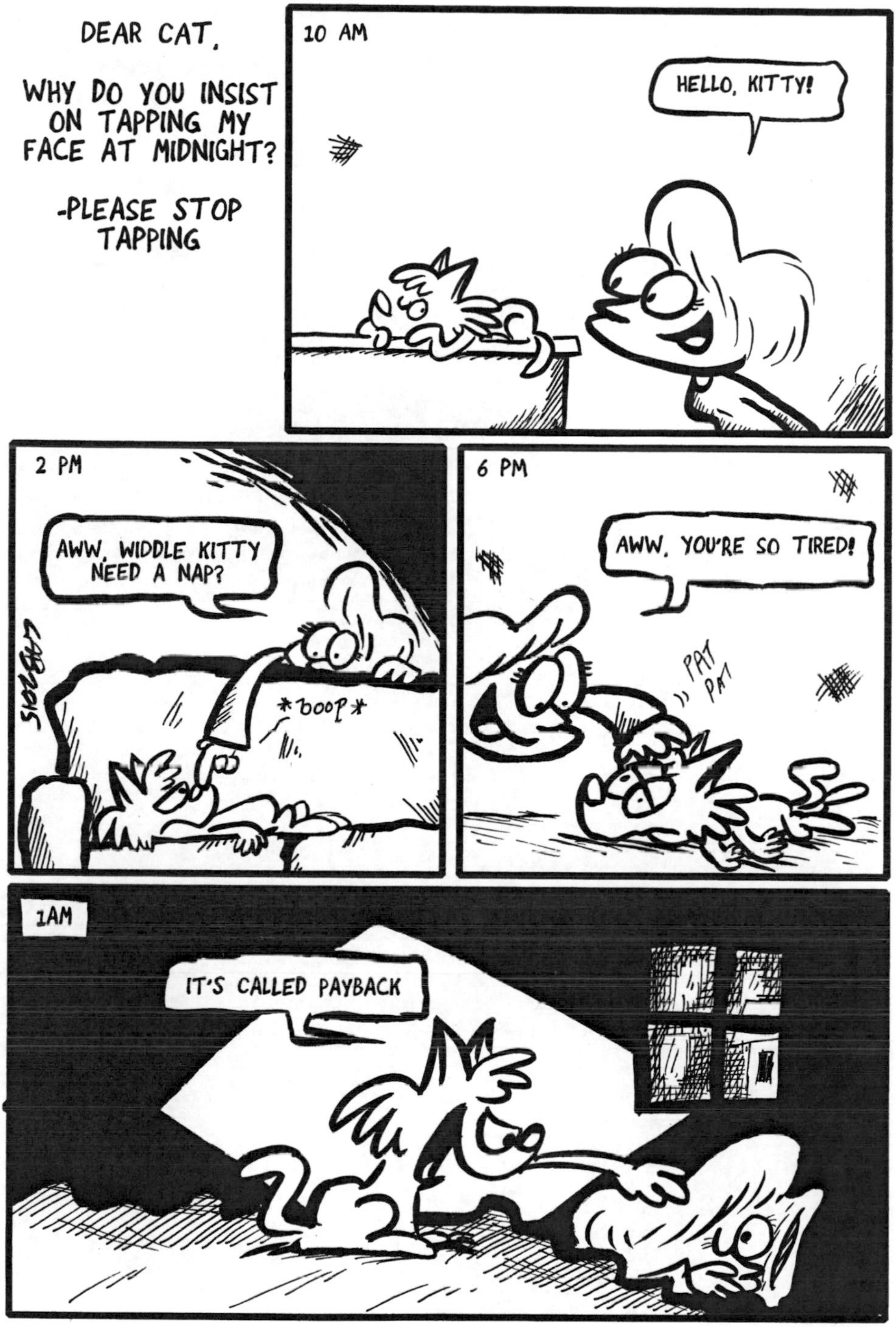
10 AM
HELLO, KITTY!
2 PM
AWW, WIDDLE KITTY NEED A NAP?
BOOP
6 PM
AWW, YOU'RE SO TIRED!
PAT PAT
1AM
IT'S CALLED PAYBACK

DEAR CAT,

WHAT ACTUALLY HAPPENED TO SCHRODINGER'S CAT?

-OUT OF THE BOX

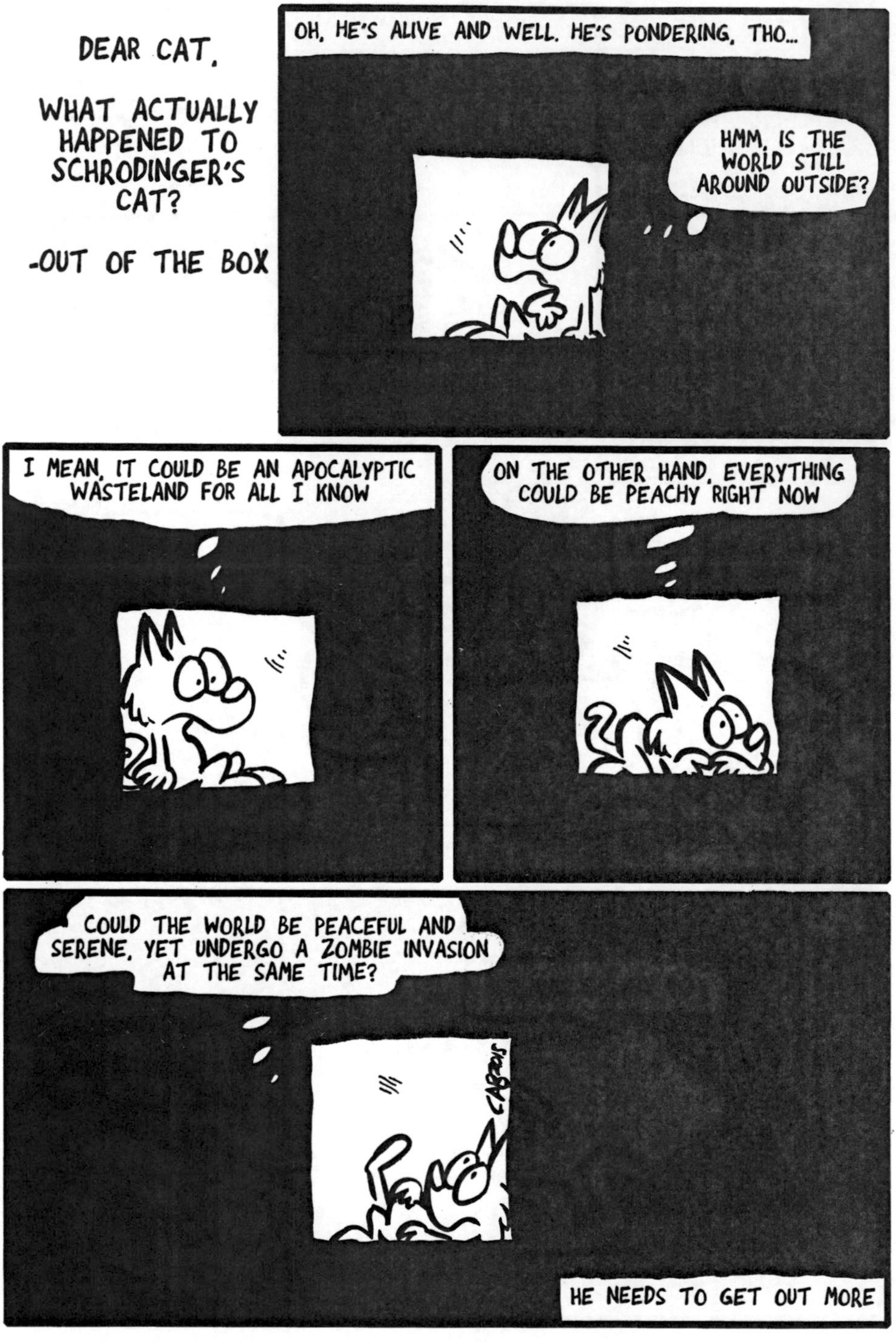

OH, HE'S ALIVE AND WELL. HE'S PONDERING, THO...
HMM, IS THE WORLD STILL AROUND OUTSIDE?
I MEAN, IT COULD BE AN APOCALYPTIC WASTELAND FOR ALL I KNOW
ON THE OTHER HAND, EVERYTHING COULD BE PEACHY RIGHT NOW
COULD THE WORLD BE PEACEFUL AND SERENE, YET UNDERGO A ZOMBIE INVASION AT THE SAME TIME?
HE NEEDS TO GET OUT MORE

DEAR CAT,

WHAT DO YOU CONSIDER TO BE YOUR GREATEST ACCOMPLISHMENT?

-DAVID, WEARING A TOGA

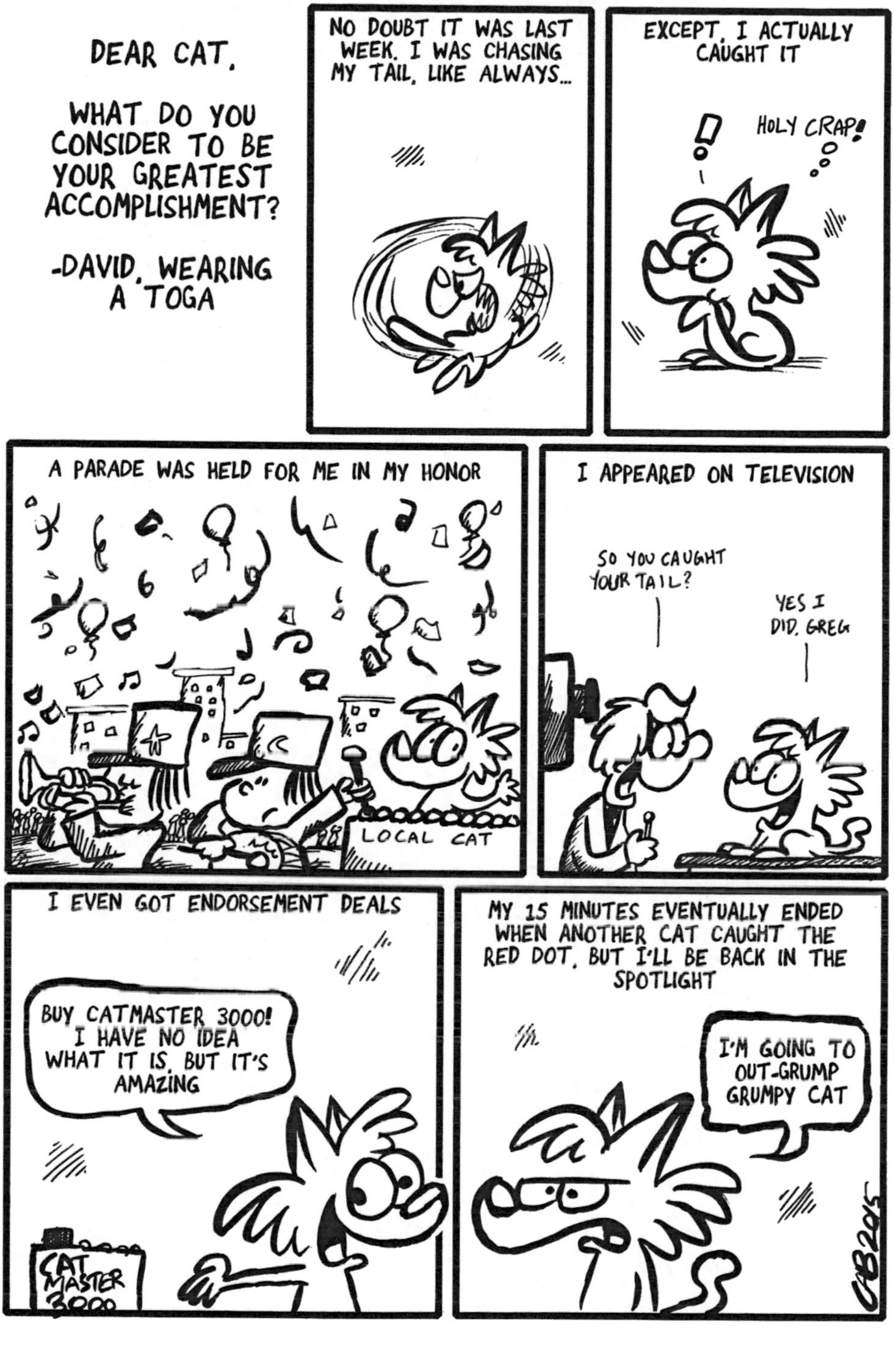

NO DOUBT IT WAS LAST WEEK. I WAS CHASING MY TAIL, LIKE ALWAYS...
EXCEPT, I ACTUALLY CAUGHT IT
!
HOLY CRAP!
A PARADE WAS HELD FOR ME IN MY HONOR
LOCAL CAT
I APPEARED ON TELEVISION
SO YOU CAUGHT YOUR TAIL?
YES I DID, GREG
I EVEN GOT ENDORSEMENT DEALS
BUY CATMASTER 3000! I HAVE NO IDEA WHAT IT IS, BUT IT'S AMAZING
CAT MASTER 3000
MY 15 MINUTES EVENTUALLY ENDED WHEN ANOTHER CAT CAUGHT THE RED DOT, BUT I'LL BE BACK IN THE SPOTLIGHT
I'M GOING TO OUT-GRUMP GRUMPY CAT
CAB2015

DEAR CAT,

EVER HAVE STRANGE DREAMS?

-SID FROM SYDNEY

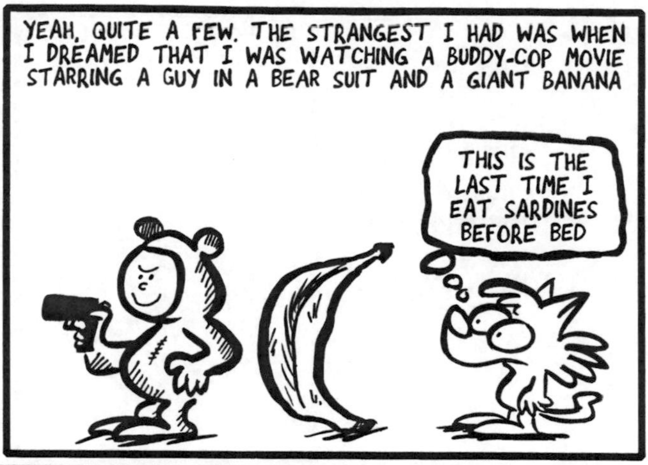
YEAH, QUITE A FEW. THE STRANGEST I HAD WAS WHEN I DREAMED THAT I WAS WATCHING A BUDDY-COP MOVIE STARRING A GUY IN A BEAR SUIT AND A GIANT BANANA
THIS IS THE LAST TIME I EAT SARDINES BEFORE BED

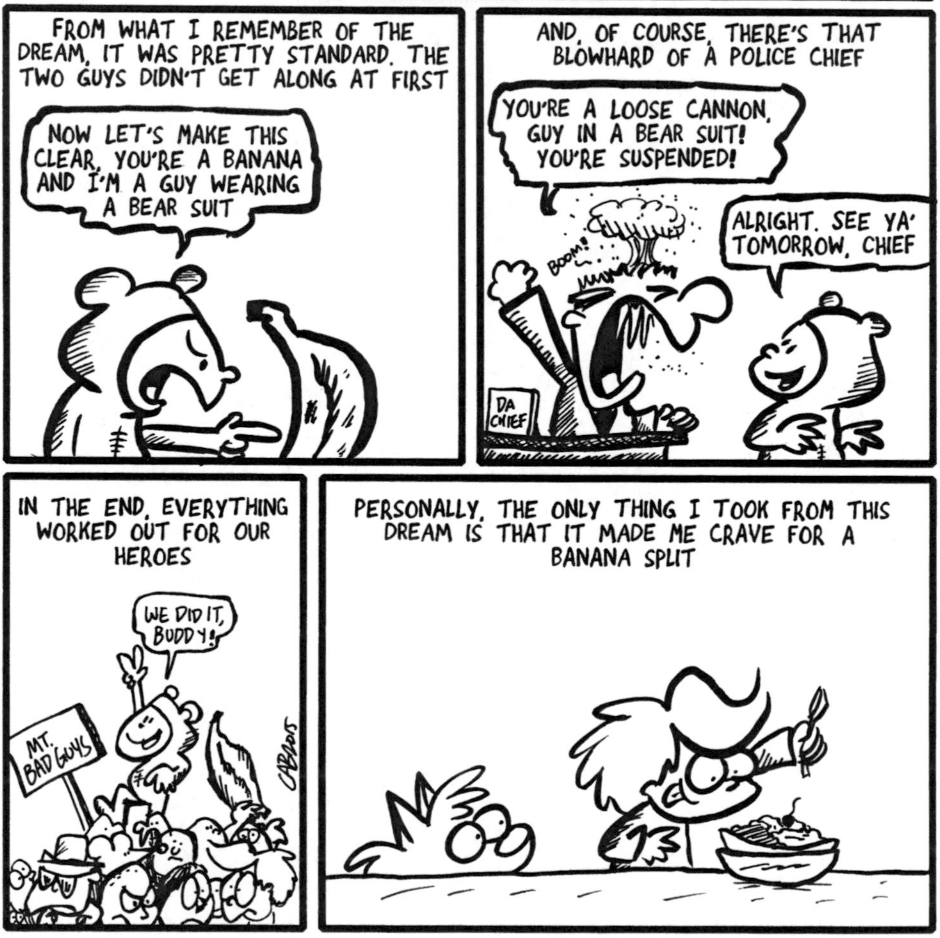
FROM WHAT I REMEMBER OF THE DREAM, IT WAS PRETTY STANDARD. THE TWO GUYS DIDN'T GET ALONG AT FIRST
NOW LET'S MAKE THIS CLEAR, YOU'RE A BANANA AND I'M A GUY WEARING A BEAR SUIT
AND, OF COURSE, THERE'S THAT BLOWHARD OF A POLICE CHIEF
YOU'RE A LOOSE CANNON, GUY IN A BEAR SUIT! YOU'RE SUSPENDED!
BOOM!
DA CHIEF
ALRIGHT. SEE YA' TOMORROW, CHIEF
IN THE END, EVERYTHING WORKED OUT FOR OUR HEROES
WE DID IT, BUDDY!
MT. BAD GUYS
PERSONALLY, THE ONLY THING I TOOK FROM THIS DREAM IS THAT IT MADE ME CRAVE FOR A BANANA SPLIT

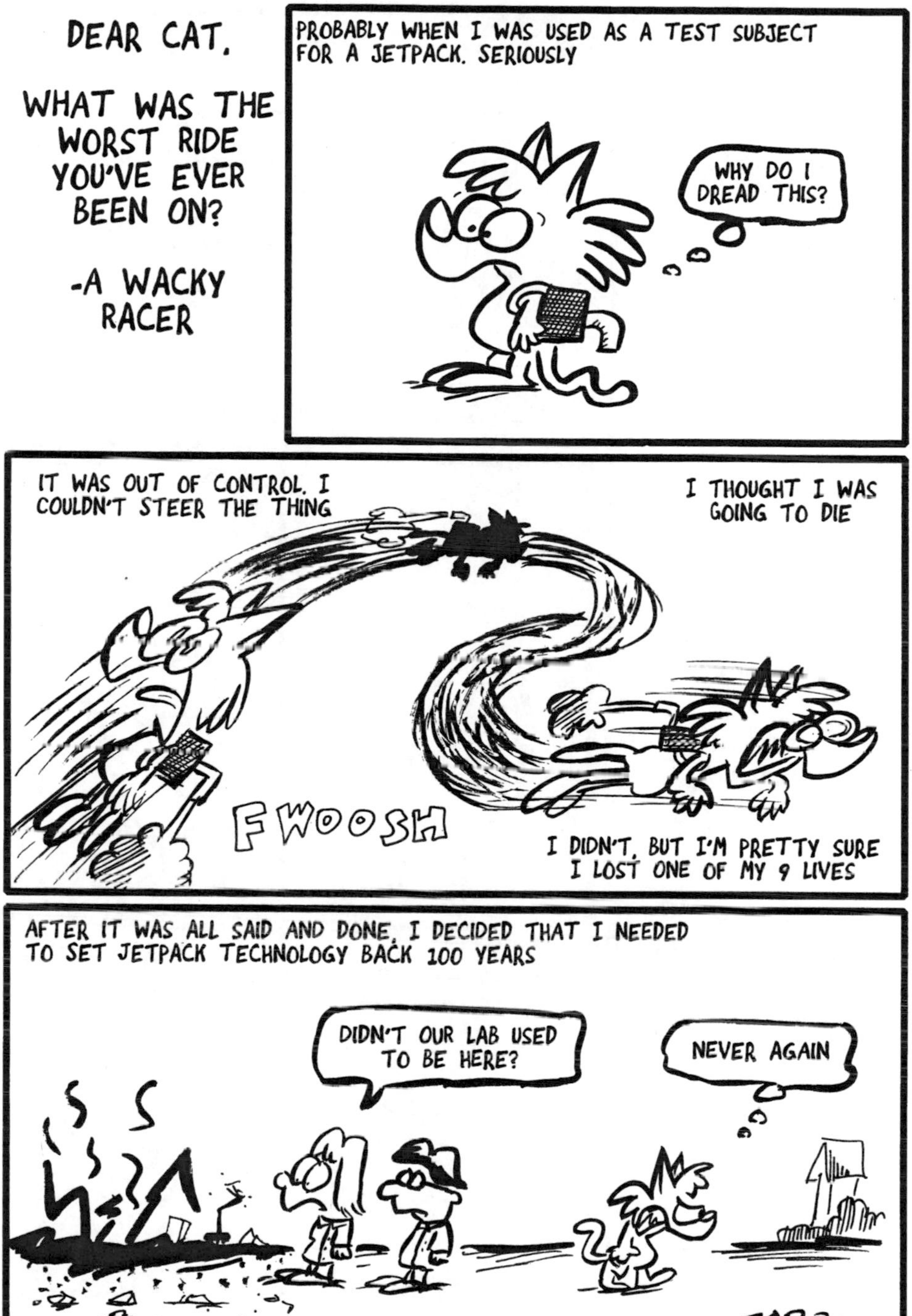
DEAR CAT,
WHAT WAS THE WORST RIDE YOU'VE EVER BEEN ON?
-A WACKY RACER
PROBABLY WHEN I WAS USED AS A TEST SUBJECT FOR A JETPACK. SERIOUSLY
WHY DO I DREAD THIS?
IT WAS OUT OF CONTROL. I COULDN'T STEER THE THING
FWOOSH
I THOUGHT I WAS GOING TO DIE
I DIDN'T, BUT I'M PRETTY SURE I LOST ONE OF MY 9 LIVES
AFTER IT WAS ALL SAID AND DONE, I DECIDED THAT I NEEDED TO SET JETPACK TECHNOLOGY BACK 100 YEARS
DIDN'T OUR LAB USED TO BE HERE?
NEVER AGAIN
CAB 2015

DEAR CAT,

CATS BLINK TO ONE ANOTHER TO SHOW THAT THEY LOVE EACH OTHER. WHAT DO THEY DO WHEN THEY WANT A DIVORCE?

-DISTRESSED CAT

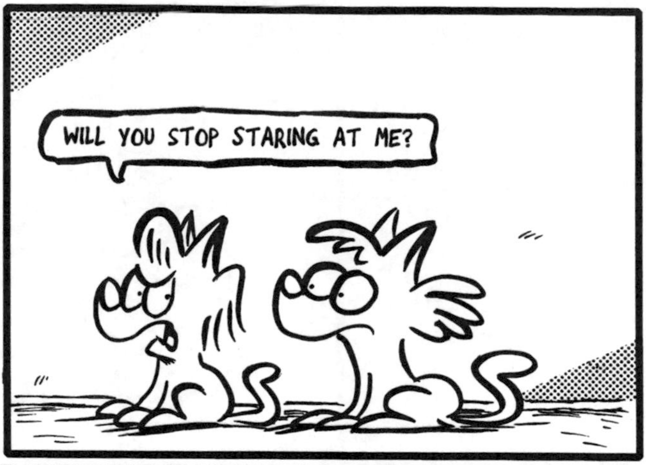
WILL YOU STOP STARING AT ME?

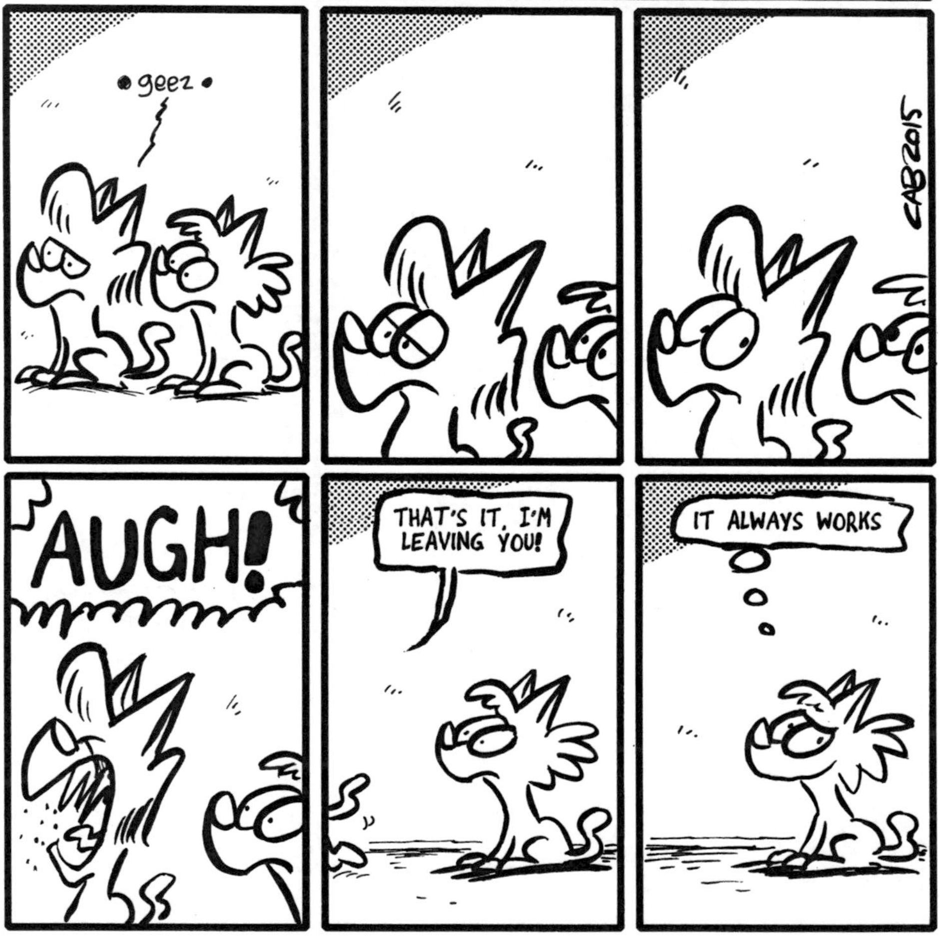
• geez •
CAB2015
AUGH!
THAT'S IT, I'M LEAVING YOU!
IT ALWAYS WORKS

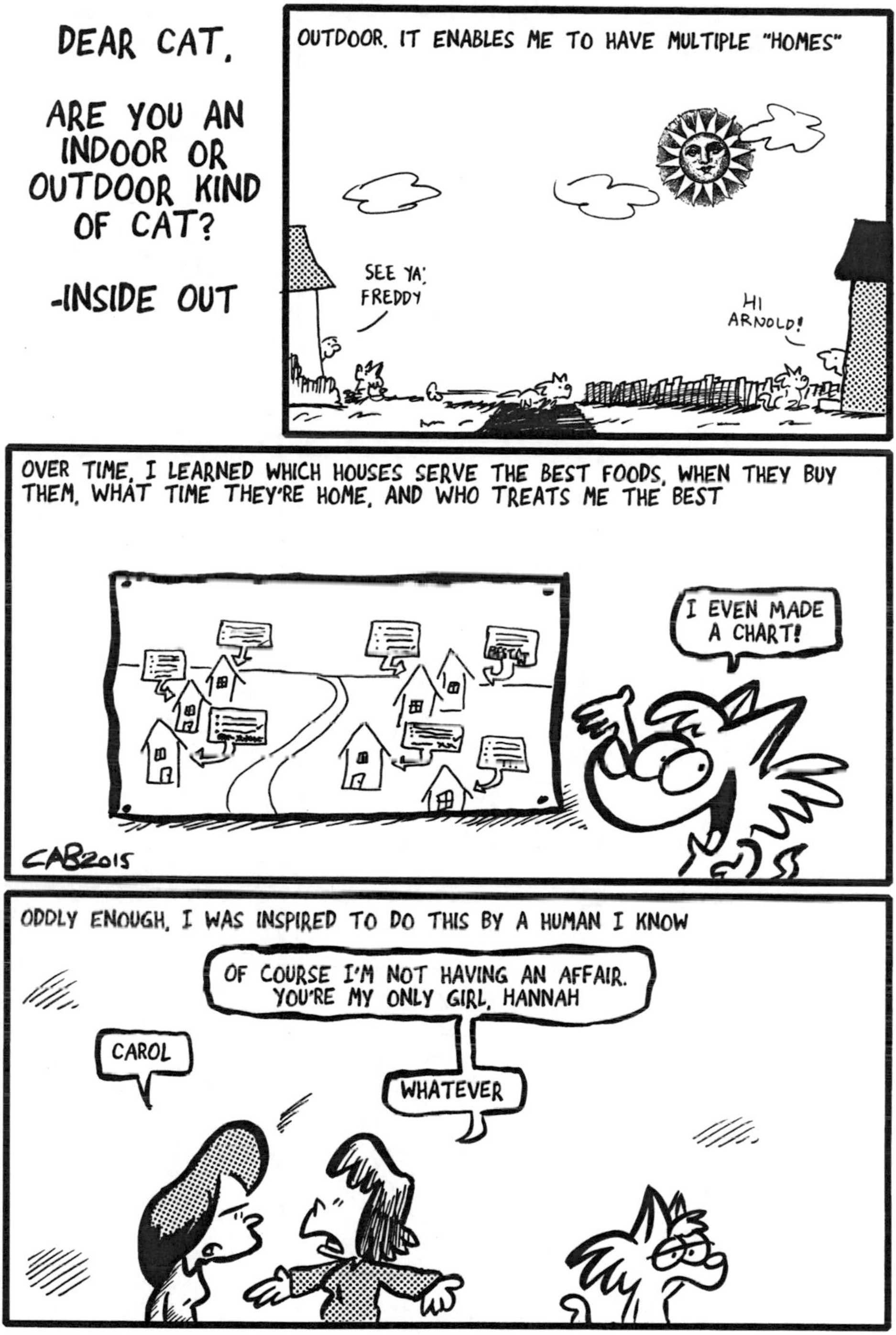
DEAR CAT,
ARE YOU AN INDOOR OR OUTDOOR KIND OF CAT?
-INSIDE OUT
OUTDOOR. IT ENABLES ME TO HAVE MULTIPLE "HOMES"
SEE YA! FREDDY
HI ARNOLD!
OVER TIME, I LEARNED WHICH HOUSES SERVE THE BEST FOODS, WHEN THEY BUY THEM, WHAT TIME THEY'RE HOME, AND WHO TREATS ME THE BEST
I EVEN MADE A CHART!
CAB2015
ODDLY ENOUGH, I WAS INSPIRED TO DO THIS BY A HUMAN I KNOW
OF COURSE I'M NOT HAVING AN AFFAIR. YOU'RE MY ONLY GIRL, HANNAH
CAROL
WHATEVER

DEAR CAT,

WHAT DO YOU THINK OF MUSTARD?

- CATSUP CAT

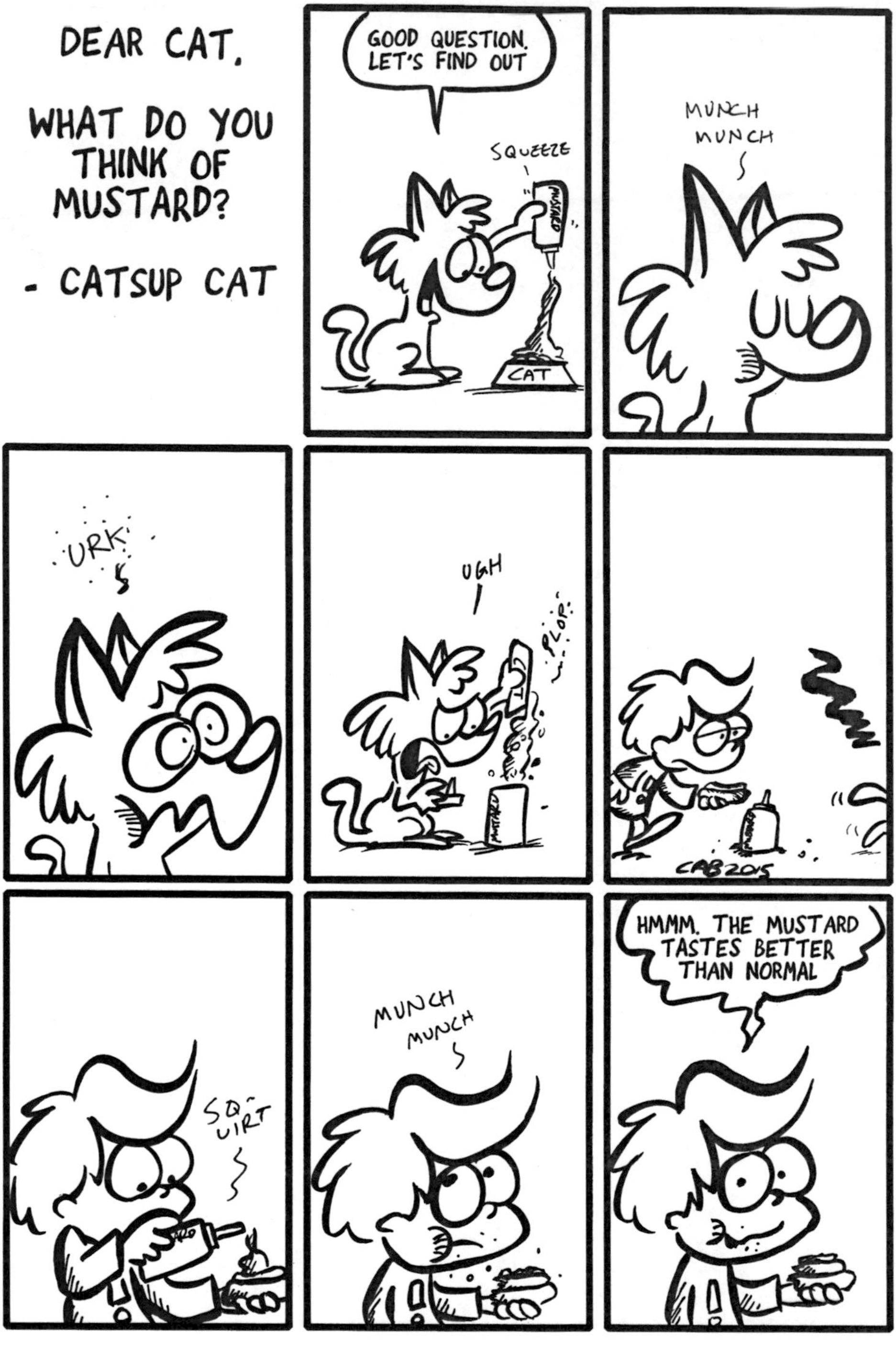

GOOD QUESTION. LET'S FIND OUT
SQUEEZE
MUSTARD
CAT
MUNCH MUNCH
URK
UGH
PLOP
MUSTARD
CAB2015
HMMM. THE MUSTARD TASTES BETTER THAN NORMAL

DEAR CAT,

HOW CAN YOU BE PROTECTED FROM OTHER CARTOONISTS STEALING YOUR CHARACTERS?

-NOT-SO-KRAZY KAT

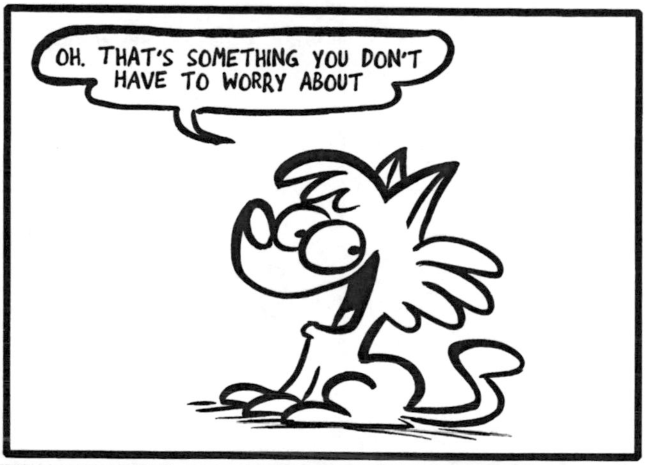
OH. THAT'S SOMETHING YOU DON'T HAVE TO WORRY ABOUT

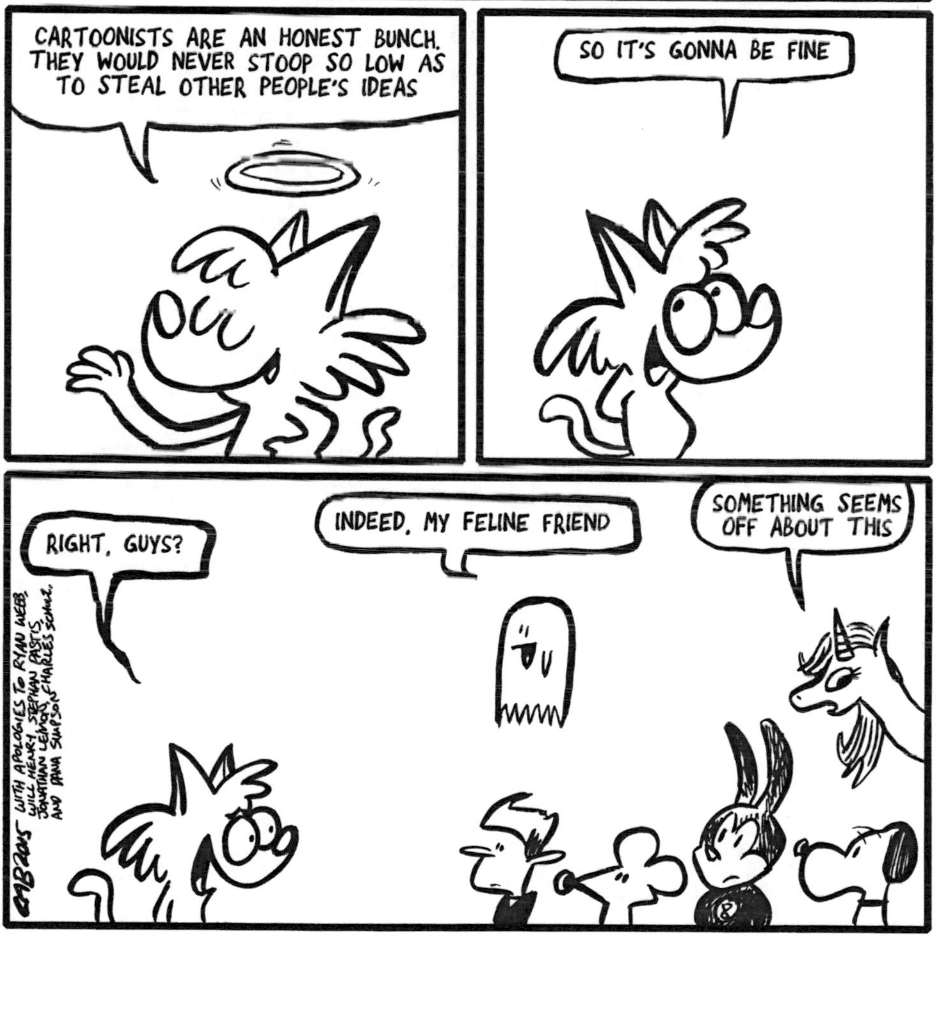
CARTOONISTS ARE AN HONEST BUNCH. THEY WOULD NEVER STOOP SO LOW AS TO STEAL OTHER PEOPLE'S IDEAS
SO IT'S GONNA BE FINE
RIGHT, GUYS?
INDEED, MY FELINE FRIEND
SOMETHING SEEMS OFF ABOUT THIS
GAB2015
WITH APOLOGIES TO RYAN WEBB, WILL HENRY, STEPHAN PASTIS, JONATHAN LEMON, CHARLES SCHULZ, AND DANA SIMPSON

DEAR CAT,

DO YOU HAVE A PET?

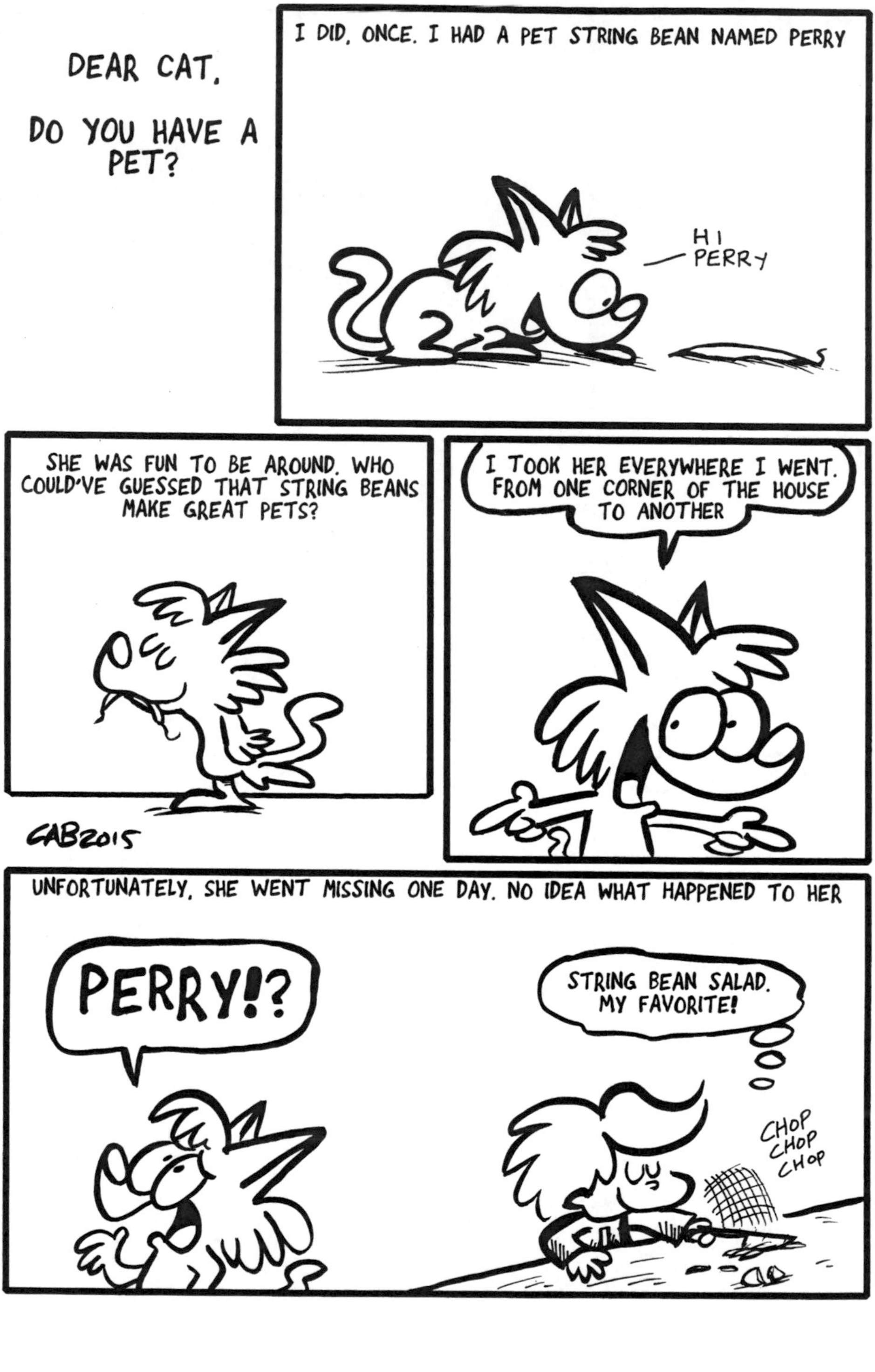

I DID, ONCE. I HAD A PET STRING BEAN NAMED PERRY
HI PERRY
SHE WAS FUN TO BE AROUND. WHO COULD'VE GUESSED THAT STRING BEANS MAKE GREAT PETS?
I TOOK HER EVERYWHERE I WENT. FROM ONE CORNER OF THE HOUSE TO ANOTHER
GAB2015
UNFORTUNATELY, SHE WENT MISSING ONE DAY. NO IDEA WHAT HAPPENED TO HER
PERRY!?
STRING BEAN SALAD. MY FAVORITE!
CHOP CHOP CHOP

DEAR CAT,

DO YOU HAVE A FAVORITE CHAIR?

-STOOL PIGEON

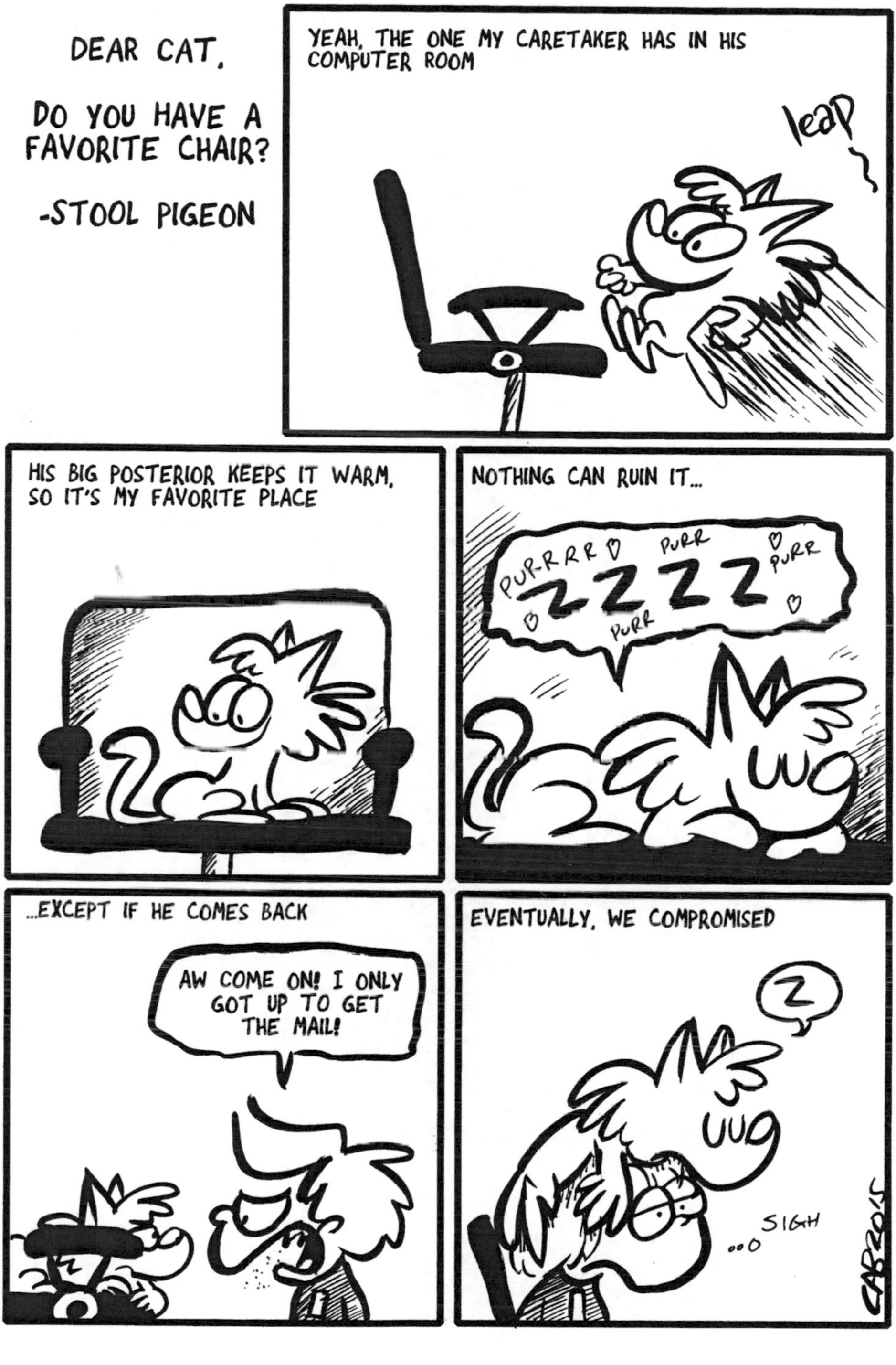
YEAH, THE ONE MY CARETAKER HAS IN HIS COMPUTER ROOM
leap
HIS BIG POSTERIOR KEEPS IT WARM, SO IT'S MY FAVORITE PLACE
NOTHING CAN RUIN IT...
PURRRR ZZZZ PURR PURR PURR
...EXCEPT IF HE COMES BACK
AW COME ON! I ONLY GOT UP TO GET THE MAIL!
EVENTUALLY, WE COMPROMISED
Z
SIGH

DEAR CAT,

WHAT ARE CAT EDITORIAL CARTOONS LIKE?

-MAN IN TOO MUCH DEBT

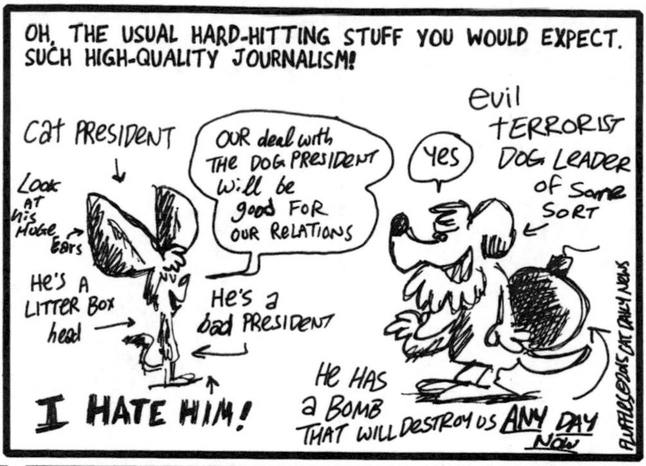
OH, THE USUAL HARD-HITTING STUFF YOU WOULD EXPECT. SUCH HIGH-QUALITY JOURNALISM!
Cat PRESIDENT
Look at his Huge Ears
He's a LITTER Box head
OUR deal with THE DOG PRESIDENT will be good FOR OUR RELATIONS
He's a bad PRESIDENT
I HATE HIM!
Yes
evil TERRORIST DOG LEADER of Some SORT
He HAS a BOMB THAT WILL DESTROY US ANY DAY NOW

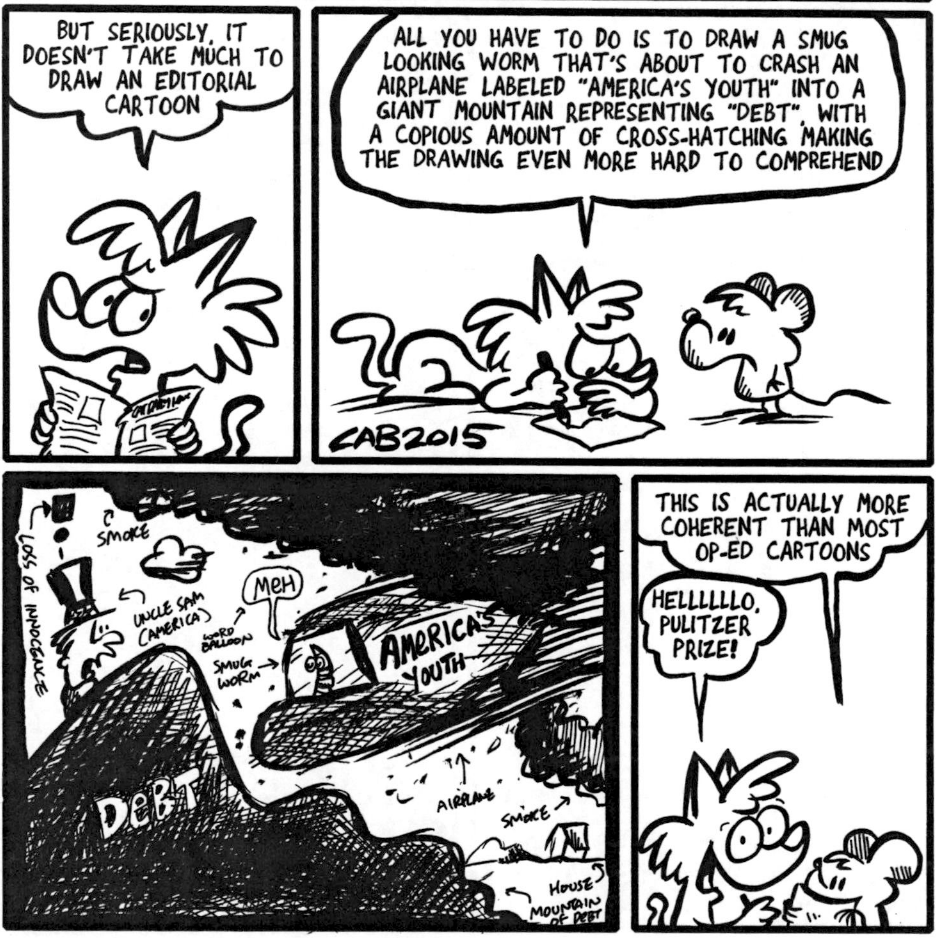
BUT SERIOUSLY, IT DOESN'T TAKE MUCH TO DRAW AN EDITORIAL CARTOON
ALL YOU HAVE TO DO IS TO DRAW A SMUG LOOKING WORM THAT'S ABOUT TO CRASH AN AIRPLANE LABELED "AMERICA'S YOUTH" INTO A GIANT MOUNTAIN REPRESENTING "DEBT", WITH A COPIOUS AMOUNT OF CROSS-HATCHING MAKING THE DRAWING EVEN MORE HARD TO COMPREHEND
CAB2015
SMOKE
LOSS OF INNOCENCE
UNCLE SAM (AMERICA)
MEH
WORD BALLOON
SMUG WORM
AMERICA'S YOUTH
DEBT
AIRPLANE
SMOKE
HOUSE
MOUNTAIN OF DEBT
THIS IS ACTUALLY MORE COHERENT THAN MOST OP-ED CARTOONS
HELLLLLLO, PULITZER PRIZE!

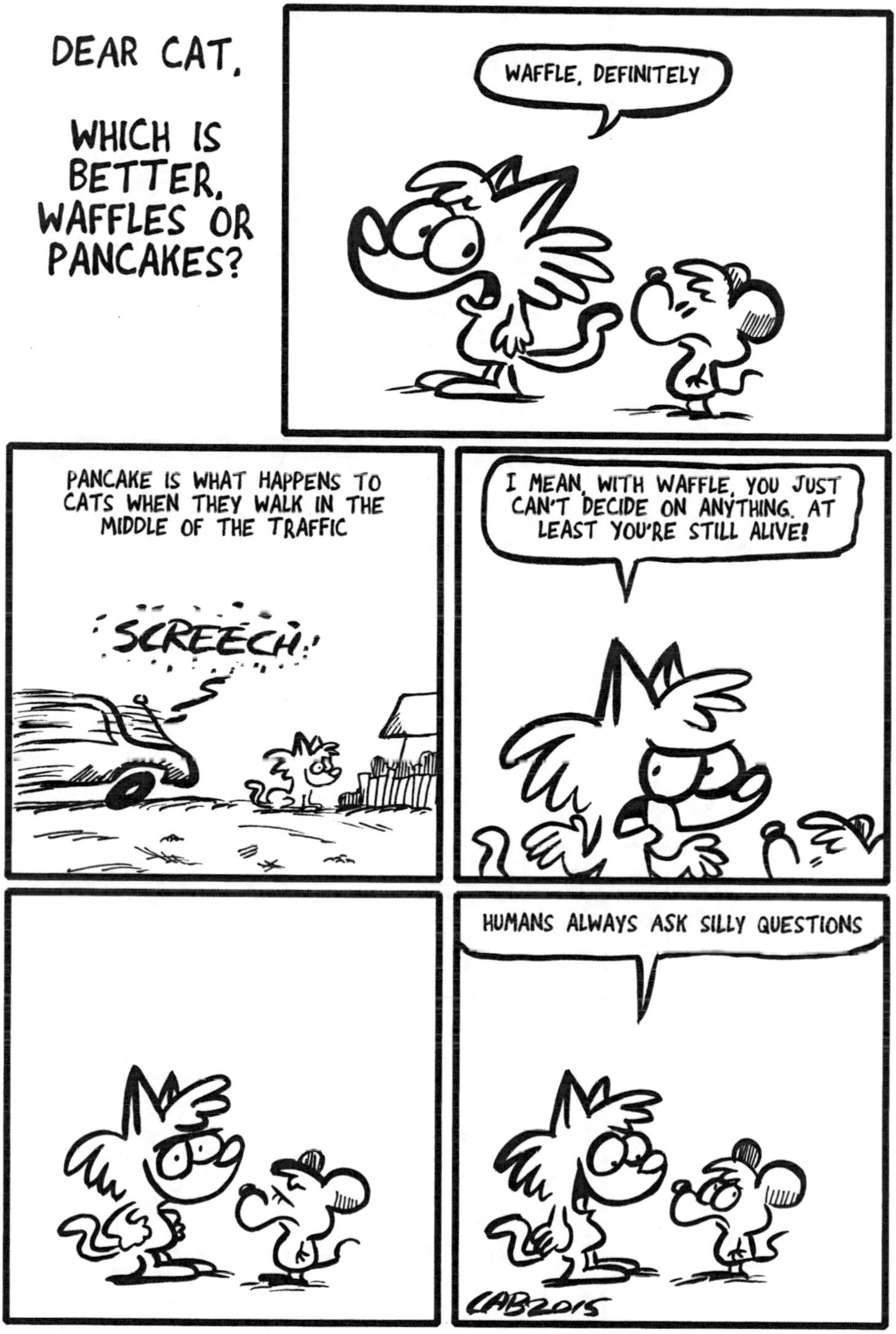
DEAR CAT,
WHICH IS BETTER, WAFFLES OR PANCAKES?
WAFFLE, DEFINITELY
PANCAKE IS WHAT HAPPENS TO CATS WHEN THEY WALK IN THE MIDDLE OF THE TRAFFIC
SCREECH
I MEAN, WITH WAFFLE, YOU JUST CAN'T DECIDE ON ANYTHING. AT LEAST YOU'RE STILL ALIVE!
HUMANS ALWAYS ASK SILLY QUESTIONS
CAB2015

DEAR CAT,

EVER MET A WALKING CATFISH?

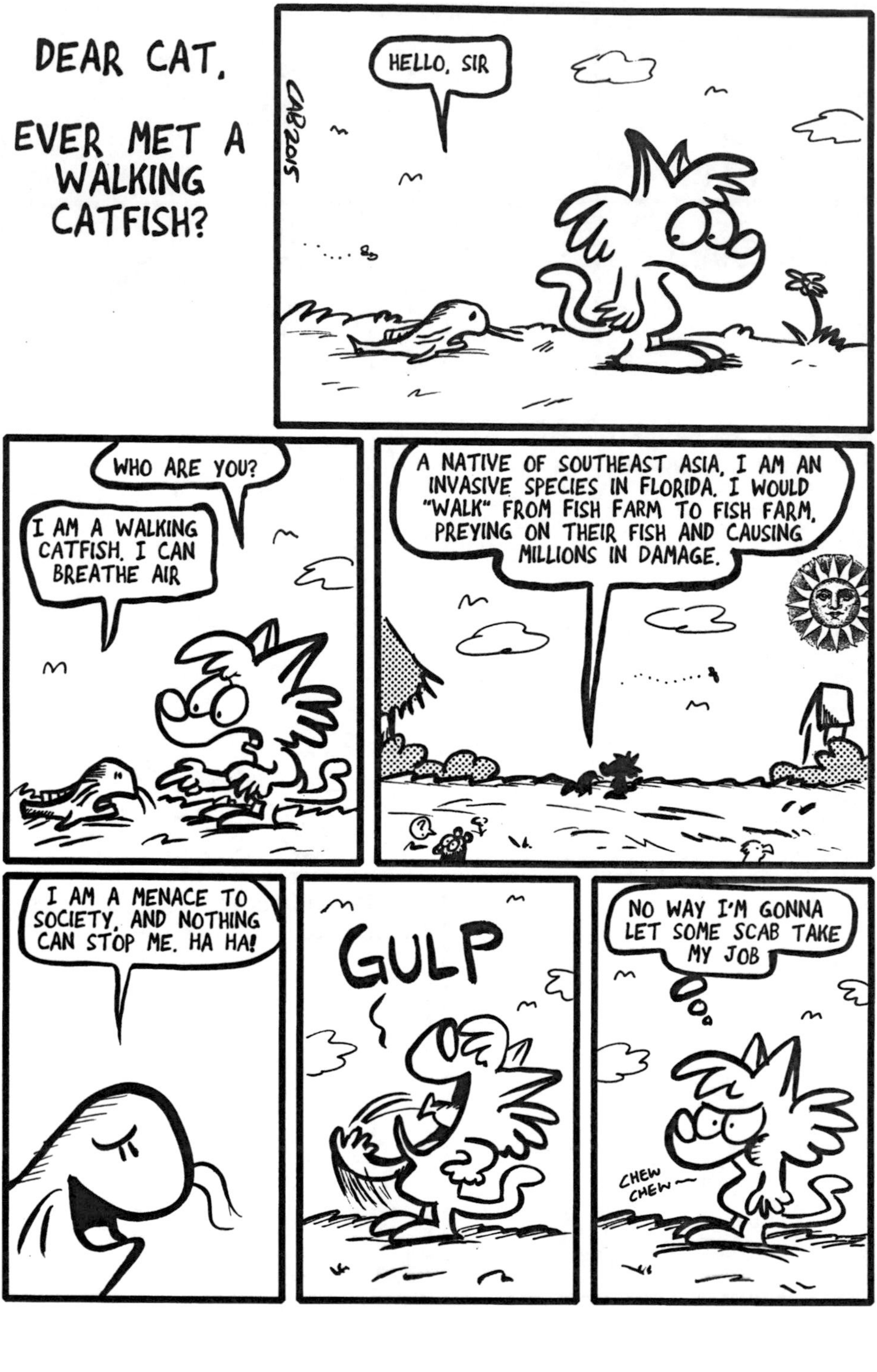
HELLO, SIR
CAB 2015
WHO ARE YOU?
I AM A WALKING CATFISH. I CAN BREATHE AIR
A NATIVE OF SOUTHEAST ASIA, I AM AN INVASIVE SPECIES IN FLORIDA. I WOULD "WALK" FROM FISH FARM TO FISH FARM, PREYING ON THEIR FISH AND CAUSING MILLIONS IN DAMAGE.
I AM A MENACE TO SOCIETY, AND NOTHING CAN STOP ME. HA HA!
GULP
NO WAY I'M GONNA LET SOME SCAB TAKE MY JOB
CHEW CHEW

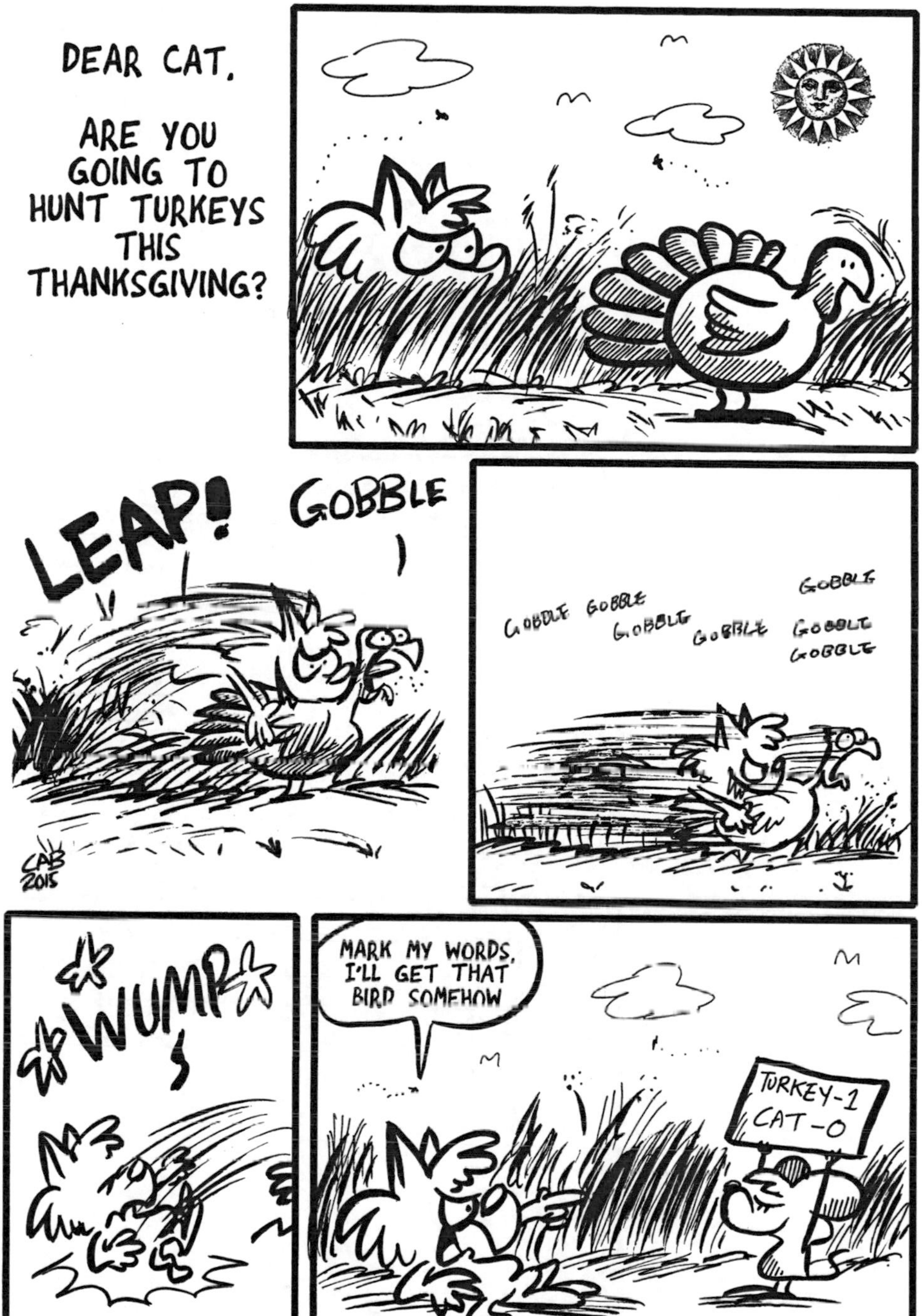
DEAR CAT,
ARE YOU GOING TO HUNT TURKEYS THIS THANKSGIVING?
LEAP!
GOBBLE
CAB 2015
GOBBLE GOBBLE GOBBLE GOBBLE GOBBLE GOBBLE GOBBLE
WUMP
MARK MY WORDS, I'LL GET THAT BIRD SOMEHOW
TURKEY-1 CAT-0

Dear Beneficiary,

kindly contact us back for your payment.

Remain Bless,
Mr.Ben Taka
Western Union

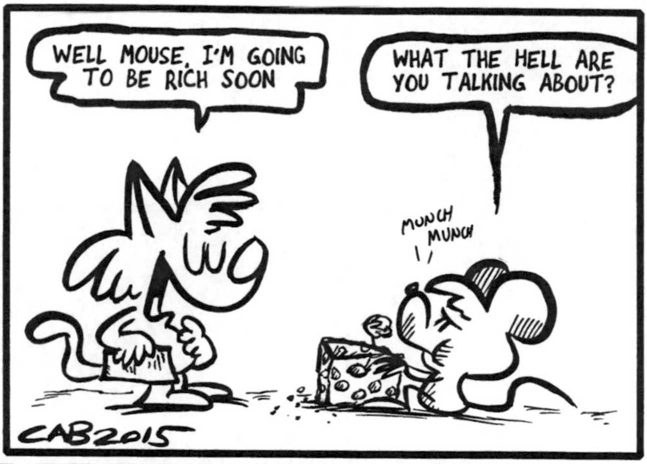
WELL MOUSE, I'M GOING TO BE RICH SOON
WHAT THE HELL ARE YOU TALKING ABOUT?
MUNCH MUNCH
CAB2015

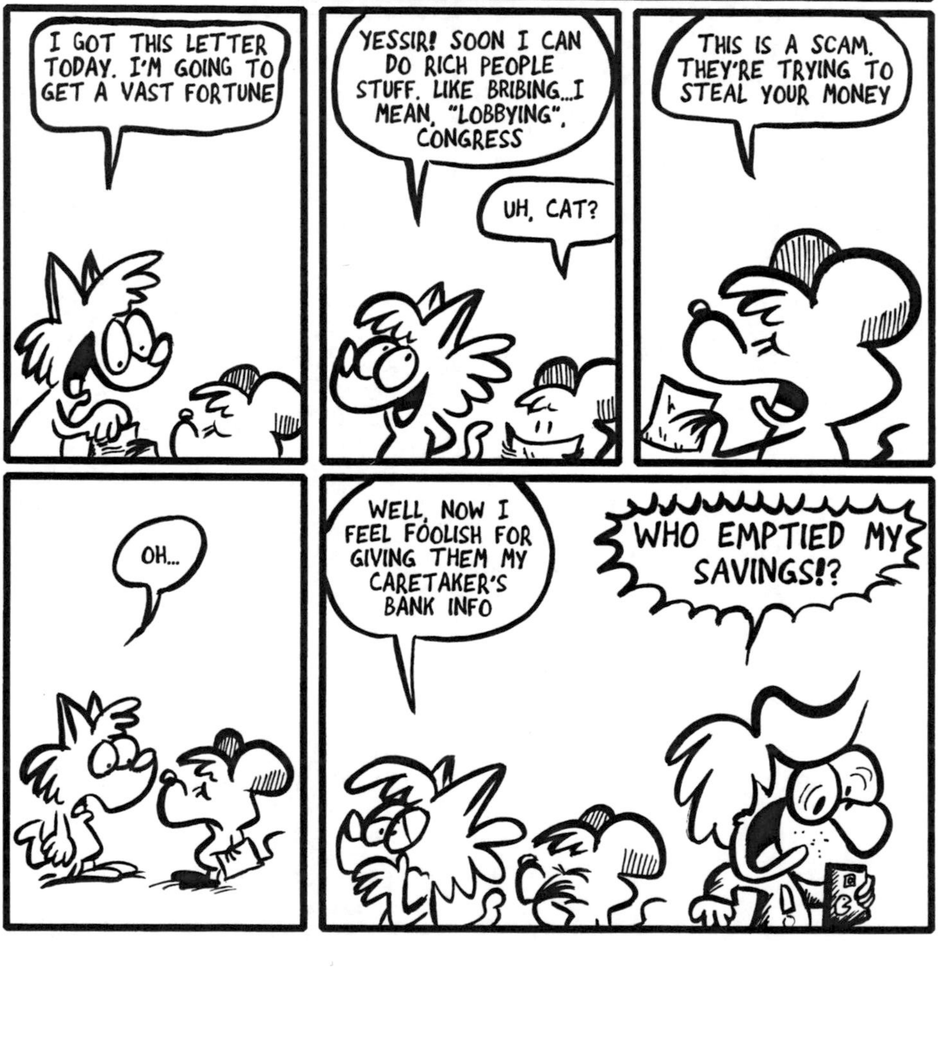
I GOT THIS LETTER TODAY. I'M GOING TO GET A VAST FORTUNE
YESSIR! SOON I CAN DO RICH PEOPLE STUFF. LIKE BRIBING...I MEAN, "LOBBYING", CONGRESS
UH, CAT?
THIS IS A SCAM. THEY'RE TRYING TO STEAL YOUR MONEY
OH...
WELL, NOW I FEEL FOOLISH FOR GIVING THEM MY CARETAKER'S BANK INFO
WHO EMPTIED MY SAVINGS!?

DEAR CAT,

DO YOU LIKE SNOW?

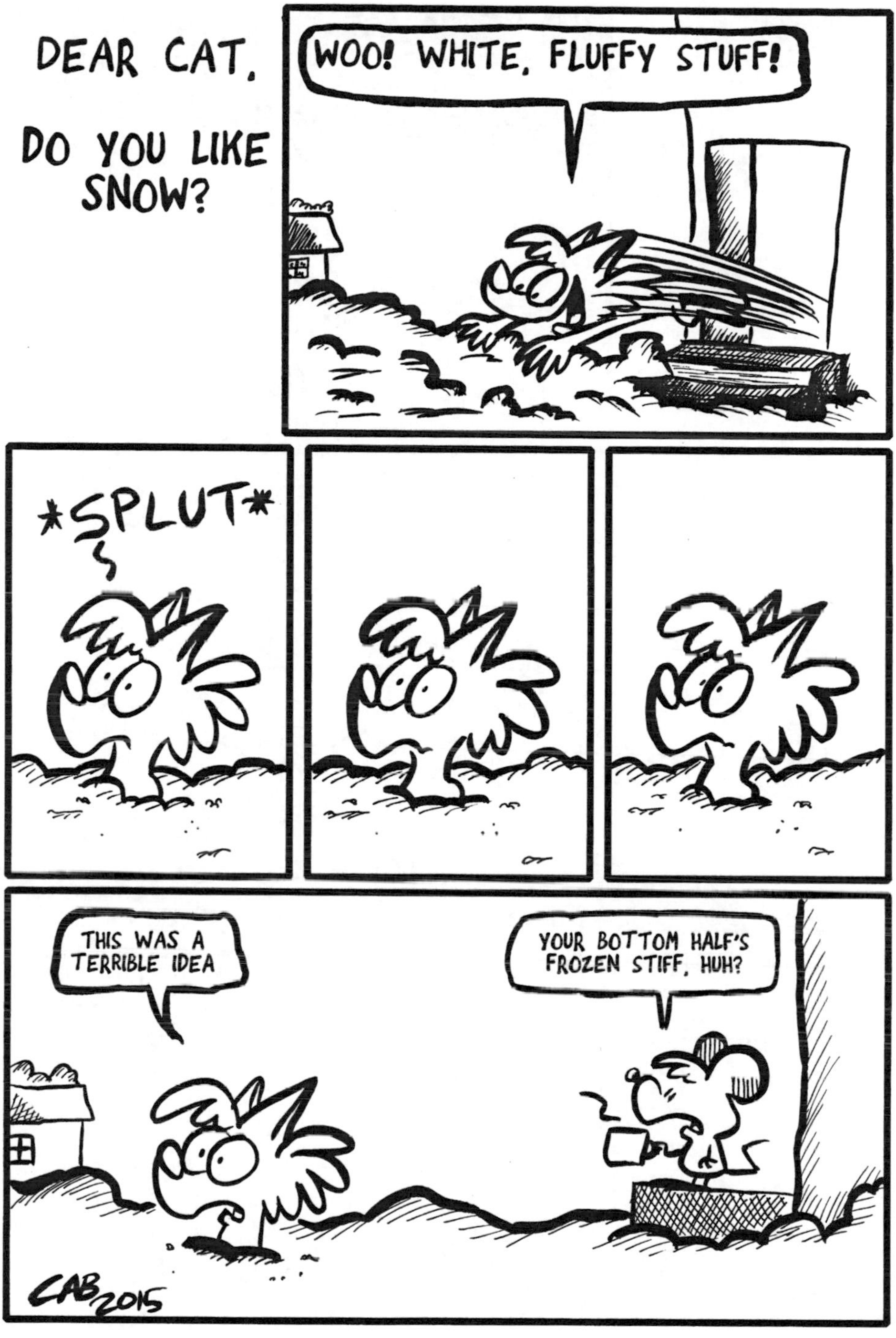
WOO! WHITE, FLUFFY STUFF!
SPLUT
THIS WAS A TERRIBLE IDEA
YOUR BOTTOM HALF'S FROZEN STIFF, HUH?
CAB 2015

DEAR CAT,

ARE YOU PREPARED FOR CHRISTMAS?

- A BASS NAMED RANKIN

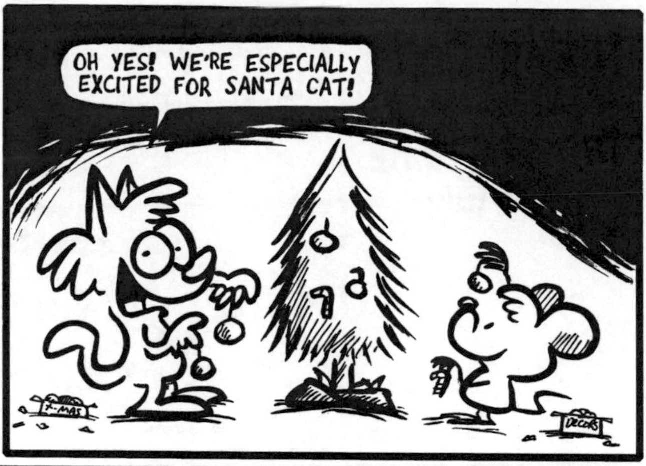
OH YES! WE'RE ESPECIALLY EXCITED FOR SANTA CAT!

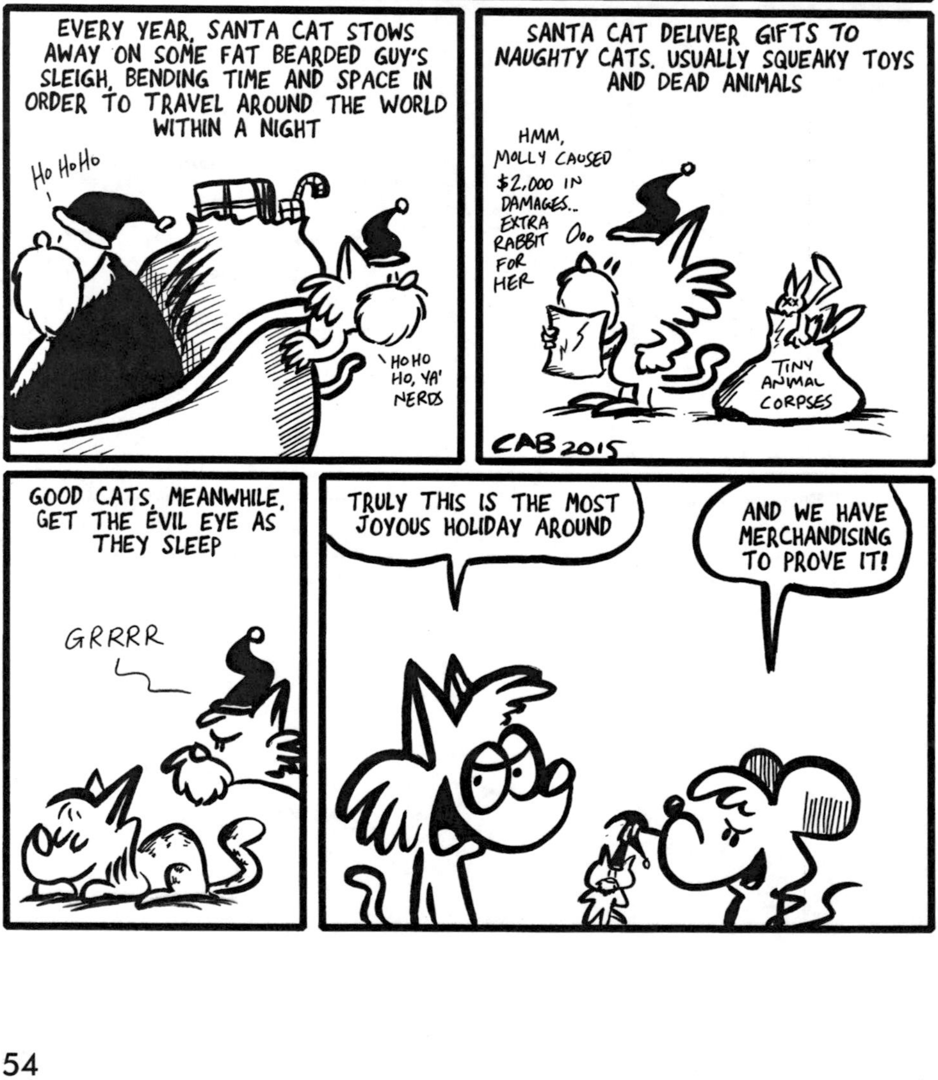
EVERY YEAR, SANTA CAT STOWS AWAY ON SOME FAT BEARDED GUY'S SLEIGH, BENDING TIME AND SPACE IN ORDER TO TRAVEL AROUND THE WORLD WITHIN A NIGHT
Ho HoHo
HO HO HO, YA' NERDS
SANTA CAT DELIVER GIFTS TO NAUGHTY CATS. USUALLY SQUEAKY TOYS AND DEAD ANIMALS
HMM, MOLLY CAUSED $2,000 IN DAMAGES.. EXTRA RABBIT FOR HER
TINY ANIMAL CORPSES
CAB 2015
GOOD CATS, MEANWHILE, GET THE EVIL EYE AS THEY SLEEP
GRRRR
TRULY THIS IS THE MOST JOYOUS HOLIDAY AROUND
AND WE HAVE MERCHANDISING TO PROVE IT!

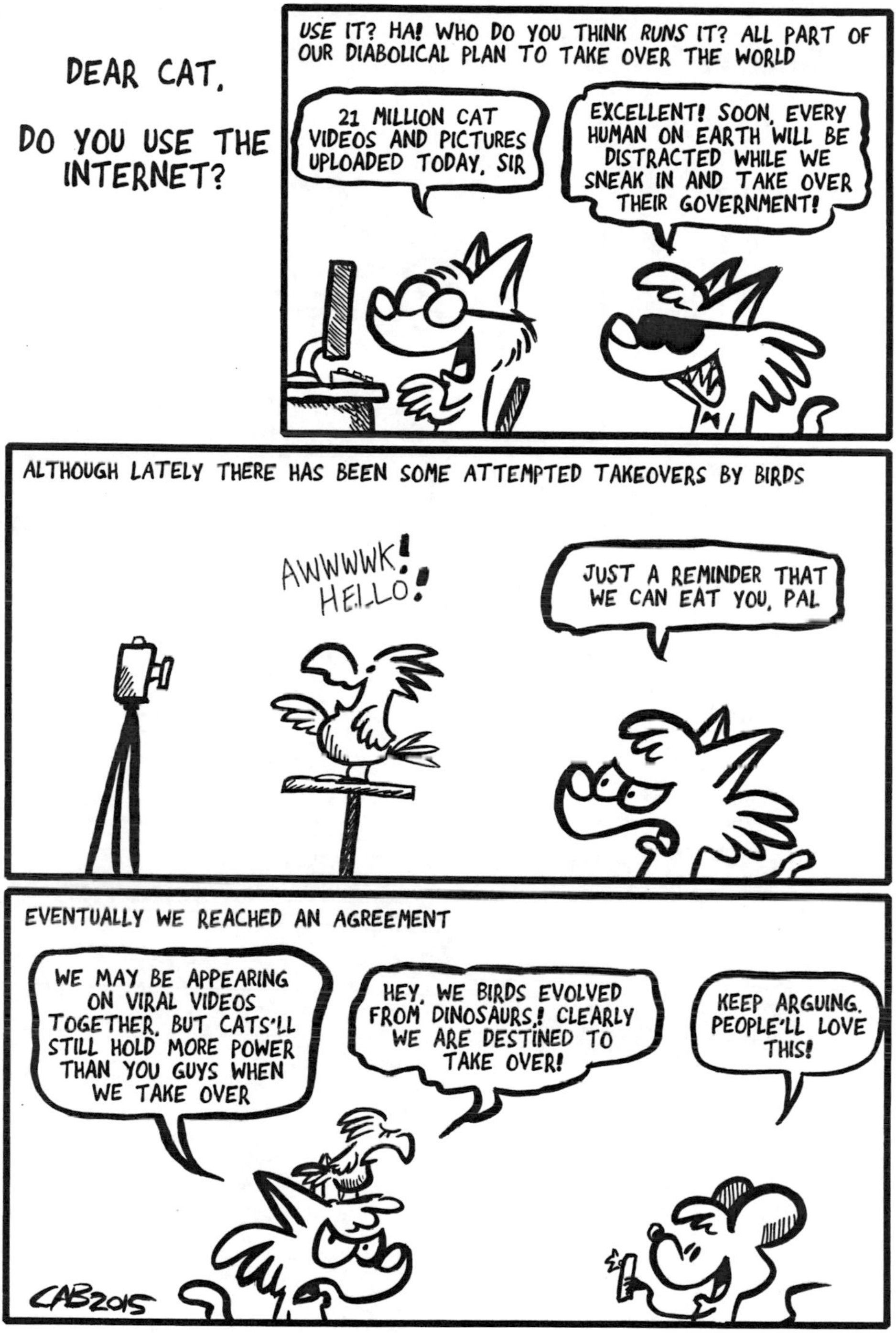
DEAR CAT,
DO YOU USE THE INTERNET?
USE IT? HA! WHO DO YOU THINK RUNS IT? ALL PART OF OUR DIABOLICAL PLAN TO TAKE OVER THE WORLD
21 MILLION CAT VIDEOS AND PICTURES UPLOADED TODAY, SIR
EXCELLENT! SOON, EVERY HUMAN ON EARTH WILL BE DISTRACTED WHILE WE SNEAK IN AND TAKE OVER THEIR GOVERNMENT!
ALTHOUGH LATELY THERE HAS BEEN SOME ATTEMPTED TAKEOVERS BY BIRDS
AWWWWK! HELLO!
JUST A REMINDER THAT WE CAN EAT YOU, PAL
EVENTUALLY WE REACHED AN AGREEMENT
WE MAY BE APPEARING ON VIRAL VIDEOS TOGETHER, BUT CATS'LL STILL HOLD MORE POWER THAN YOU GUYS WHEN WE TAKE OVER
HEY, WE BIRDS EVOLVED FROM DINOSAURS! CLEARLY WE ARE DESTINED TO TAKE OVER!
KEEP ARGUING. PEOPLE'LL LOVE THIS!
CAB2015

DEAR CAT,

HOW DO CATS ALWAYS LAND ON THEIR FEET?

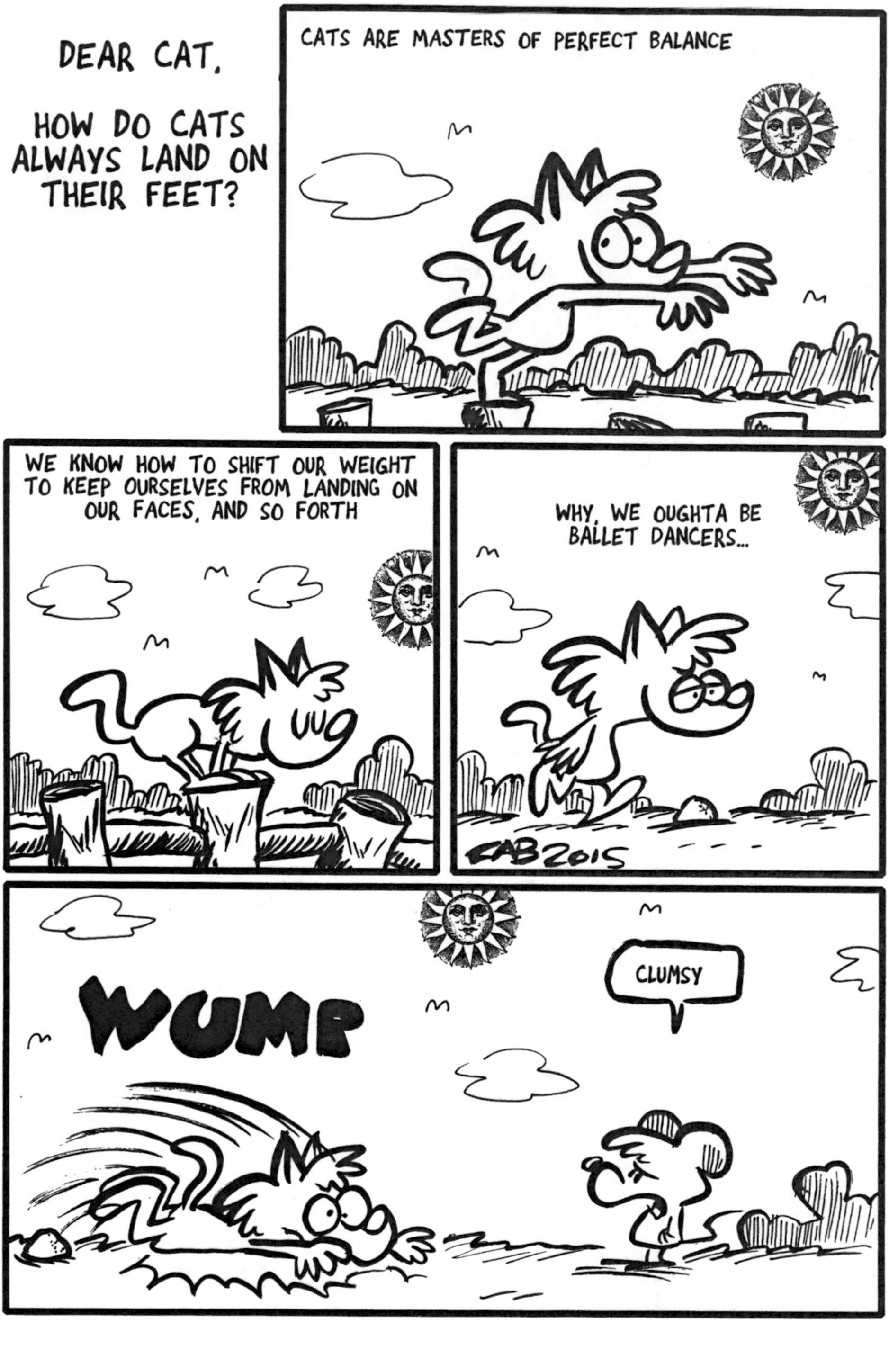
CATS ARE MASTERS OF PERFECT BALANCE
WE KNOW HOW TO SHIFT OUR WEIGHT TO KEEP OURSELVES FROM LANDING ON OUR FACES, AND SO FORTH
WHY, WE OUGHTA BE BALLET DANCERS...
CAB 2015
WUMP
CLUMSY

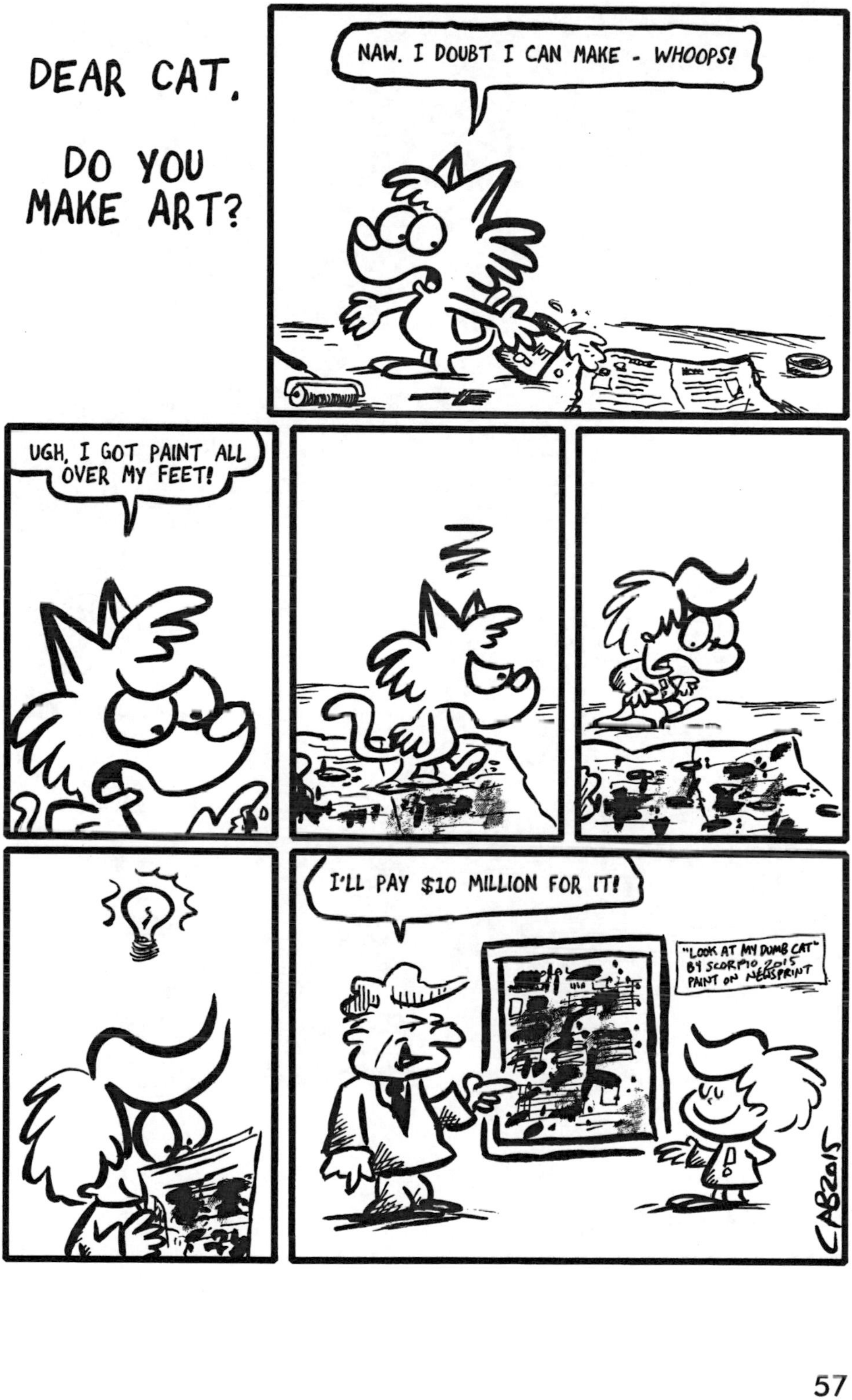
DEAR CAT,
DO YOU MAKE ART?
NAW. I DOUBT I CAN MAKE - WHOOPS!
UGH, I GOT PAINT ALL OVER MY FEET!
I'LL PAY $10 MILLION FOR IT!
"LOOK AT MY DUMB CAT"
BY SCORPIO 2015
PAINT ON NEWSPRINT
CAB2015

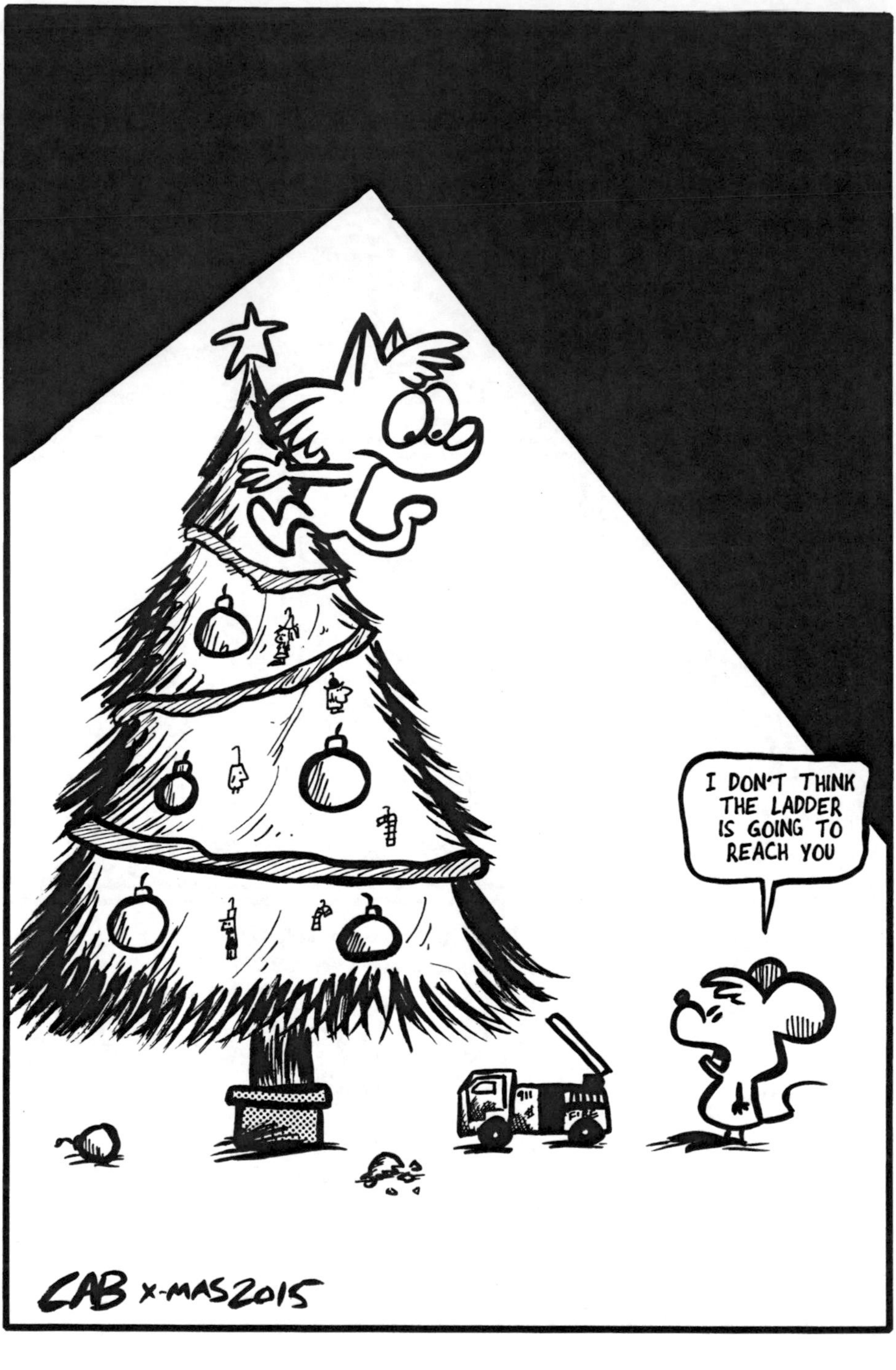
I DON'T THINK THE LADDER IS GOING TO REACH YOU
CAB X-MAS 2015

DEAR CAT,

DO YOU REALLY EXIST OR NOT?

-MR. SHRODINGER

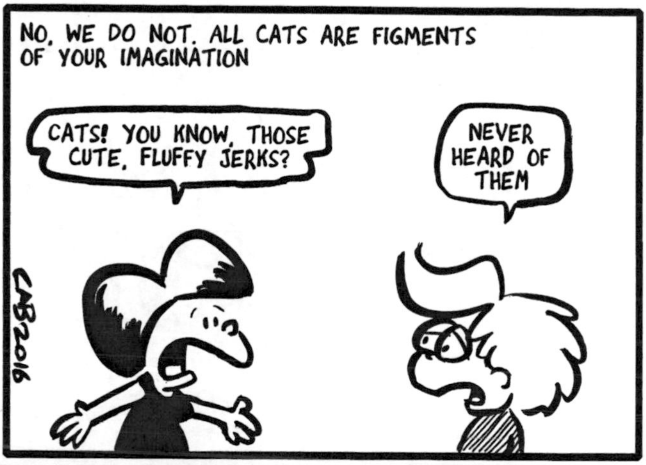
NO, WE DO NOT. ALL CATS ARE FIGMENTS OF YOUR IMAGINATION
CATS! YOU KNOW, THOSE CUTE, FLUFFY JERKS?
NEVER HEARD OF THEM
CAB 2016

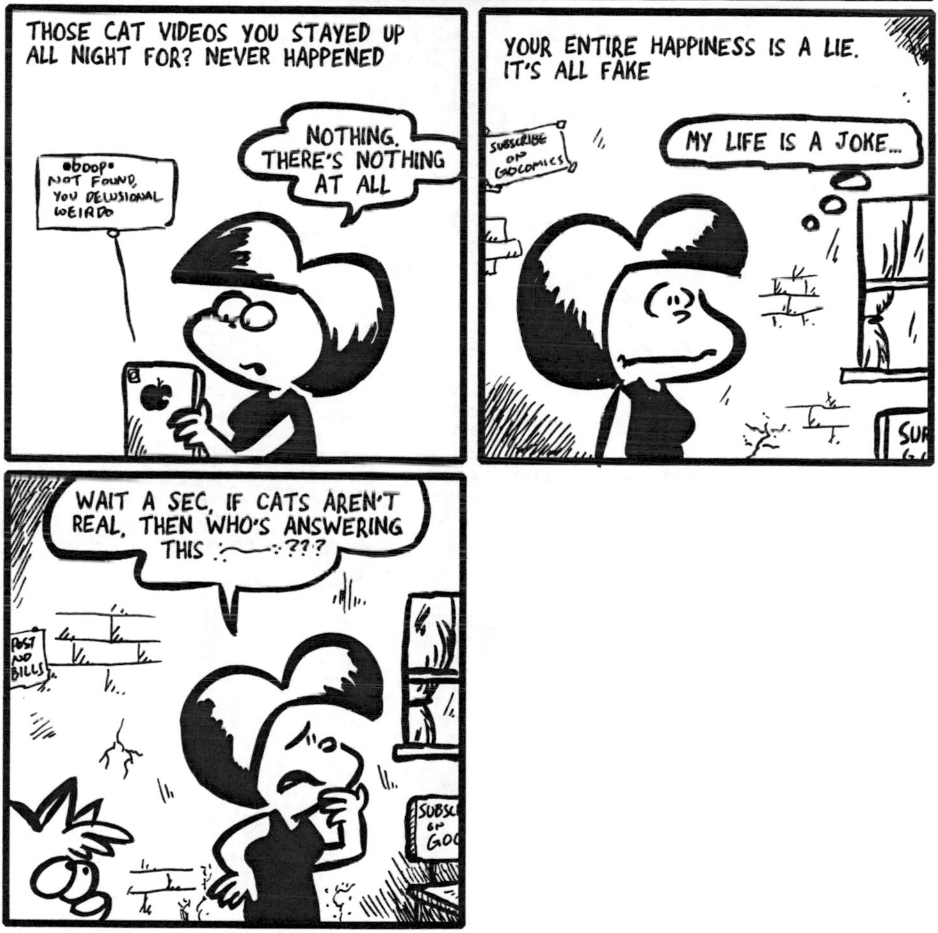
THOSE CAT VIDEOS YOU STAYED UP ALL NIGHT FOR? NEVER HAPPENED
•boop• NOT FOUND, YOU DELUSIONAL WEIRDO
NOTHING. THERE'S NOTHING AT ALL
YOUR ENTIRE HAPPINESS IS A LIE. IT'S ALL FAKE
SUBSCRIBE ON GOCOMICS
MY LIFE IS A JOKE...
WAIT A SEC, IF CATS AREN'T REAL, THEN WHO'S ANSWERING THIS ???
POST NO BILLS

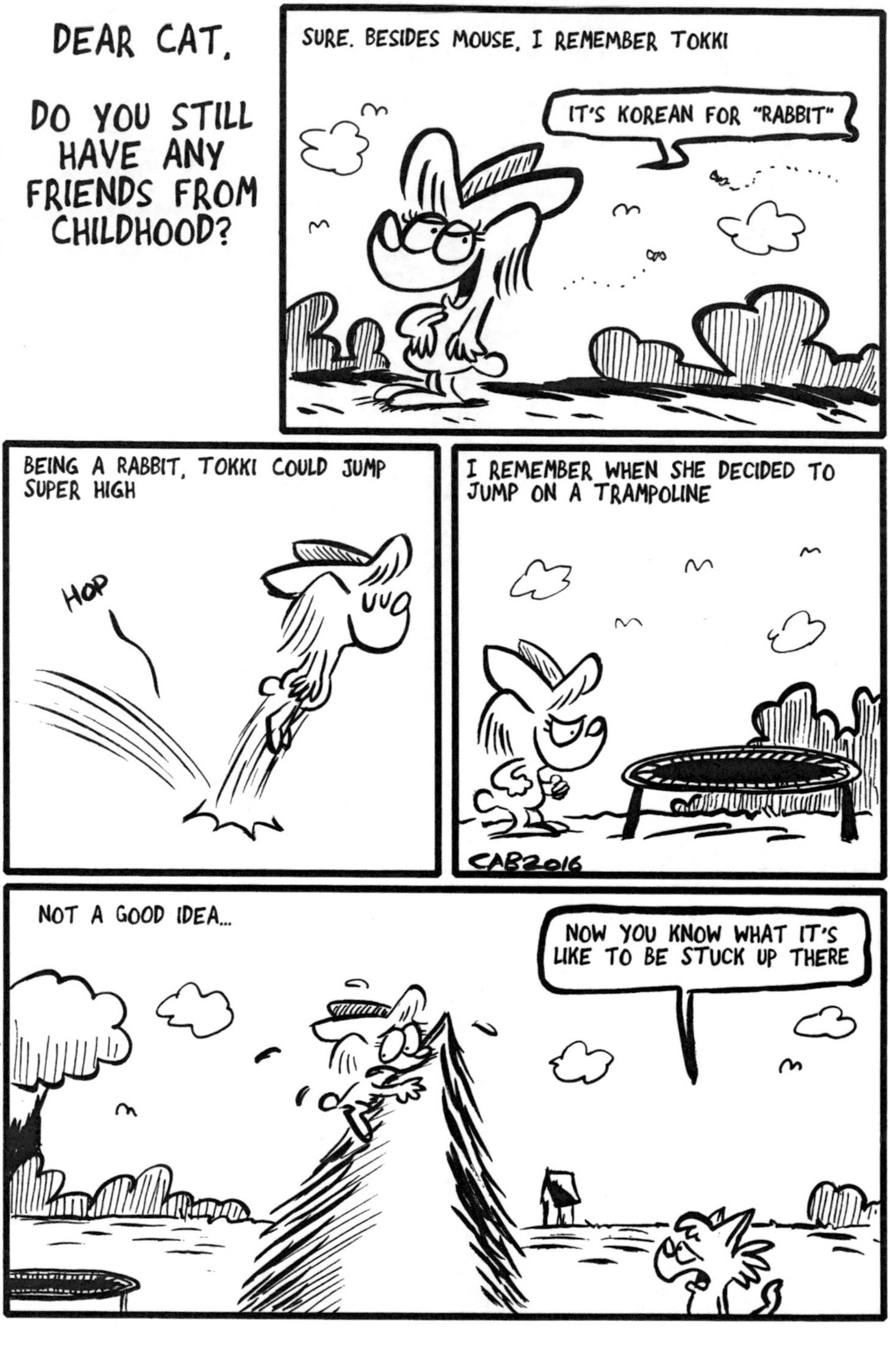
DEAR CAT,
DO YOU STILL HAVE ANY FRIENDS FROM CHILDHOOD?
SURE. BESIDES MOUSE, I REMEMBER TOKKI
IT'S KOREAN FOR "RABBIT"
BEING A RABBIT, TOKKI COULD JUMP SUPER HIGH
HOP
I REMEMBER WHEN SHE DECIDED TO JUMP ON A TRAMPOLINE
CAB2016
NOT A GOOD IDEA...
NOW YOU KNOW WHAT IT'S LIKE TO BE STUCK UP THERE

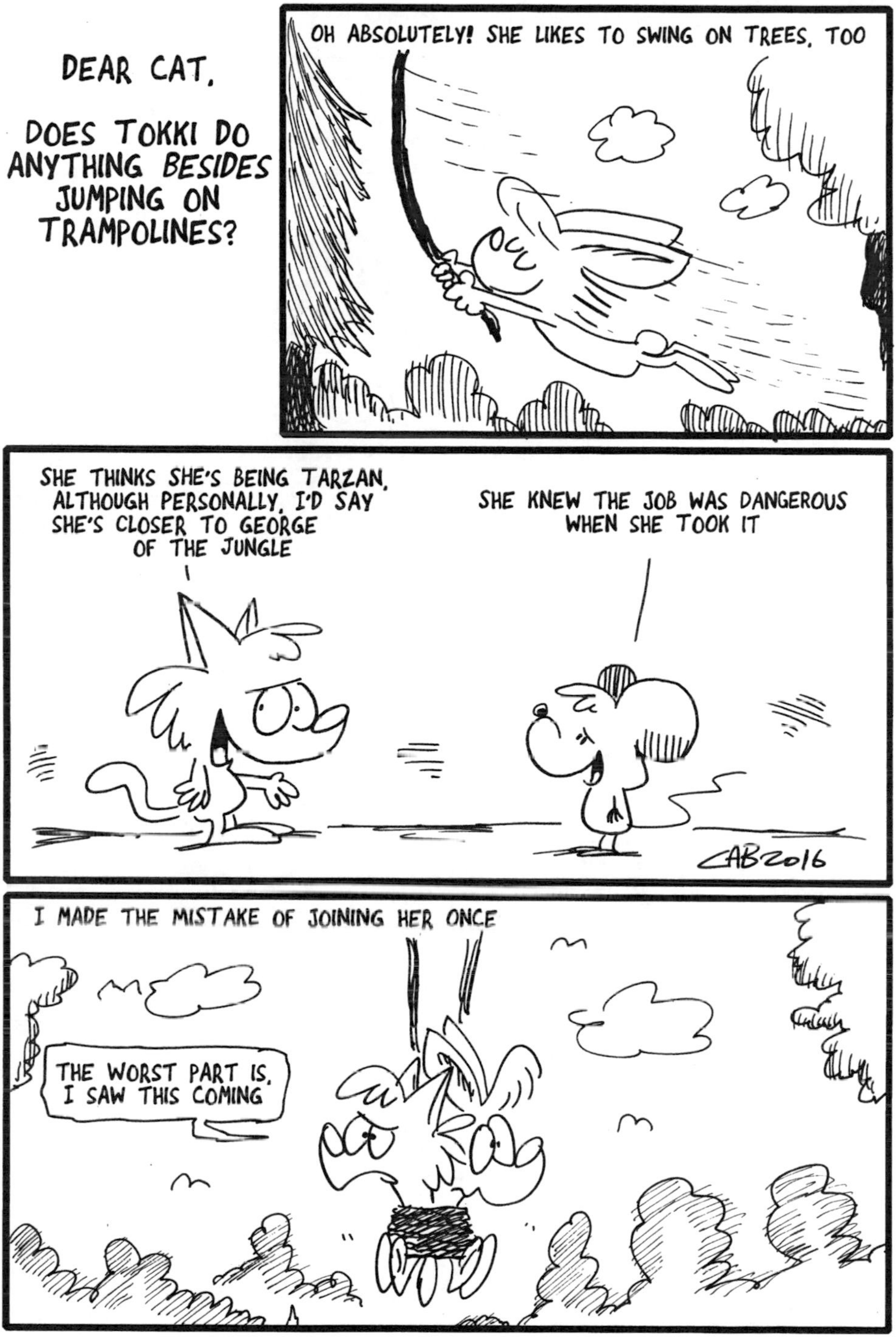
DEAR CAT,
DOES TOKKI DO ANYTHING BESIDES JUMPING ON TRAMPOLINES?
OH ABSOLUTELY! SHE LIKES TO SWING ON TREES, TOO
SHE THINKS SHE'S BEING TARZAN, ALTHOUGH PERSONALLY, I'D SAY SHE'S CLOSER TO GEORGE OF THE JUNGLE
SHE KNEW THE JOB WAS DANGEROUS WHEN SHE TOOK IT
CAB 2016
I MADE THE MISTAKE OF JOINING HER ONCE
THE WORST PART IS, I SAW THIS COMING

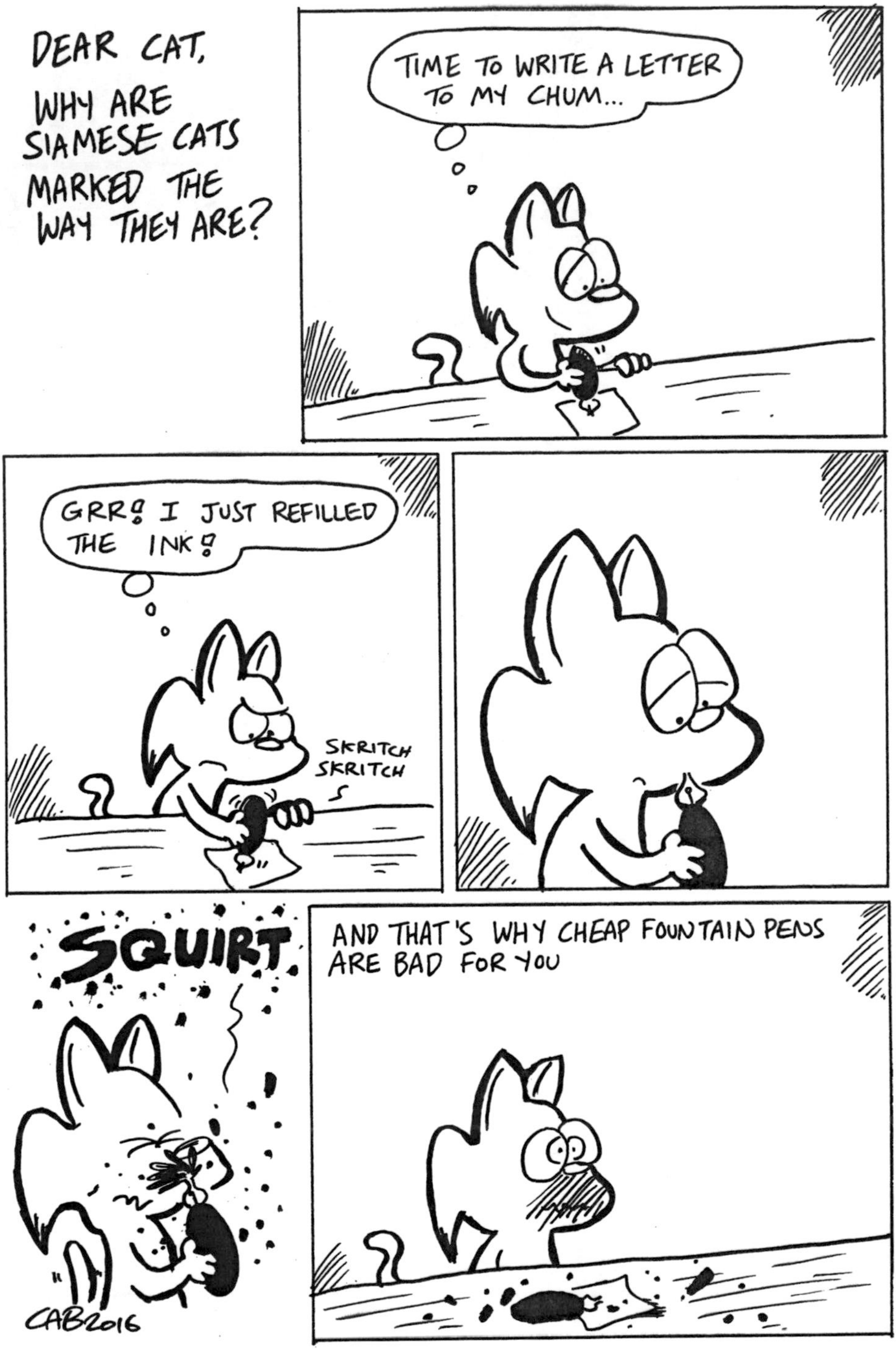
DEAR CAT,
WHY ARE SIAMESE CATS MARKED THE WAY THEY ARE?
TIME TO WRITE A LETTER TO MY CHUM...
GRR! I JUST REFILLED THE INK!
SKRITCH SKRITCH
SQUIRT
CAB2016
AND THAT'S WHY CHEAP FOUNTAIN PENS ARE BAD FOR YOU

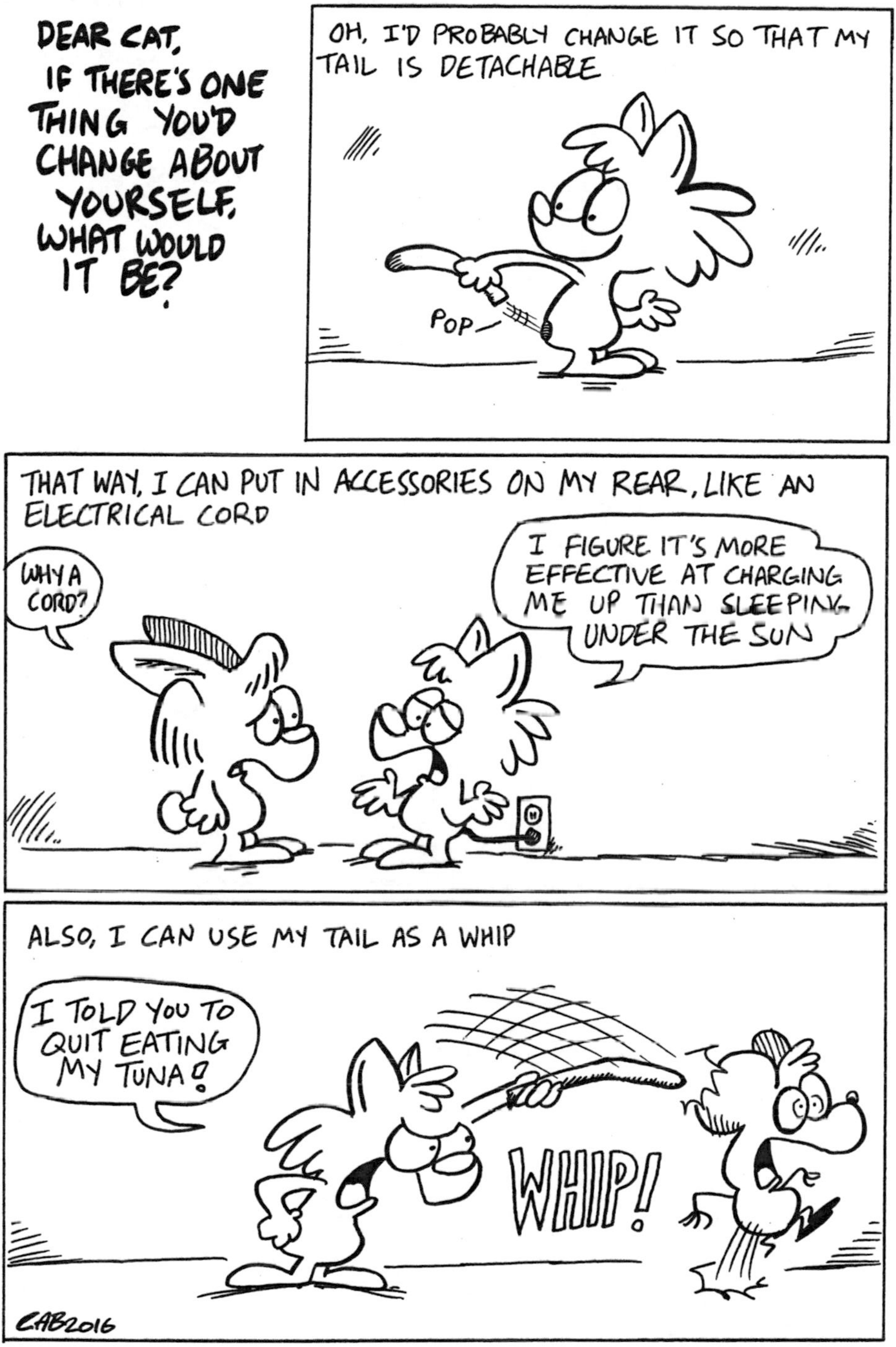
DEAR CAT, IF THERE'S ONE THING YOU'D CHANGE ABOUT YOURSELF, WHAT WOULD IT BE?
OH, I'D PROBABLY CHANGE IT SO THAT MY TAIL IS DETACHABLE
POP
THAT WAY, I CAN PUT IN ACCESSORIES ON MY REAR, LIKE AN ELECTRICAL CORD
WHY A CORD?
I FIGURE IT'S MORE EFFECTIVE AT CHARGING ME UP THAN SLEEPING UNDER THE SUN
ALSO, I CAN USE MY TAIL AS A WHIP
I TOLD YOU TO QUIT EATING MY TUNA!
WHIP!
CAB2016

DEAR CAT,
WHATEVER HAPPENED TO YOUR MOM AND LITTERMATES?

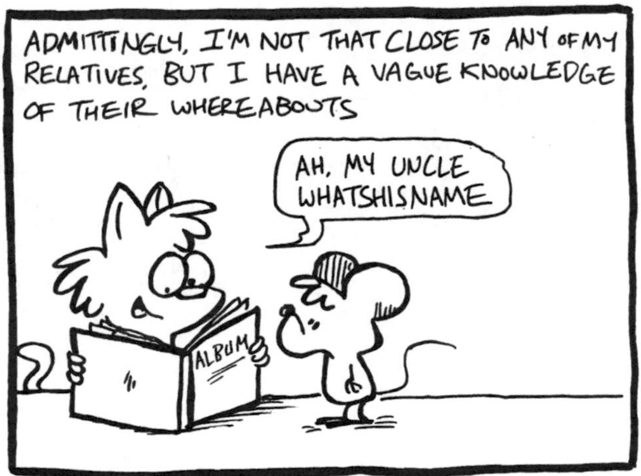

ADMITTINGLY, I'M NOT THAT CLOSE TO ANY OF MY RELATIVES, BUT I HAVE A VAGUE KNOWLEDGE OF THEIR WHEREABOUTS
AH, MY UNCLE WHATSHISNAME
ALBUM

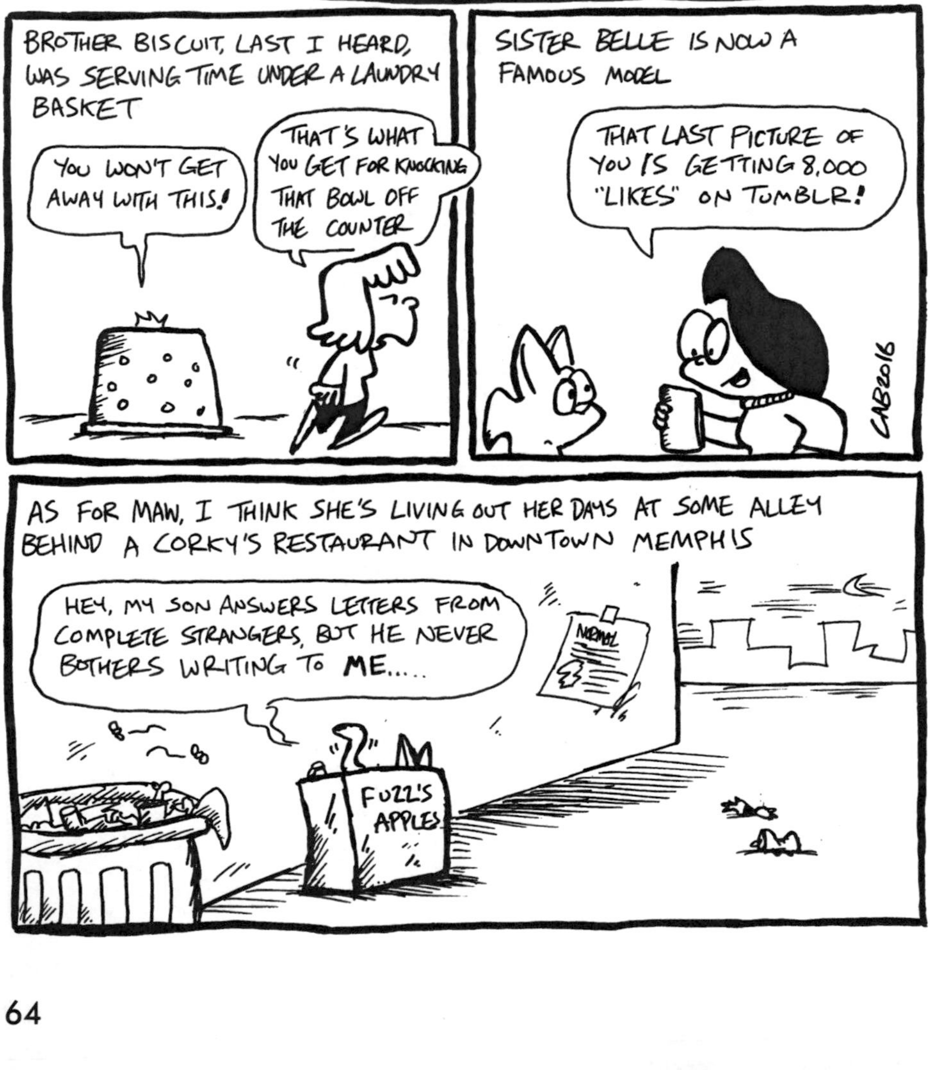

BROTHER BISCUIT, LAST I HEARD, WAS SERVING TIME UNDER A LAUNDRY BASKET
YOU WON'T GET AWAY WITH THIS!
THAT'S WHAT YOU GET FOR KNOCKING THAT BOWL OFF THE COUNTER
SISTER BELLE IS NOW A FAMOUS MODEL
THAT LAST PICTURE OF YOU IS GETTING 8,000 "LIKES" ON TUMBLR!
CAB2016
AS FOR MAW, I THINK SHE'S LIVING OUT HER DAYS AT SOME ALLEY BEHIND A CORKY'S RESTAURANT IN DOWNTOWN MEMPHIS
HEY, MY SON ANSWERS LETTERS FROM COMPLETE STRANGERS, BUT HE NEVER BOTHERS WRITING TO ME.....
NORMAL
FUZZ'S APPLES

DEAR CAT,

WHO IS TACOCAT?

- BURRITO BUNNY

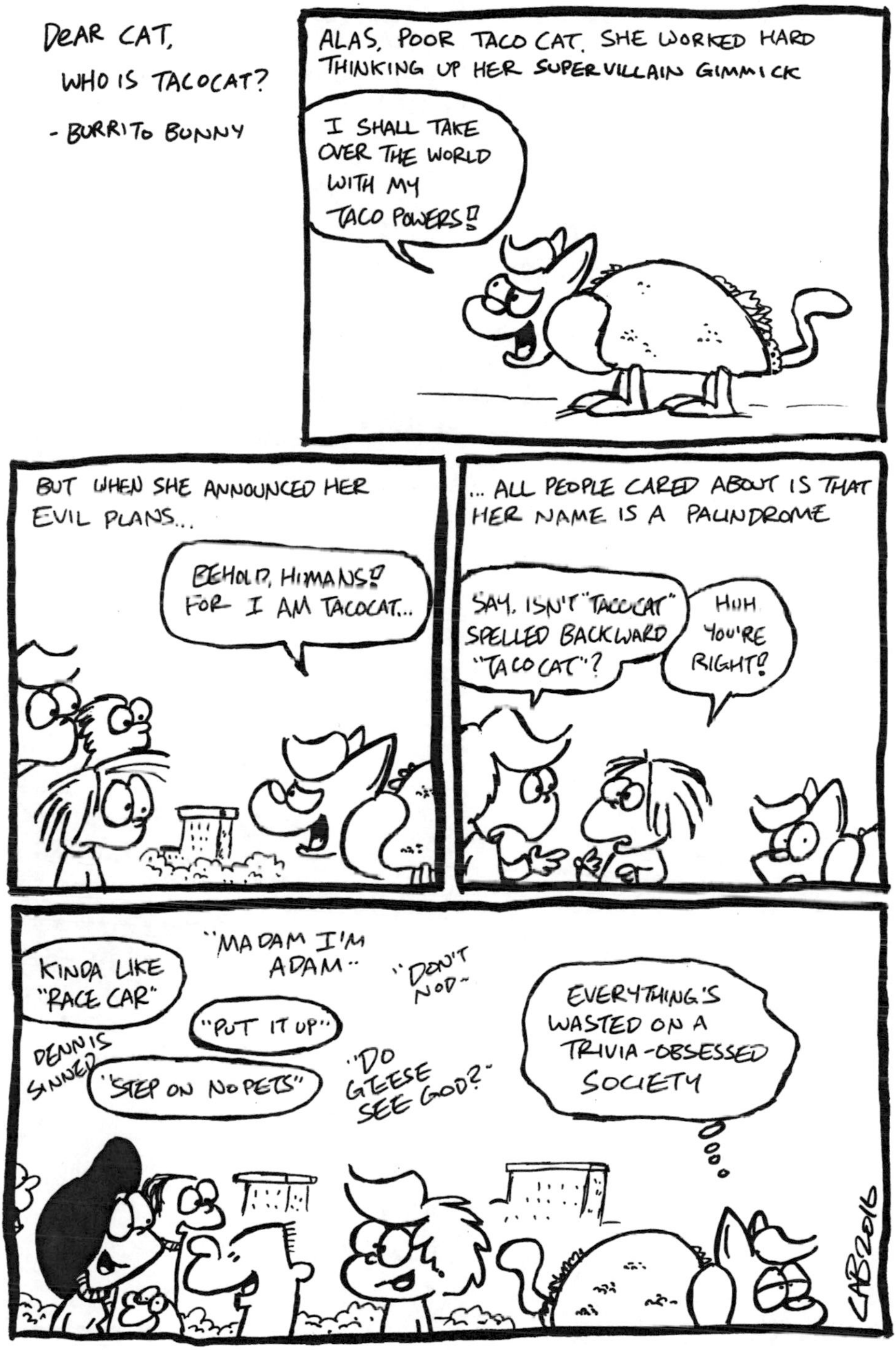

ALAS, POOR TACO CAT. SHE WORKED HARD THINKING UP HER SUPERVILLAIN GIMMICK
I SHALL TAKE OVER THE WORLD WITH MY TACO POWERS!!
BUT WHEN SHE ANNOUNCED HER EVIL PLANS...
BEHOLD, HUMANS!! FOR I AM TACOCAT...
... ALL PEOPLE CARED ABOUT IS THAT HER NAME IS A PALINDROME
SAY, ISN'T "TACOCAT" SPELLED BACKWARD "TACOCAT"?
HUH YOU'RE RIGHT!!
KINDA LIKE "RACE CAR"
"MADAM I'M ADAM"
"DON'T NOD"
"PUT IT UP"
DENNIS SINNED
"STEP ON NO PETS"
"DO GEESE SEE GOD?"
EVERYTHING'S WASTED ON A TRIVIA-OBSESSED SOCIETY
CAB2016

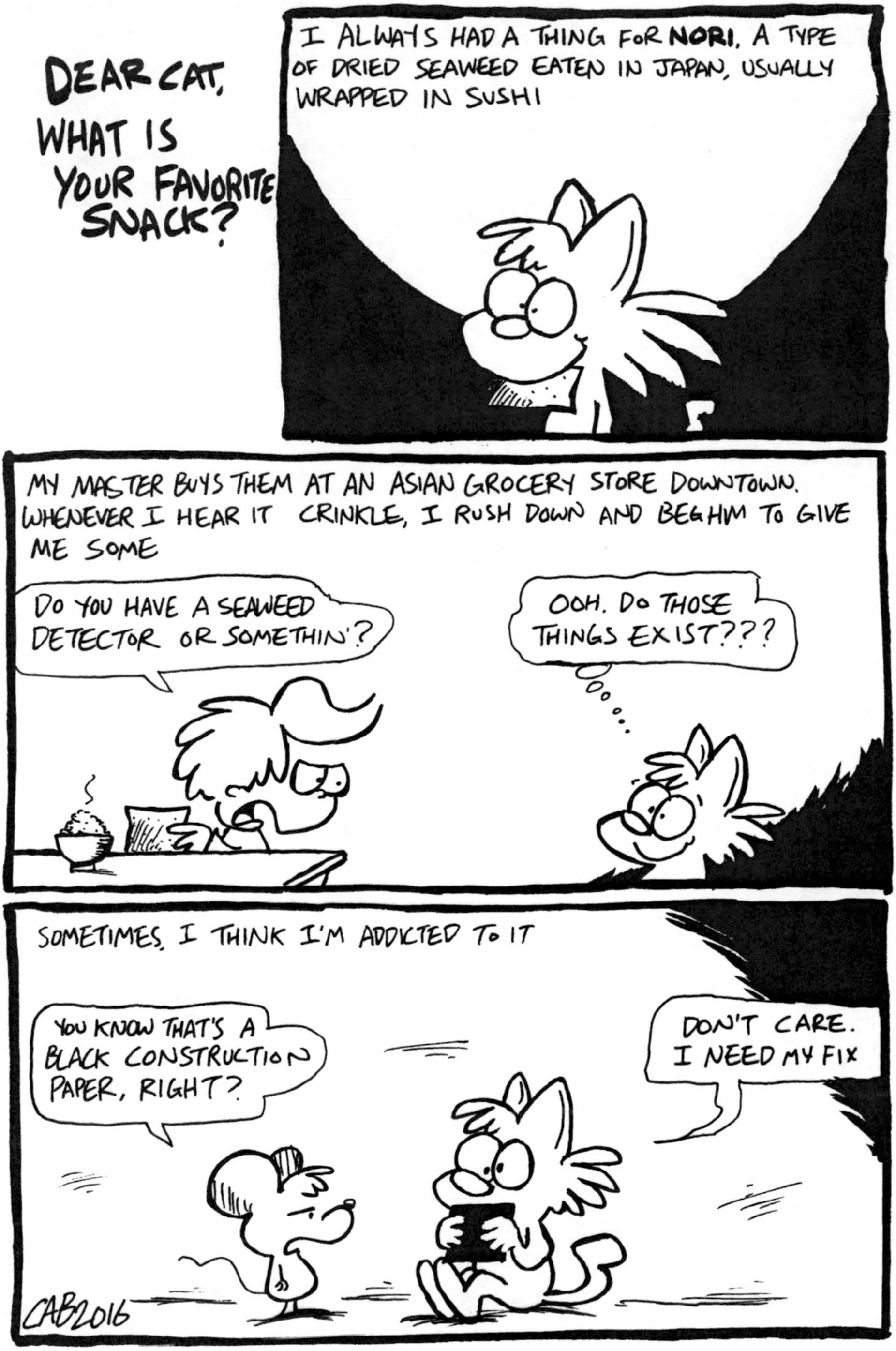
DEAR CAT, WHAT IS YOUR FAVORITE SNACK?
I ALWAYS HAD A THING FOR **NORI**. A TYPE OF DRIED SEAWEED EATEN IN JAPAN, USUALLY WRAPPED IN SUSHI
MY MASTER BUYS THEM AT AN ASIAN GROCERY STORE DOWNTOWN. WHENEVER I HEAR IT CRINKLE, I RUSH DOWN AND BEG HIM TO GIVE ME SOME
DO YOU HAVE A SEAWEED DETECTOR OR SOMETHIN'?
OOH. DO THOSE THINGS EXIST???
SOMETIMES, I THINK I'M ADDICTED TO IT
YOU KNOW THAT'S A BLACK CONSTRUCTION PAPER, RIGHT?
DON'T CARE. I NEED MY FIX
CAB2016

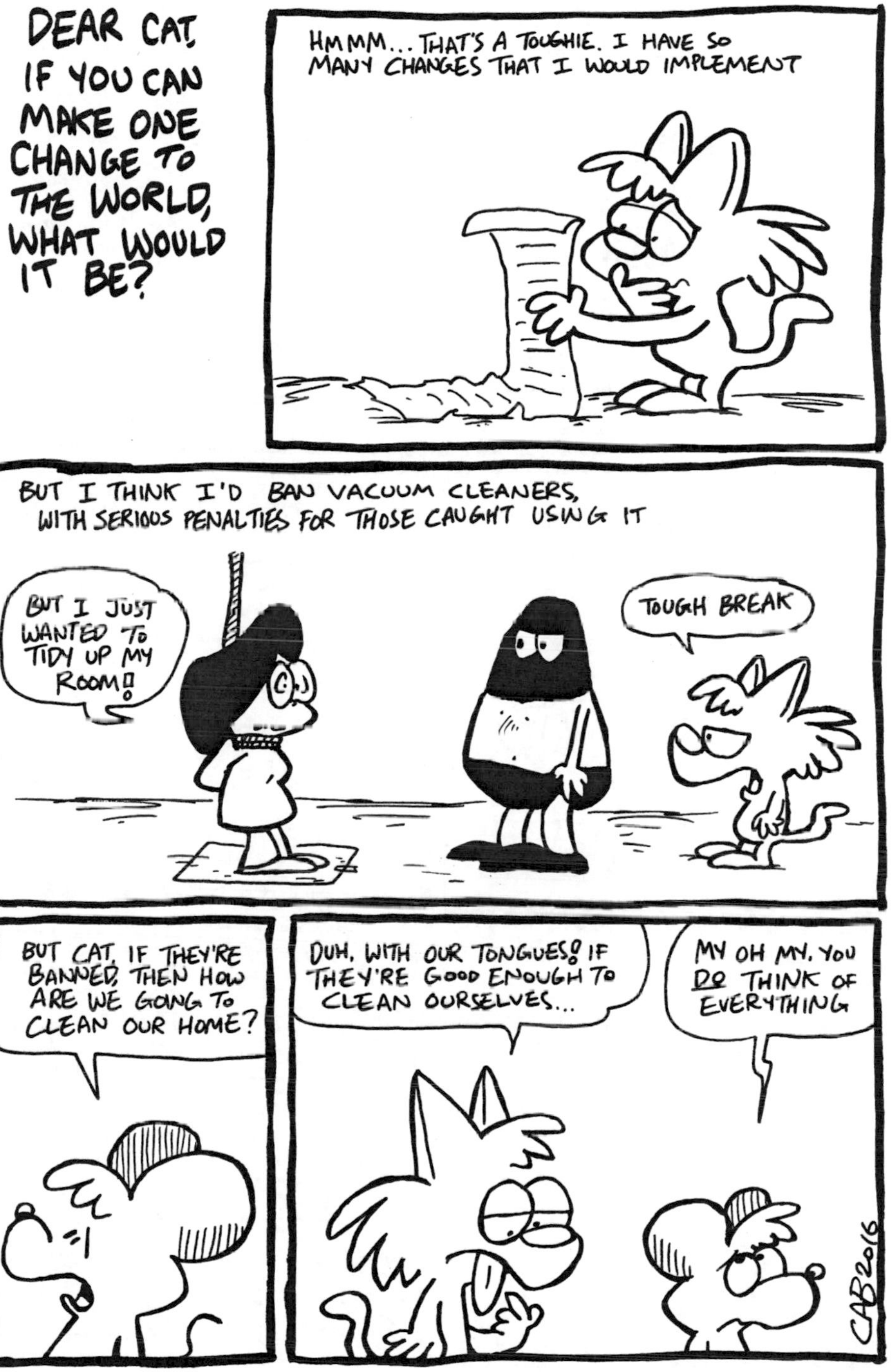
DEAR CAT, IF YOU CAN MAKE ONE CHANGE TO THE WORLD, WHAT WOULD IT BE?
HMMM... THAT'S A TOUGHIE. I HAVE SO MANY CHANGES THAT I WOULD IMPLEMENT
BUT I THINK I'D BAN VACUUM CLEANERS, WITH SERIOUS PENALTIES FOR THOSE CAUGHT USING IT
BUT I JUST WANTED TO TIDY UP MY ROOM!!
TOUGH BREAK
BUT CAT, IF THEY'RE BANNED, THEN HOW ARE WE GOING TO CLEAN OUR HOME?
DUH, WITH OUR TONGUES! IF THEY'RE GOOD ENOUGH TO CLEAN OURSELVES...
MY OH MY. YOU DO THINK OF EVERYTHING
CAB 2016

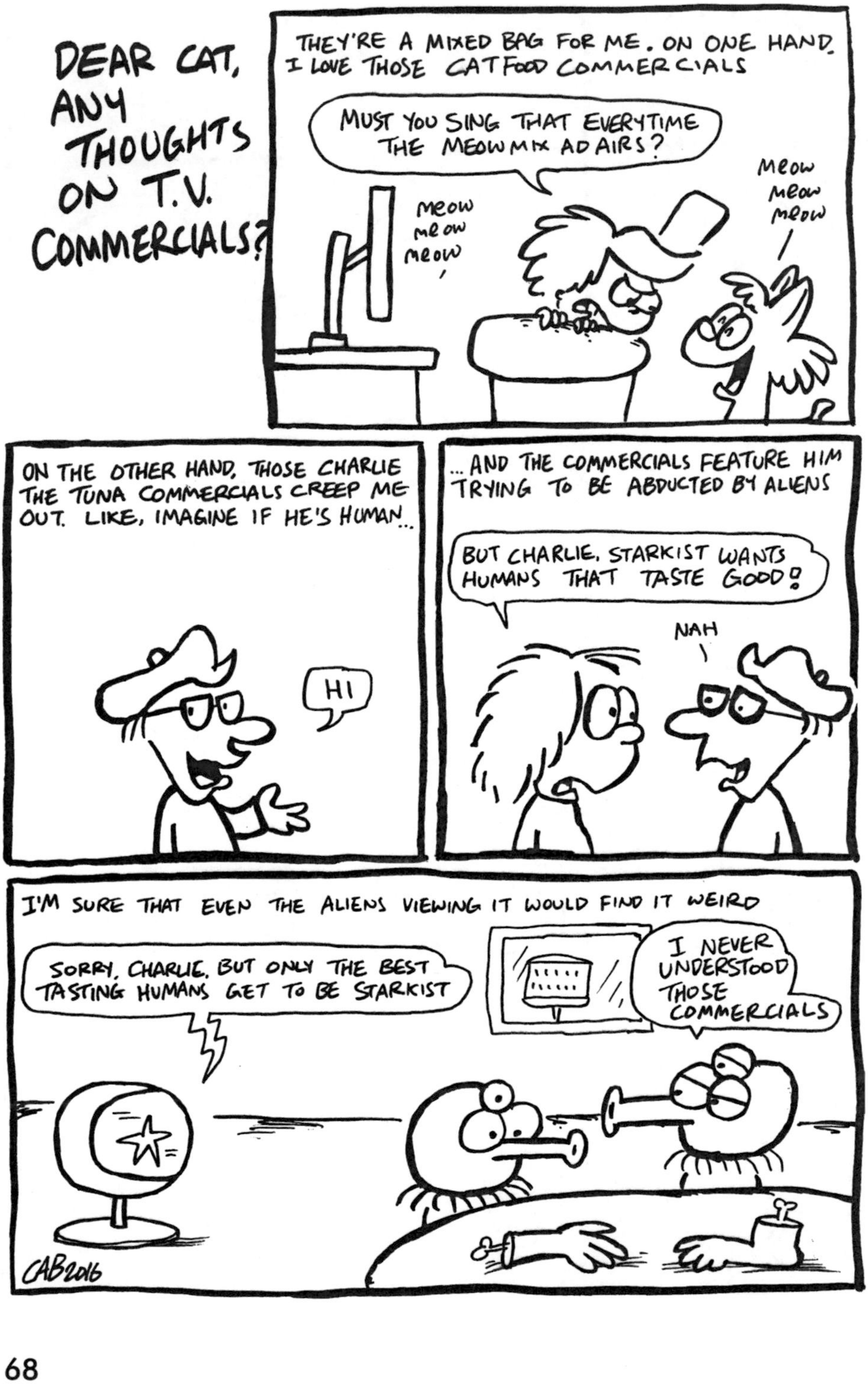
DEAR CAT, ANY THOUGHTS ON T.V. COMMERCIALS?
THEY'RE A MIXED BAG FOR ME. ON ONE HAND, I LOVE THOSE CATFOOD COMMERCIALS
MUST YOU SING THAT EVERYTIME THE MEOWMIX AD AIRS?
MEOW MEOW MEOW
MEOW MEOW MEOW
ON THE OTHER HAND, THOSE CHARLIE THE TUNA COMMERCIALS CREEP ME OUT. LIKE, IMAGINE IF HE'S HUMAN...
HI
...AND THE COMMERCIALS FEATURE HIM TRYING TO BE ABDUCTED BY ALIENS
BUT CHARLIE, STARKIST WANTS HUMANS THAT TASTE GOOD!
NAH
I'M SURE THAT EVEN THE ALIENS VIEWING IT WOULD FIND IT WEIRD
SORRY, CHARLIE, BUT ONLY THE BEST TASTING HUMANS GET TO BE STARKIST
I NEVER UNDERSTOOD THOSE COMMERCIALS
CAB 2016

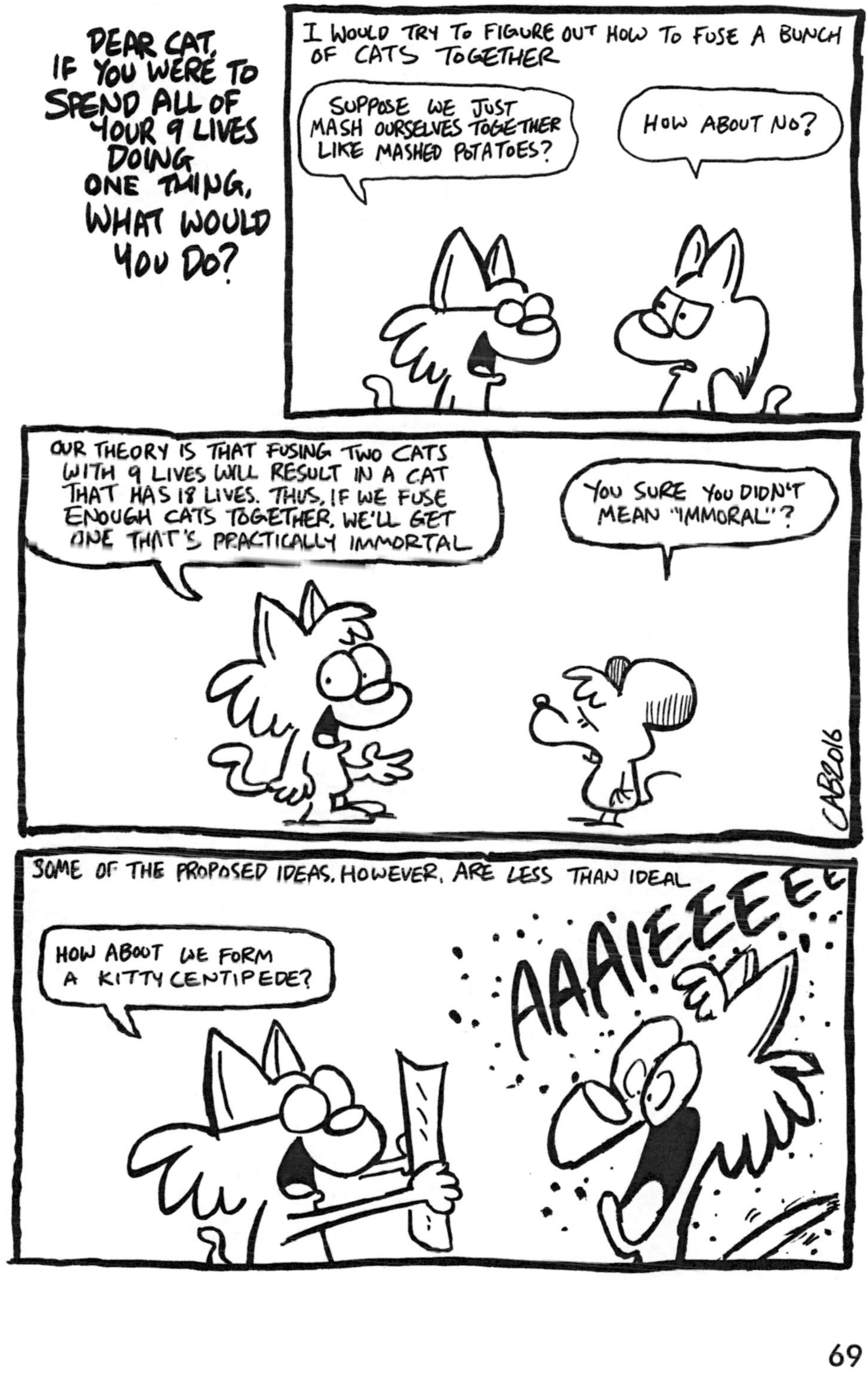
DEAR CAT, IF YOU WERE TO SPEND ALL OF YOUR 9 LIVES DOING ONE THING, WHAT WOULD YOU DO?
I WOULD TRY TO FIGURE OUT HOW TO FUSE A BUNCH OF CATS TOGETHER
SUPPOSE WE JUST MASH OURSELVES TOGETHER LIKE MASHED POTATOES?
HOW ABOUT NO?
OUR THEORY IS THAT FUSING TWO CATS WITH 9 LIVES WILL RESULT IN A CAT THAT HAS 18 LIVES. THUS, IF WE FUSE ENOUGH CATS TOGETHER, WE'LL GET ONE THAT'S PRACTICALLY IMMORTAL
YOU SURE YOU DIDN'T MEAN "IMMORAL"?
CABRO16
SOME OF THE PROPOSED IDEAS, HOWEVER, ARE LESS THAN IDEAL
HOW ABOUT WE FORM A KITTY CENTIPEDE?
AAAIEEEEEE

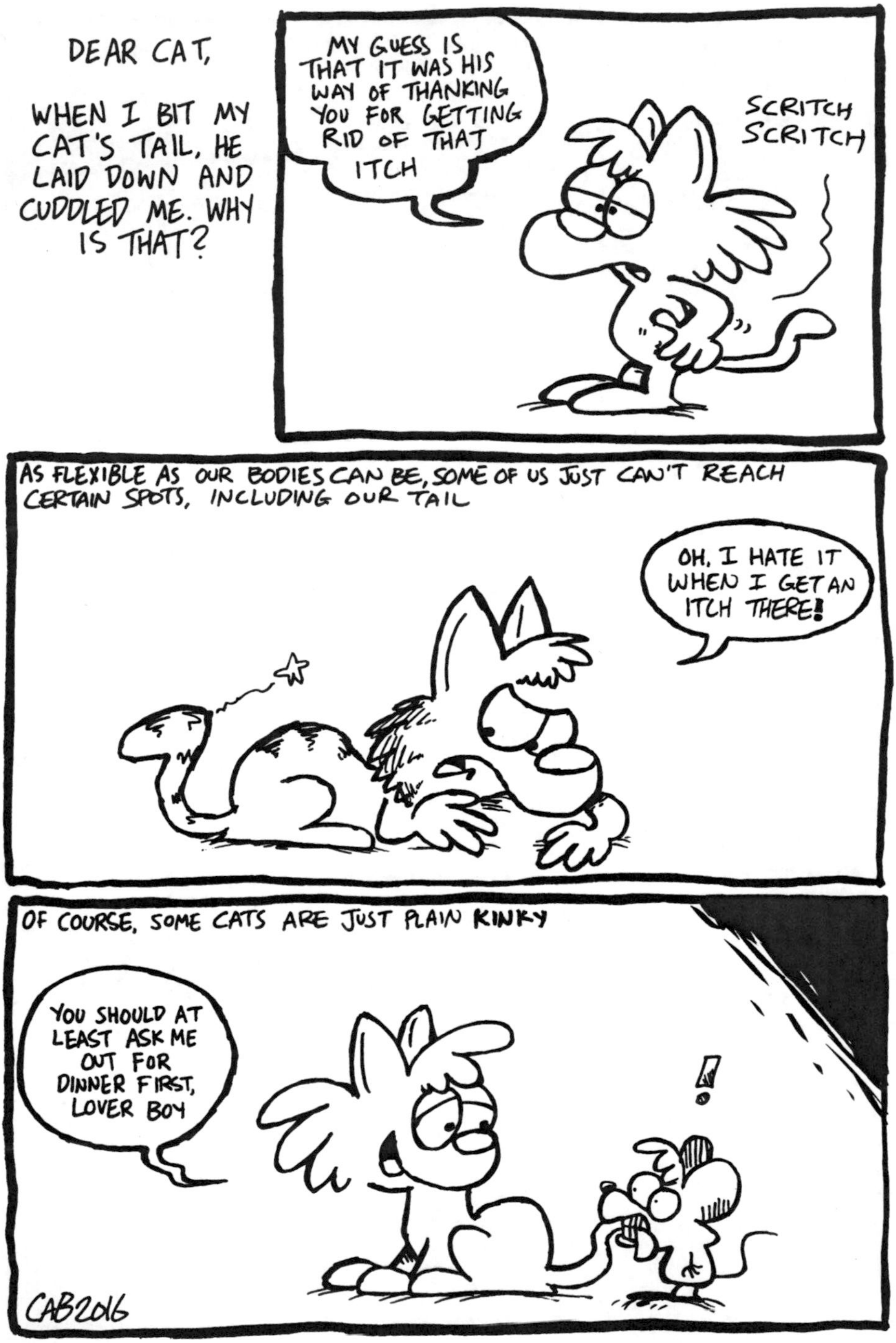
DEAR CAT,
WHEN I BIT MY CAT'S TAIL, HE LAID DOWN AND CUDDLED ME. WHY IS THAT?
MY GUESS IS THAT IT WAS HIS WAY OF THANKING YOU FOR GETTING RID OF THAT ITCH
SCRITCH SCRITCH
AS FLEXIBLE AS OUR BODIES CAN BE, SOME OF US JUST CAN'T REACH CERTAIN SPOTS, INCLUDING OUR TAIL
OH, I HATE IT WHEN I GET AN ITCH THERE!
OF COURSE, SOME CATS ARE JUST PLAIN KINKY
YOU SHOULD AT LEAST ASK ME OUT FOR DINNER FIRST, LOVER BOY
!
CAB2016

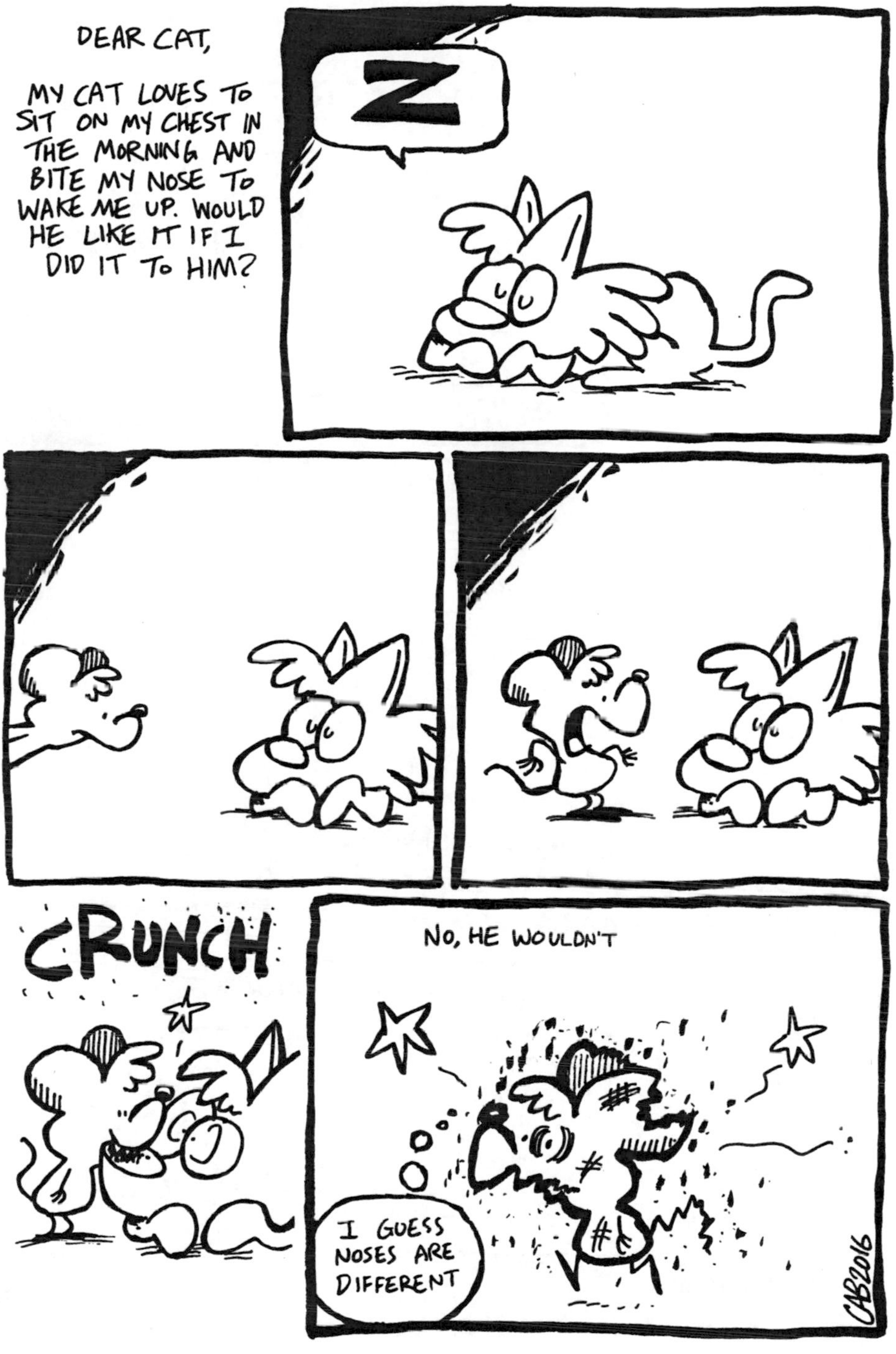
DEAR CAT,
MY CAT LOVES TO SIT ON MY CHEST IN THE MORNING AND BITE MY NOSE TO WAKE ME UP. WOULD HE LIKE IT IF I DID IT TO HIM?
Z
CRUNCH
NO, HE WOULDN'T
I GUESS NOSES ARE DIFFERENT
CAB2016

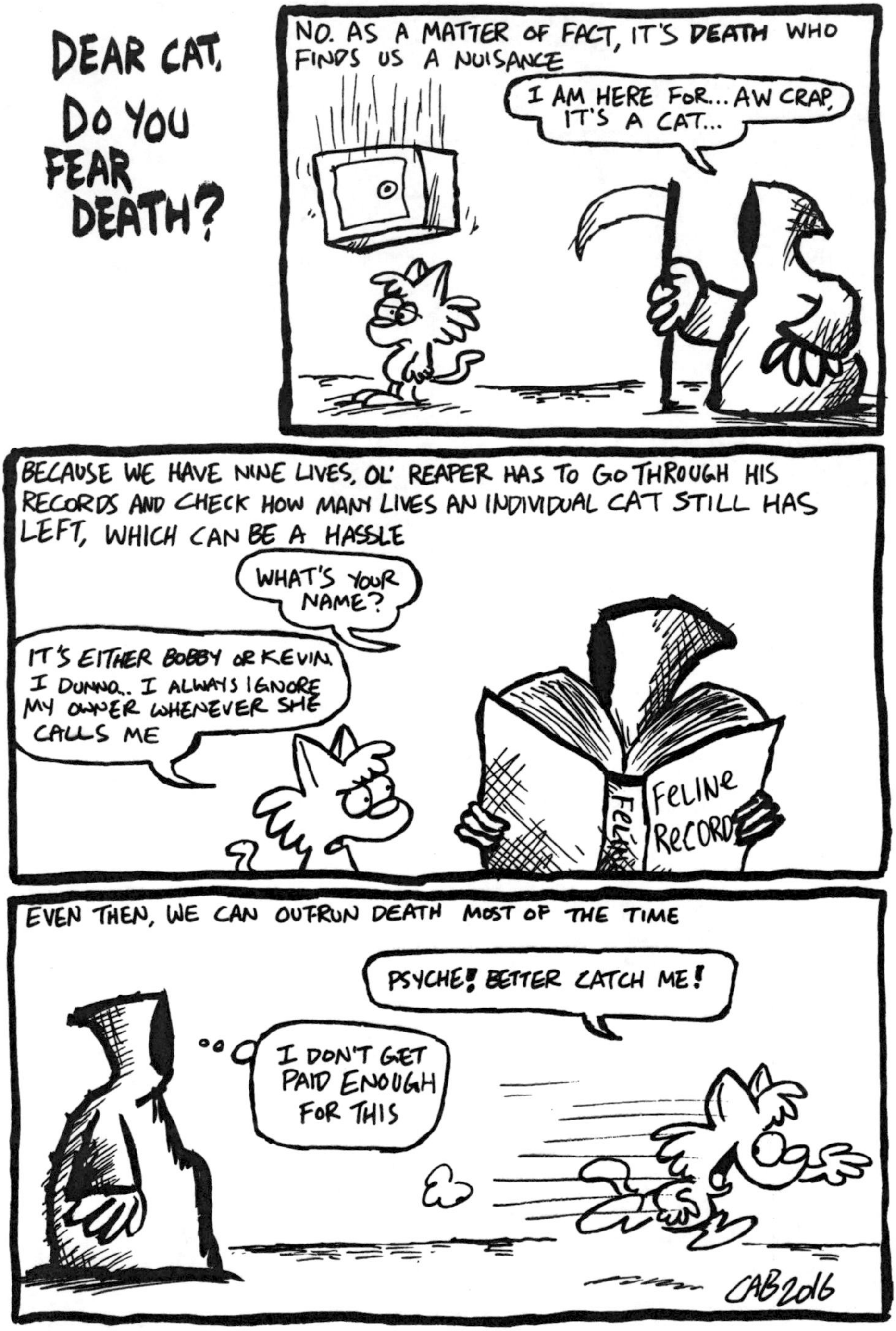
DEAR CAT, DO YOU FEAR DEATH?
NO. AS A MATTER OF FACT, IT'S DEATH WHO FINDS US A NUISANCE
I AM HERE FOR... AW CRAP, IT'S A CAT...
BECAUSE WE HAVE NINE LIVES, OL' REAPER HAS TO GO THROUGH HIS RECORDS AND CHECK HOW MANY LIVES AN INDIVIDUAL CAT STILL HAS LEFT, WHICH CAN BE A HASSLE
WHAT'S YOUR NAME?
IT'S EITHER BOBBY OR KEVIN. I DUNNO.. I ALWAYS IGNORE MY OWNER WHENEVER SHE CALLS ME
FELINE RECORDS
EVEN THEN, WE CAN OUT-RUN DEATH MOST OF THE TIME
PSYCHE! BETTER CATCH ME!
I DON'T GET PAID ENOUGH FOR THIS
CAB 2016

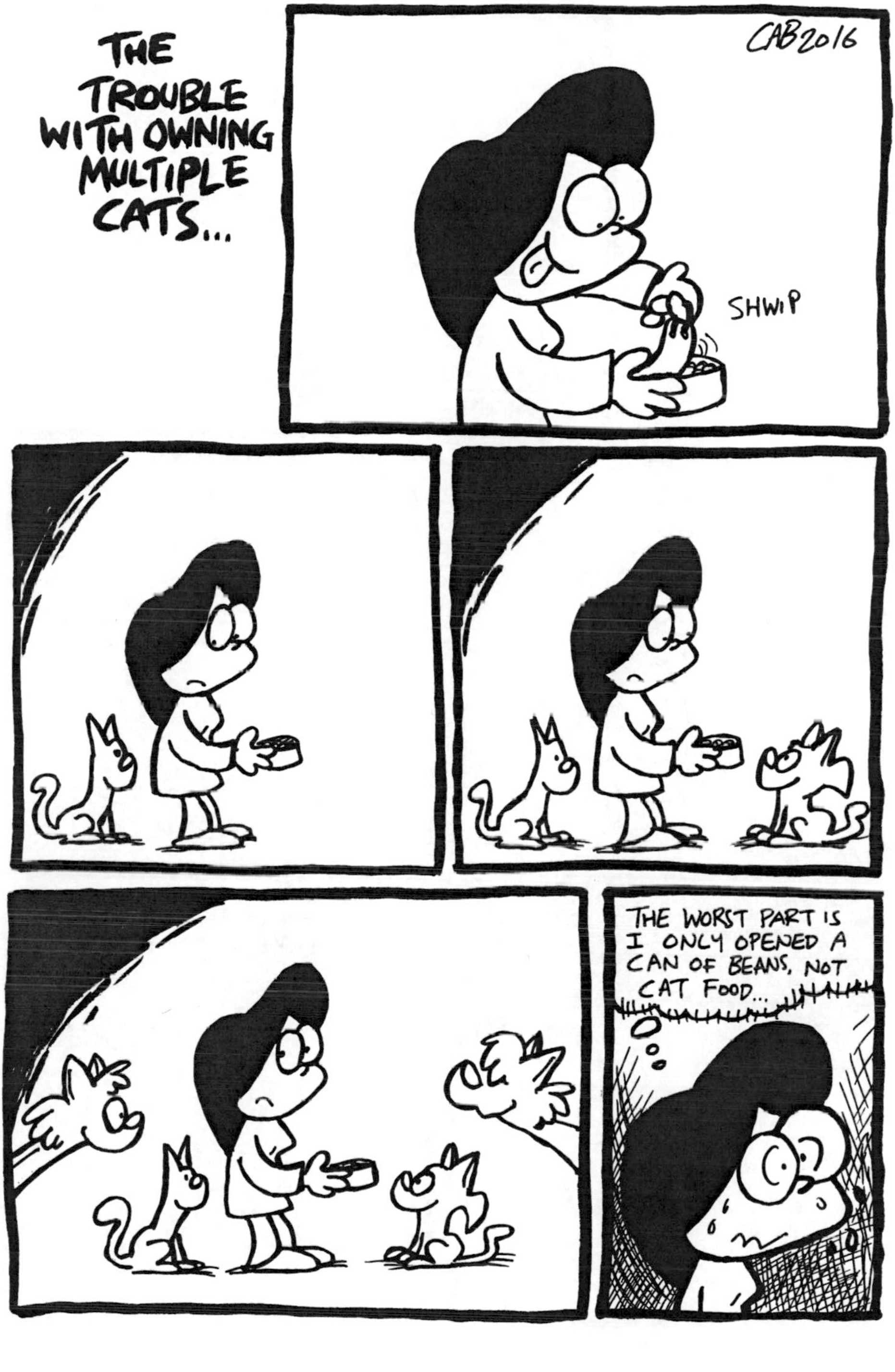
THE TROUBLE WITH OWNING MULTIPLE CATS...
CAB2016
SHWIP
THE WORST PART IS I ONLY OPENED A CAN OF BEANS, NOT CAT FOOD...

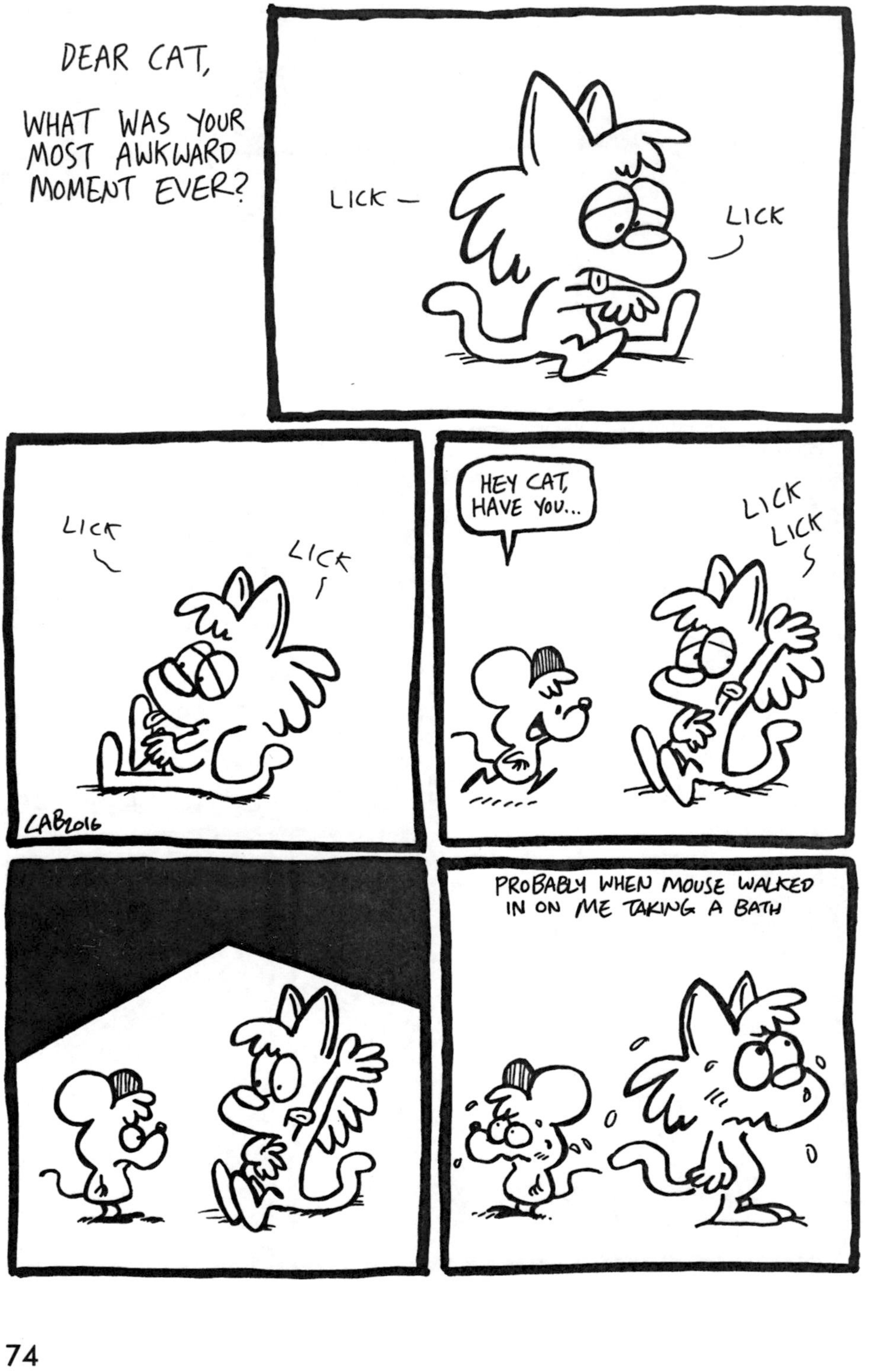
DEAR CAT,
WHAT WAS YOUR MOST AWKWARD MOMENT EVER?
LICK —
LICK
LICK
LICK
CAB2016
HEY CAT, HAVE YOU...
LICK
LICK
PROBABLY WHEN MOUSE WALKED IN ON ME TAKING A BATH

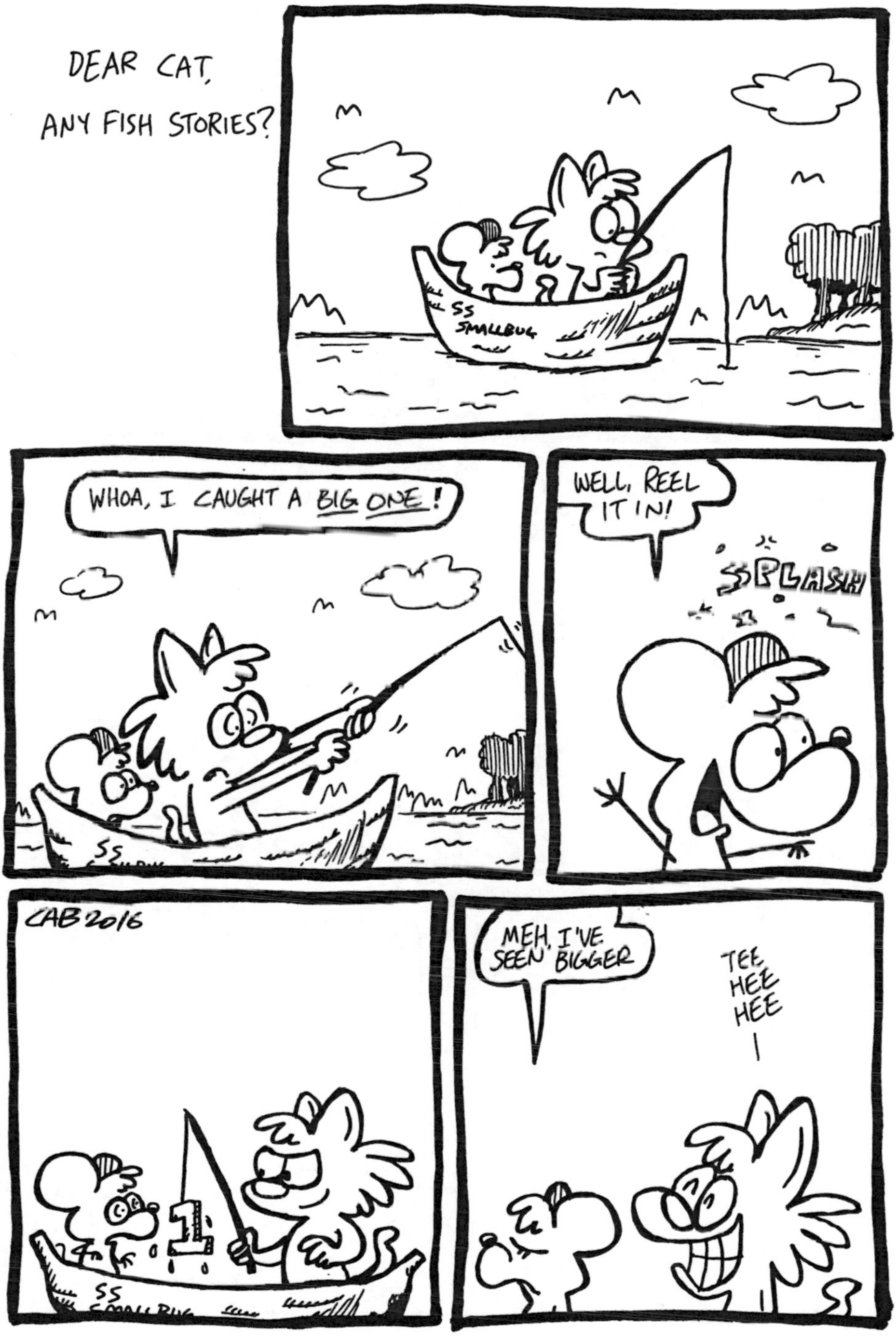
DEAR CAT,
ANY FISH STORIES?
SS SMALLBUG
WHOA, I CAUGHT A BIG ONE!
WELL, REEL IT IN!
SPLASH
CAB 2016
SS
MEH, I'VE SEEN BIGGER
TEE HEE HEE

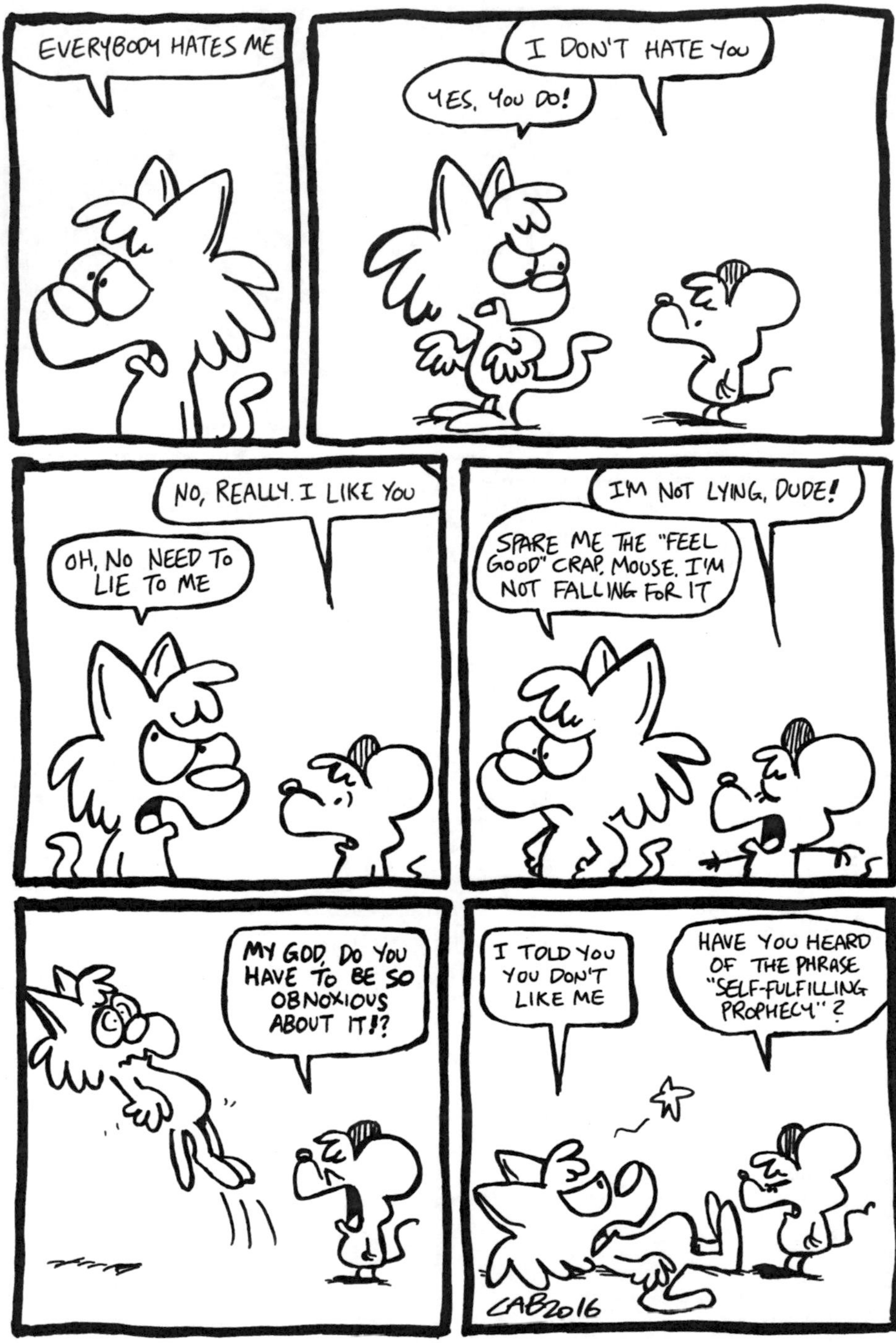
EVERYBODY HATES ME
I DON'T HATE YOU
YES, YOU DO!
NO, REALLY. I LIKE YOU
OH, NO NEED TO LIE TO ME
I'M NOT LYING, DUDE!
SPARE ME THE "FEEL GOOD" CRAP, MOUSE. I'M NOT FALLING FOR IT
MY GOD, DO YOU HAVE TO BE SO OBNOXIOUS ABOUT IT!?
I TOLD YOU YOU DON'T LIKE ME
HAVE YOU HEARD OF THE PHRASE "SELF-FULFILLING PROPHECY"?
CAB 2016

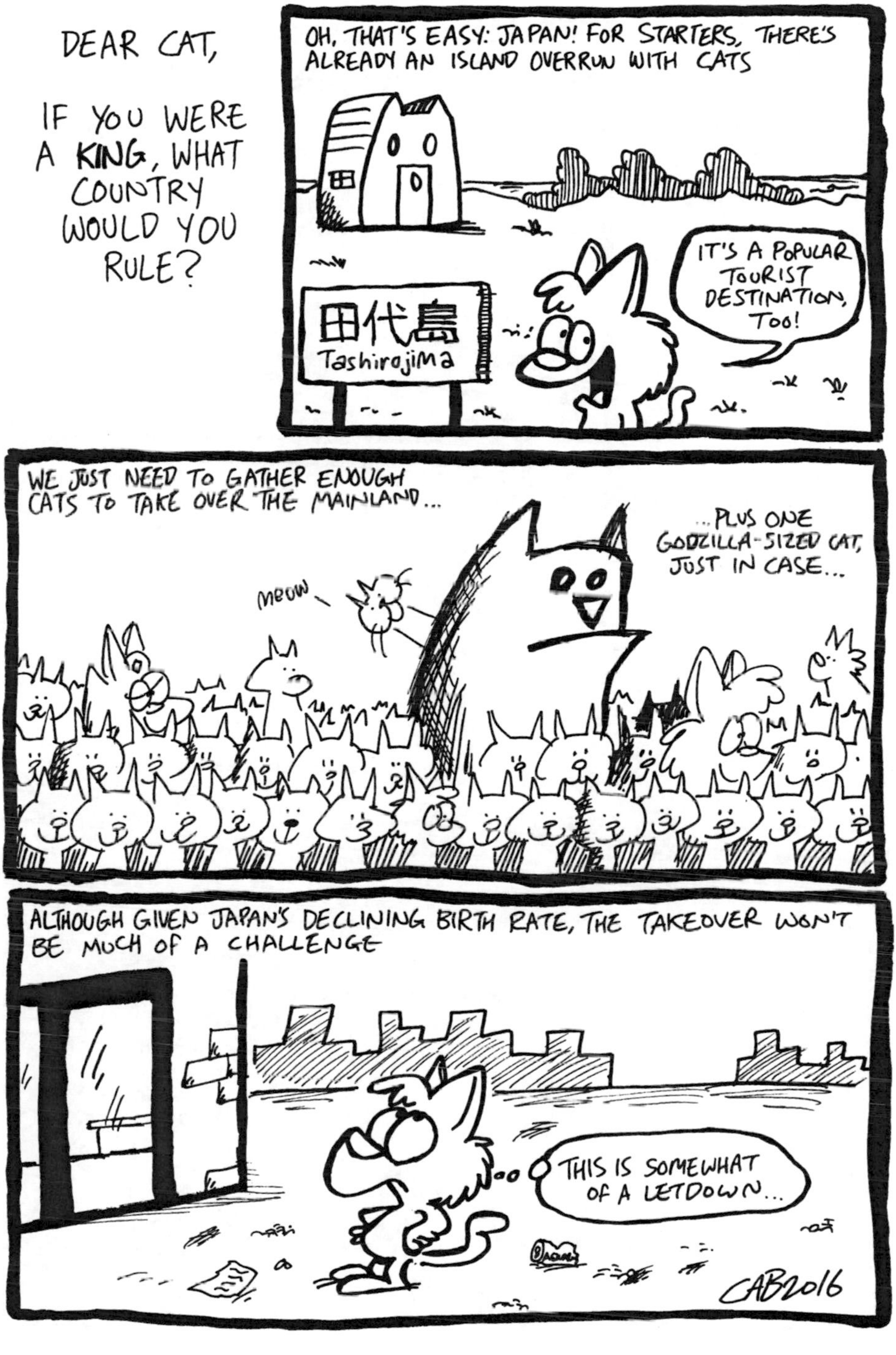
DEAR CAT,
IF YOU WERE A **KING**, WHAT COUNTRY WOULD YOU RULE?
OH, THAT'S EASY: JAPAN! FOR STARTERS, THERE'S ALREADY AN ISLAND OVERRUN WITH CATS
田代島
Tashirojima
IT'S A POPULAR TOURIST DESTINATION, TOO!
WE JUST NEED TO GATHER ENOUGH CATS TO TAKE OVER THE MAINLAND...
MEOW
...PLUS ONE GODZILLA-SIZED CAT, JUST IN CASE...
ALTHOUGH GIVEN JAPAN'S DECLINING BIRTH RATE, THE TAKEOVER WON'T BE MUCH OF A CHALLENGE
THIS IS SOMEWHAT OF A LETDOWN...
CAB2016

DEAR CAT,

HAVE YOU EVER HAD A RUN-IN WITH CURIOSITY?

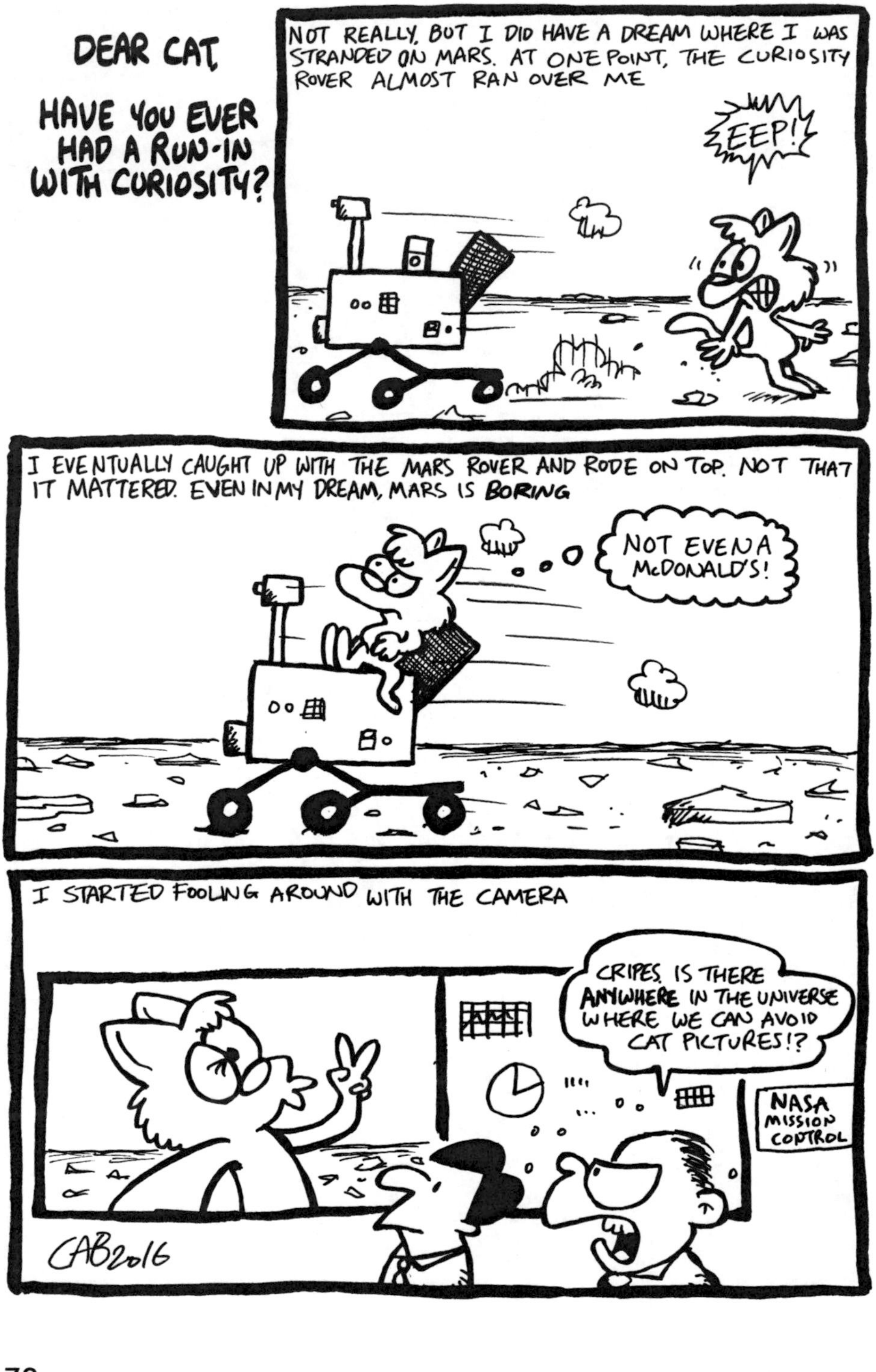
NOT REALLY, BUT I DID HAVE A DREAM WHERE I WAS STRANDED ON MARS. AT ONE POINT, THE CURIOSITY ROVER ALMOST RAN OVER ME
EEP!
I EVENTUALLY CAUGHT UP WITH THE MARS ROVER AND RODE ON TOP. NOT THAT IT MATTERED. EVEN IN MY DREAM, MARS IS BORING
NOT EVEN A McDONALD'S!
I STARTED FOOLING AROUND WITH THE CAMERA
CRIPES. IS THERE ANYWHERE IN THE UNIVERSE WHERE WE CAN AVOID CAT PICTURES!?
NASA MISSION CONTROL
CAB 2016

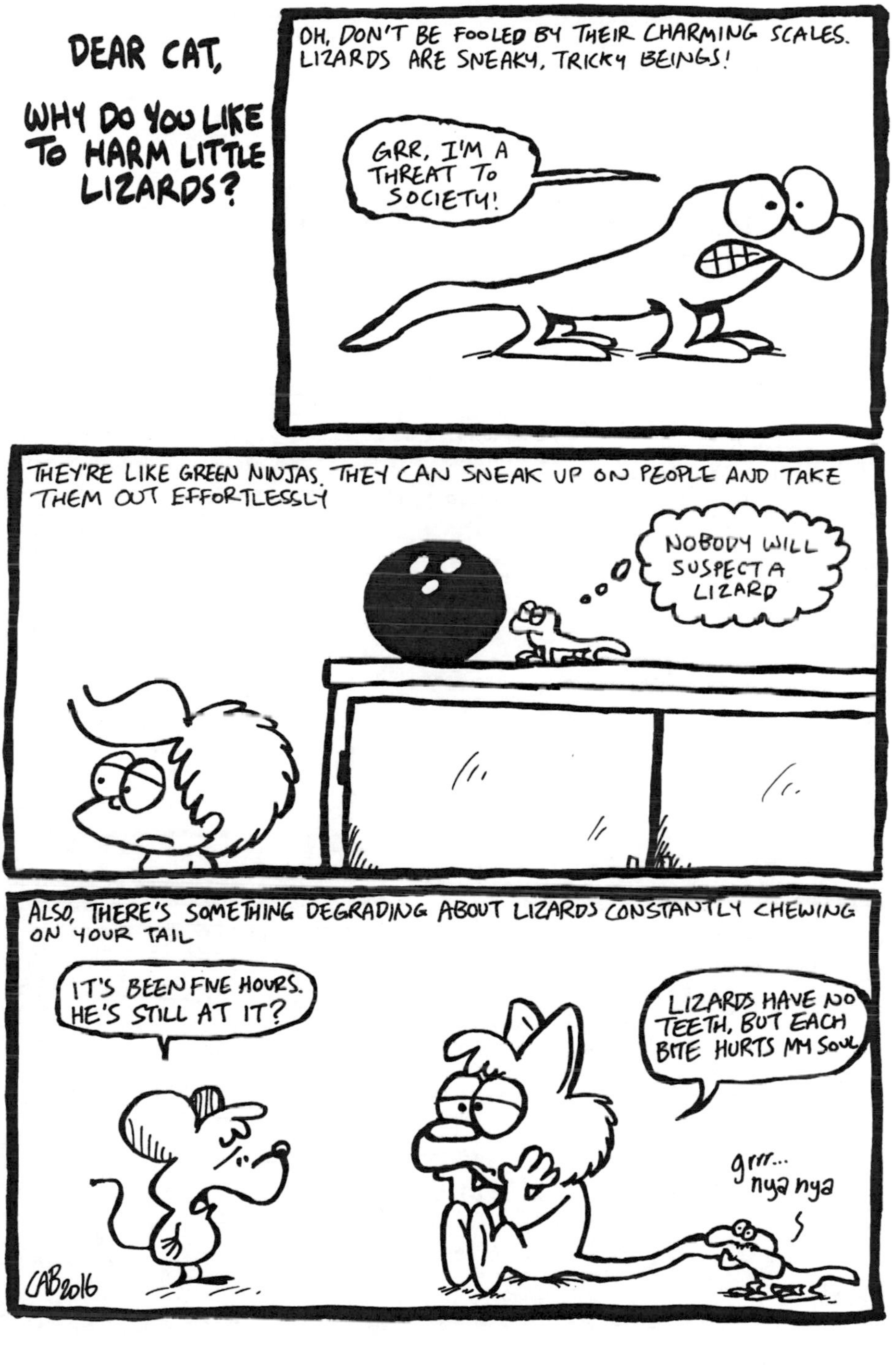
DEAR CAT,
WHY DO YOU LIKE TO HARM LITTLE LIZARDS?
OH, DON'T BE FOOLED BY THEIR CHARMING SCALES. LIZARDS ARE SNEAKY, TRICKY BEINGS!
GRR, I'M A THREAT TO SOCIETY!
THEY'RE LIKE GREEN NINJAS. THEY CAN SNEAK UP ON PEOPLE AND TAKE THEM OUT EFFORTLESSLY
NOBODY WILL SUSPECT A LIZARD
ALSO, THERE'S SOMETHING DEGRADING ABOUT LIZARDS CONSTANTLY CHEWING ON YOUR TAIL
IT'S BEEN FIVE HOURS. HE'S STILL AT IT?
LIZARDS HAVE NO TEETH, BUT EACH BITE HURTS MY SOUL
grrr... nya nya
CAB 2016

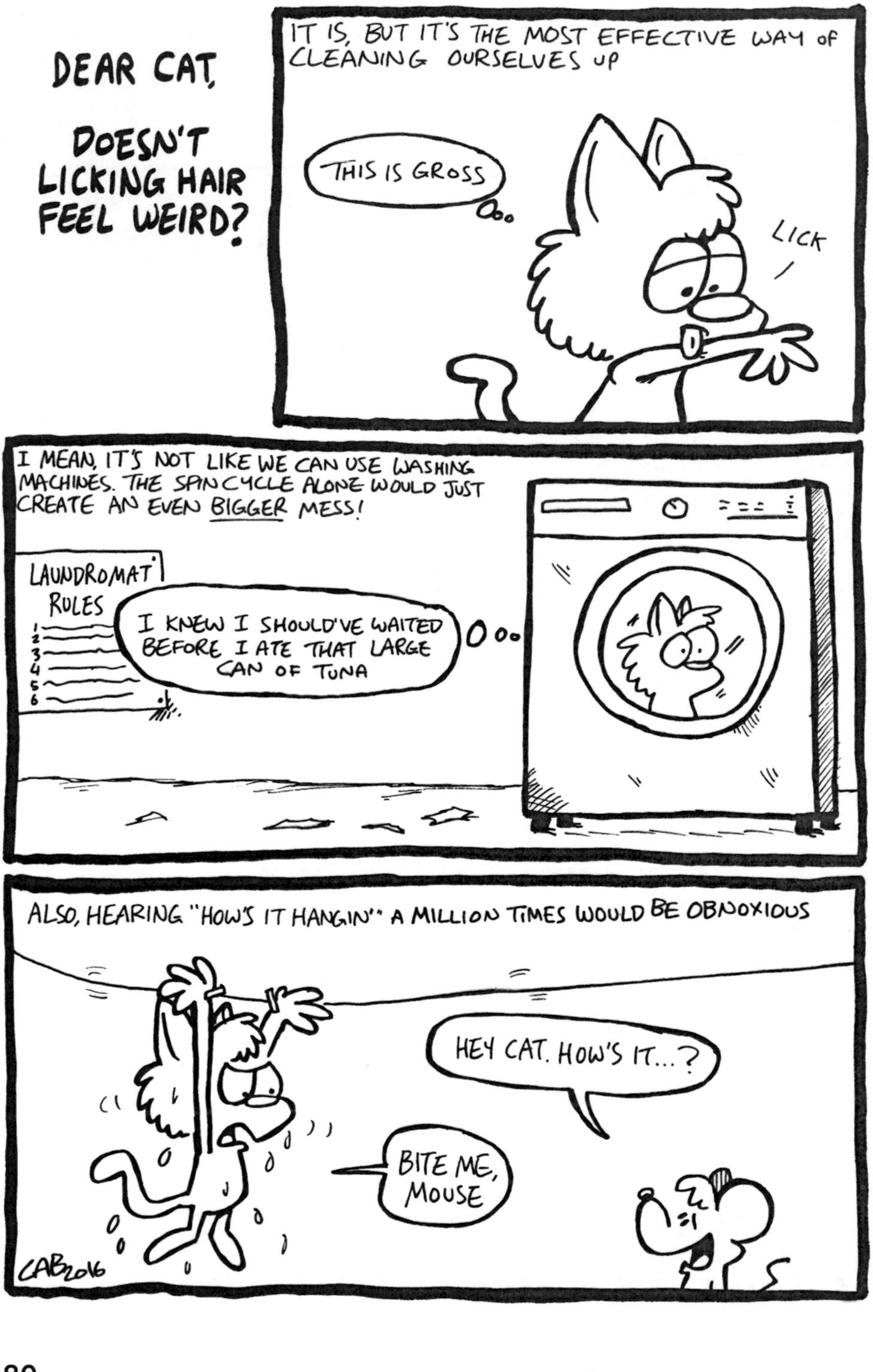
DEAR CAT,
DOESN'T LICKING HAIR FEEL WEIRD?
IT IS, BUT IT'S THE MOST EFFECTIVE WAY OF CLEANING OURSELVES UP
THIS IS GROSS
LICK
I MEAN, IT'S NOT LIKE WE CAN USE WASHING MACHINES. THE SPIN CYCLE ALONE WOULD JUST CREATE AN EVEN BIGGER MESS!
LAUNDROMAT RULES
I KNEW I SHOULD'VE WAITED BEFORE I ATE THAT LARGE CAN OF TUNA
ALSO, HEARING "HOW'S IT HANGIN'" A MILLION TIMES WOULD BE OBNOXIOUS
HEY CAT. HOW'S IT...?
BITE ME, MOUSE
CAB 2016

DEAR CAT,

HAVE YOU EVER DUELED WITH AN UNDERWATER CREATURE?

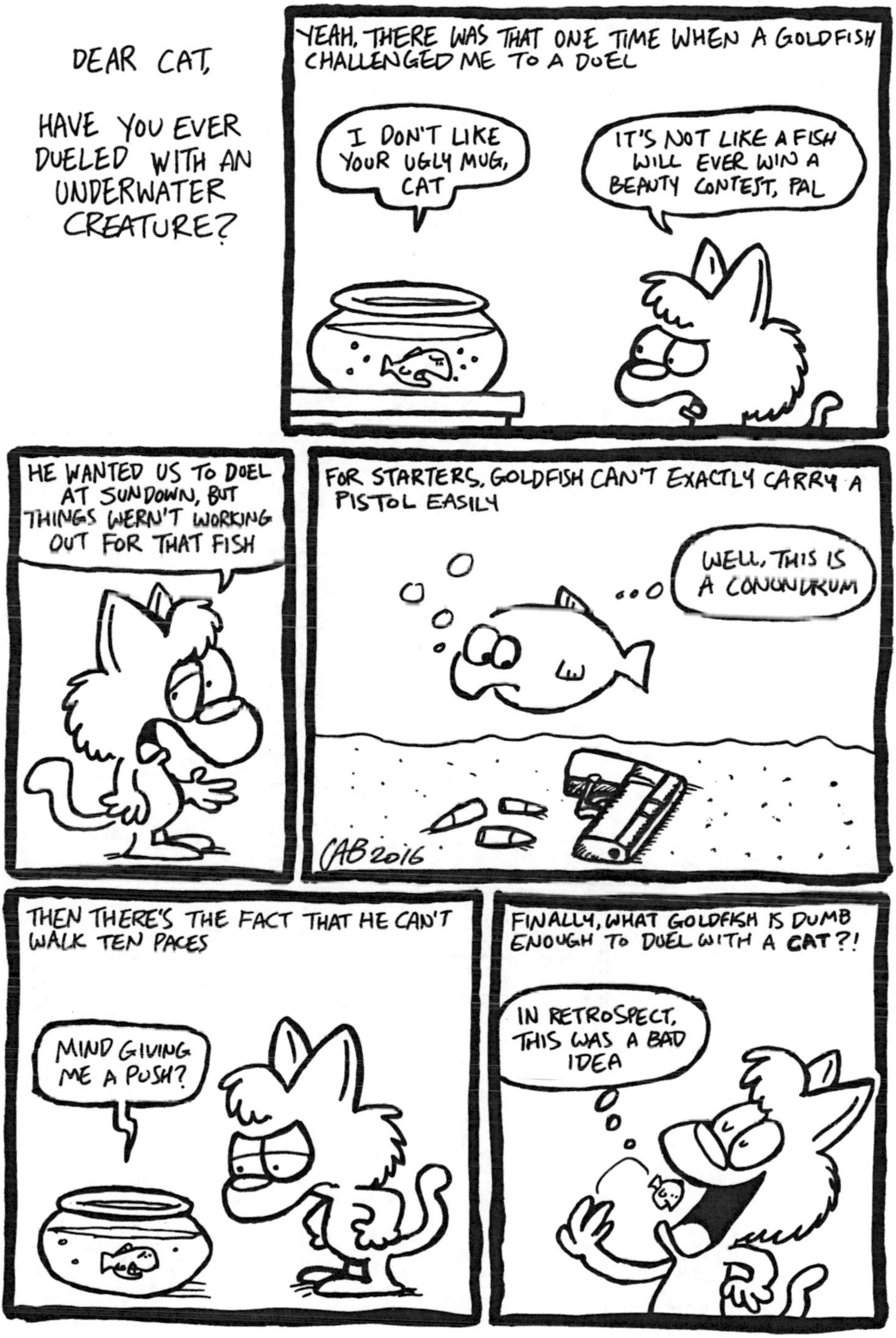

YEAH, THERE WAS THAT ONE TIME WHEN A GOLDFISH CHALLENGED ME TO A DUEL
I DON'T LIKE YOUR UGLY MUG, CAT
IT'S NOT LIKE A FISH WILL EVER WIN A BEAUTY CONTEST, PAL
HE WANTED US TO DUEL AT SUNDOWN, BUT THINGS WERN'T WORKING OUT FOR THAT FISH
FOR STARTERS, GOLDFISH CAN'T EXACTLY CARRY A PISTOL EASILY
WELL, THIS IS A CONUNDRUM
CAB 2016
THEN THERE'S THE FACT THAT HE CAN'T WALK TEN PACES
MIND GIVING ME A PUSH?
FINALLY, WHAT GOLDFISH IS DUMB ENOUGH TO DUEL WITH A CAT?!
IN RETROSPECT, THIS WAS A BAD IDEA

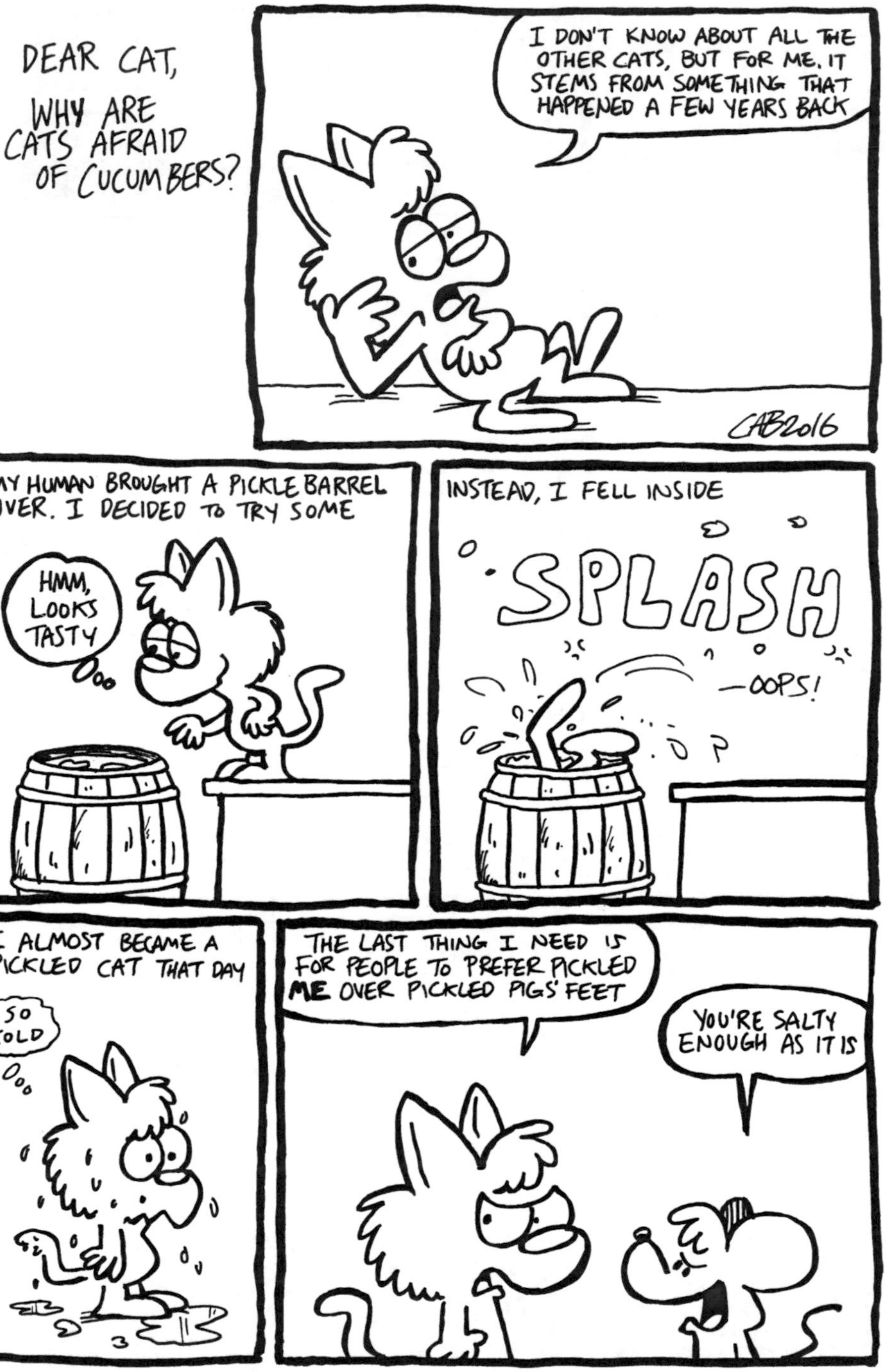
DEAR CAT,
WHY ARE CATS AFRAID OF CUCUMBERS?
I DON'T KNOW ABOUT ALL THE OTHER CATS, BUT FOR ME, IT STEMS FROM SOMETHING THAT HAPPENED A FEW YEARS BACK
CAB2016
MY HUMAN BROUGHT A PICKLE BARREL OVER. I DECIDED TO TRY SOME
HMM, LOOKS TASTY
INSTEAD, I FELL INSIDE
SPLASH
—OOPS!
I ALMOST BECAME A PICKLED CAT THAT DAY
SO COLD
THE LAST THING I NEED IS FOR PEOPLE TO PREFER PICKLED ME OVER PICKLED PIGS' FEET
YOU'RE SALTY ENOUGH AS IT IS

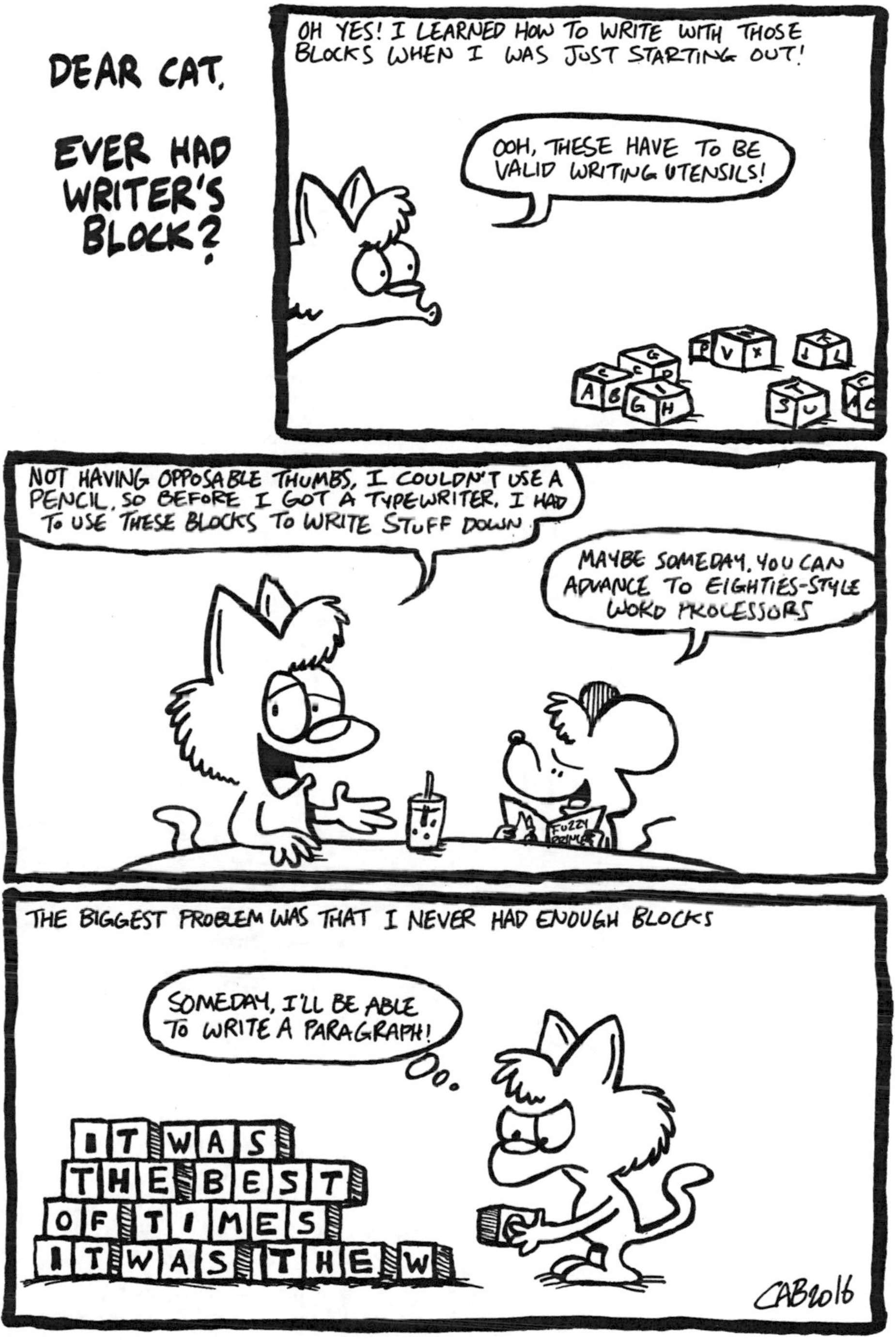
DEAR CAT,
EVER HAD WRITER'S BLOCK?
OH YES! I LEARNED HOW TO WRITE WITH THOSE BLOCKS WHEN I WAS JUST STARTING OUT!
OOH, THESE HAVE TO BE VALID WRITING UTENSILS!
NOT HAVING OPPOSABLE THUMBS, I COULDN'T USE A PENCIL, SO BEFORE I GOT A TYPEWRITER, I HAD TO USE THESE BLOCKS TO WRITE STUFF DOWN.
MAYBE SOMEDAY, YOU CAN ADVANCE TO EIGHTIES-STYLE WORD PROCESSORS
FUZZY PRIMER
THE BIGGEST PROBLEM WAS THAT I NEVER HAD ENOUGH BLOCKS
SOMEDAY, I'LL BE ABLE TO WRITE A PARAGRAPH!
IT WAS THE BEST OF TIMES IT WAS THE W
CAB2016

DEAR CAT,

HOW DO YOU MARK YOUR TERRITORY?

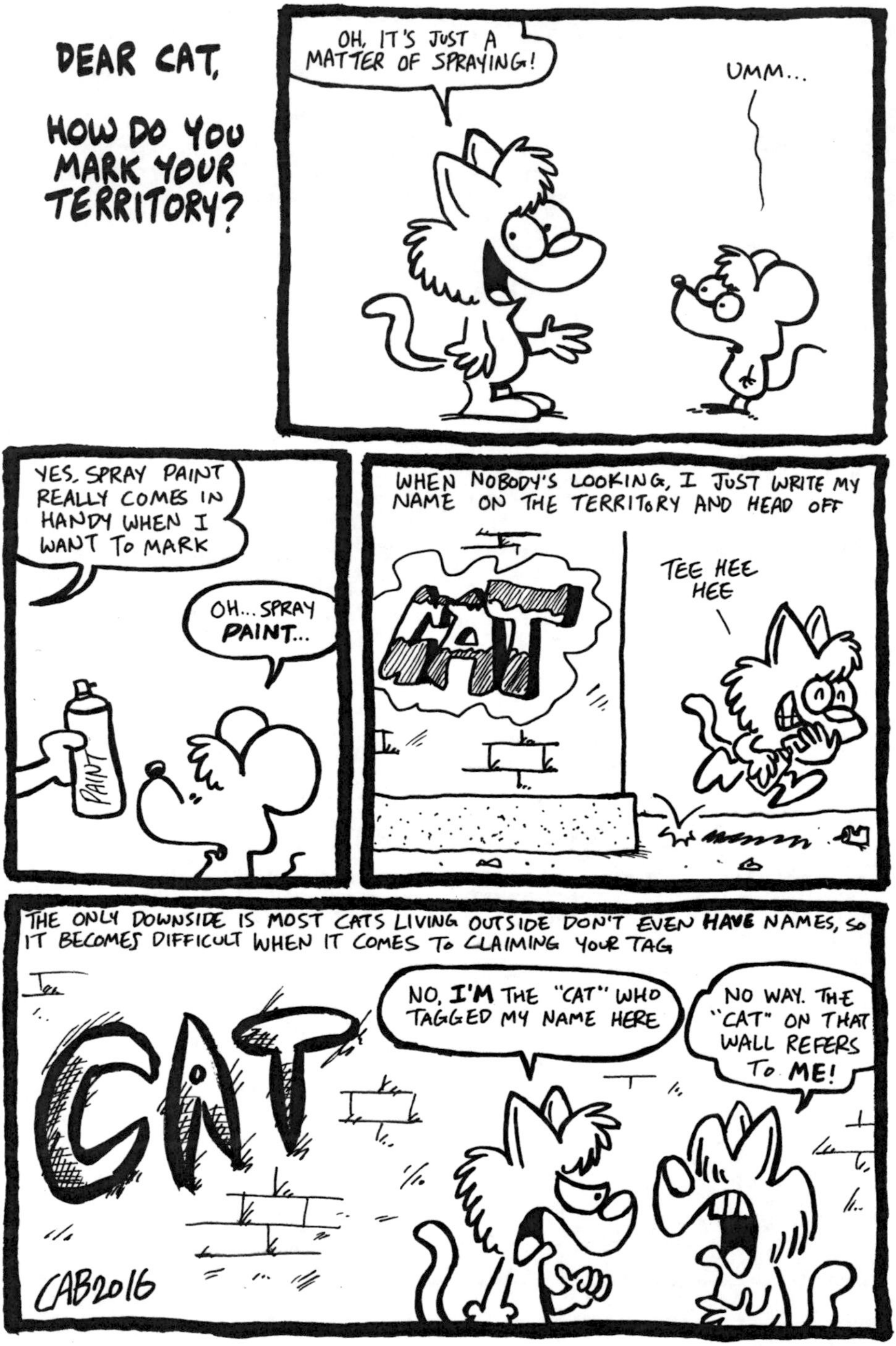
OH, IT'S JUST A MATTER OF SPRAYING!
UMM...
YES, SPRAY PAINT REALLY COMES IN HANDY WHEN I WANT TO MARK
OH... SPRAY **PAINT**...
PAINT
WHEN NOBODY'S LOOKING, I JUST WRITE MY NAME ON THE TERRITORY AND HEAD OFF
CAT
TEE HEE HEE
THE ONLY DOWNSIDE IS MOST CATS LIVING OUTSIDE DON'T EVEN **HAVE** NAMES, SO IT BECOMES DIFFICULT WHEN IT COMES TO CLAIMING YOUR TAG
CAT
NO, **I'M** THE "CAT" WHO TAGGED MY NAME HERE
NO WAY. THE "CAT" ON THAT WALL REFERS TO **ME**!
CAB2016

DEAR CAT,

HAVE YOU EVER APPEARED IN A CAT VIDEO?

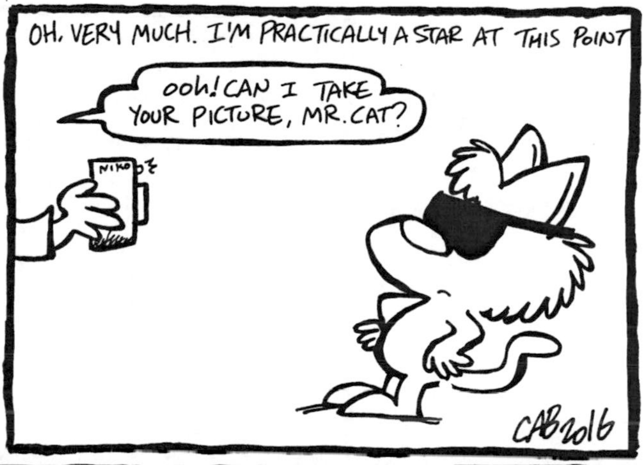
OH, VERY MUCH. I'M PRACTICALLY A STAR AT THIS POINT
OOH! CAN I TAKE YOUR PICTURE, MR. CAT?
CAB 2016

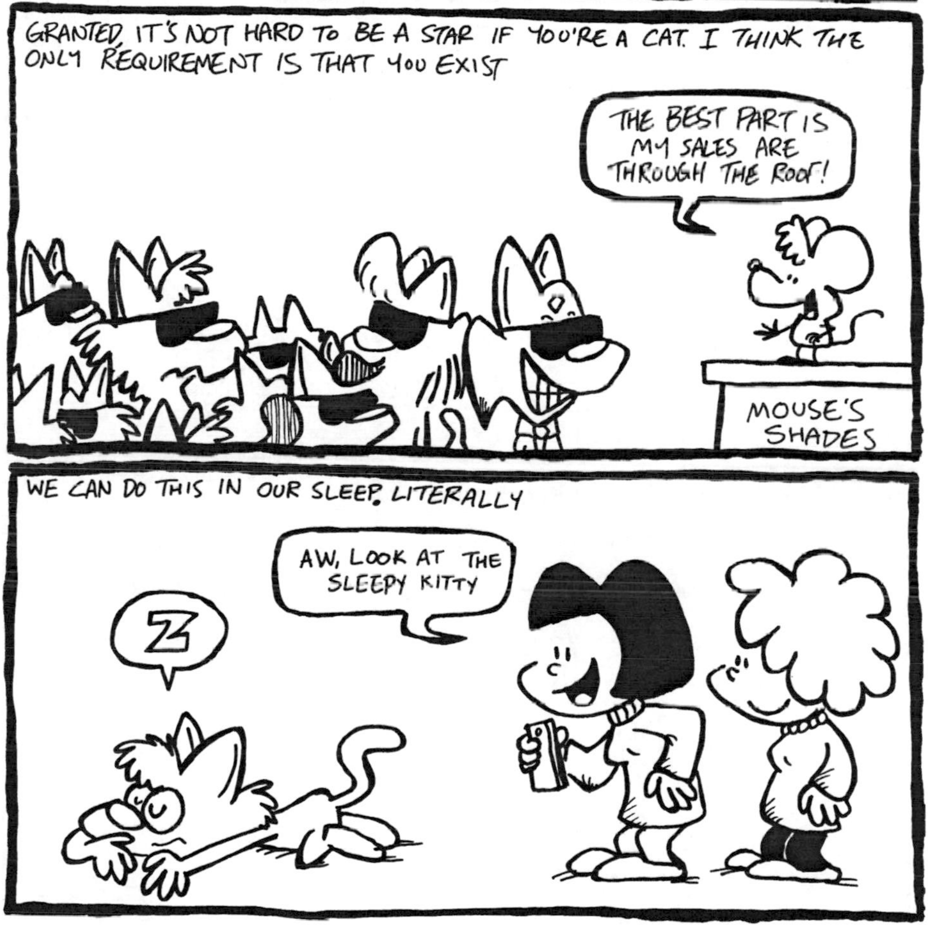
GRANTED, IT'S NOT HARD TO BE A STAR IF YOU'RE A CAT. I THINK THE ONLY REQUIREMENT IS THAT YOU EXIST
THE BEST PART IS MY SALES ARE THROUGH THE ROOF!
MOUSE'S SHADES
WE CAN DO THIS IN OUR SLEEP. LITERALLY
AW, LOOK AT THE SLEEPY KITTY
Z

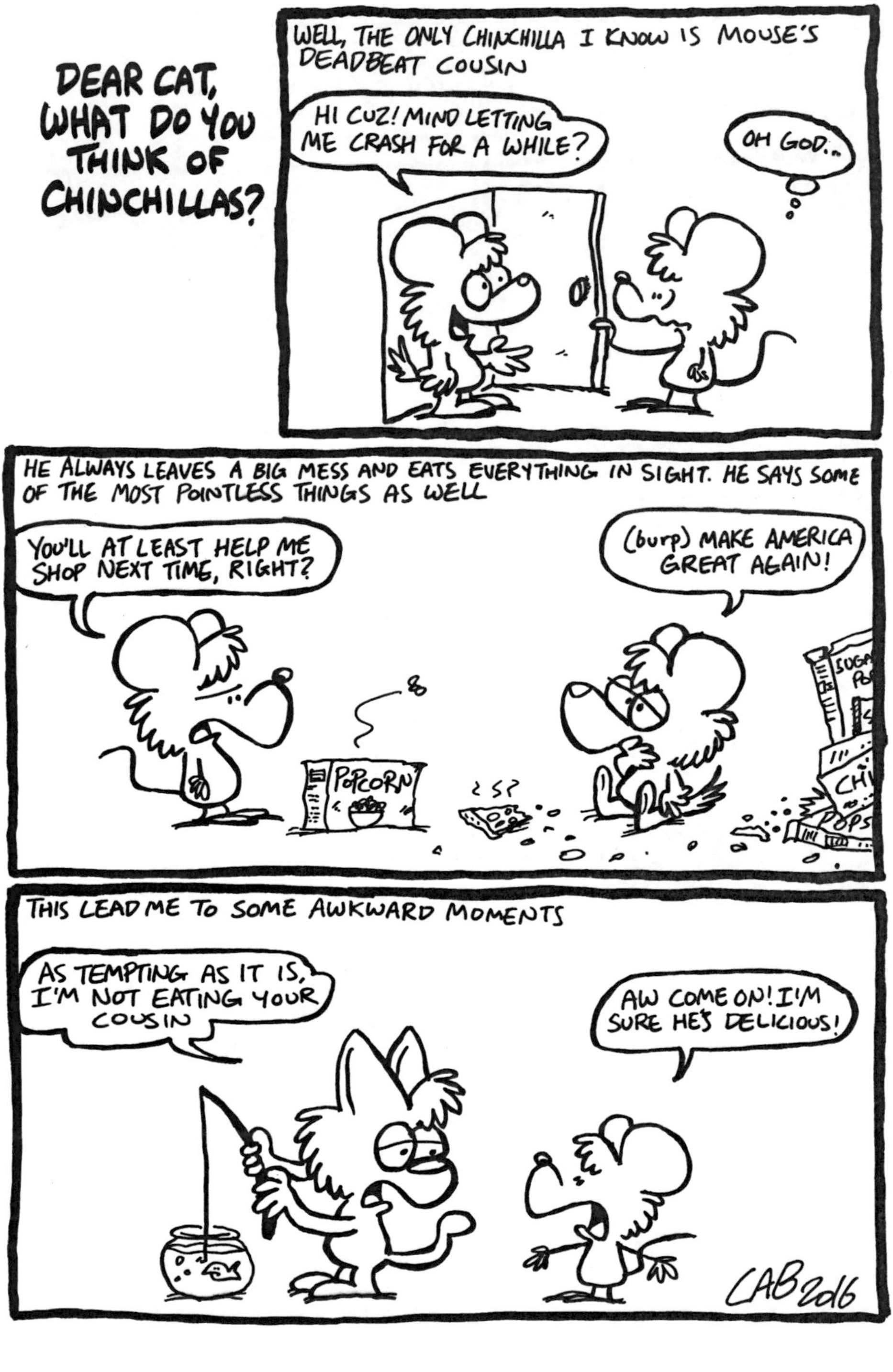
DEAR CAT, WHAT DO YOU THINK OF CHINCHILLAS?
WELL, THE ONLY CHINCHILLA I KNOW IS MOUSE'S DEADBEAT COUSIN
HI CUZ! MIND LETTING ME CRASH FOR A WHILE?
OH GOD...
HE ALWAYS LEAVES A BIG MESS AND EATS EVERYTHING IN SIGHT. HE SAYS SOME OF THE MOST POINTLESS THINGS AS WELL
YOU'LL AT LEAST HELP ME SHOP NEXT TIME, RIGHT?
(burp) MAKE AMERICA GREAT AGAIN!
POPCORN
THIS LEAD ME TO SOME AWKWARD MOMENTS
AS TEMPTING AS IT IS, I'M NOT EATING YOUR COUSIN
AW COME ON! I'M SURE HE'S DELICIOUS!
CAB 2016

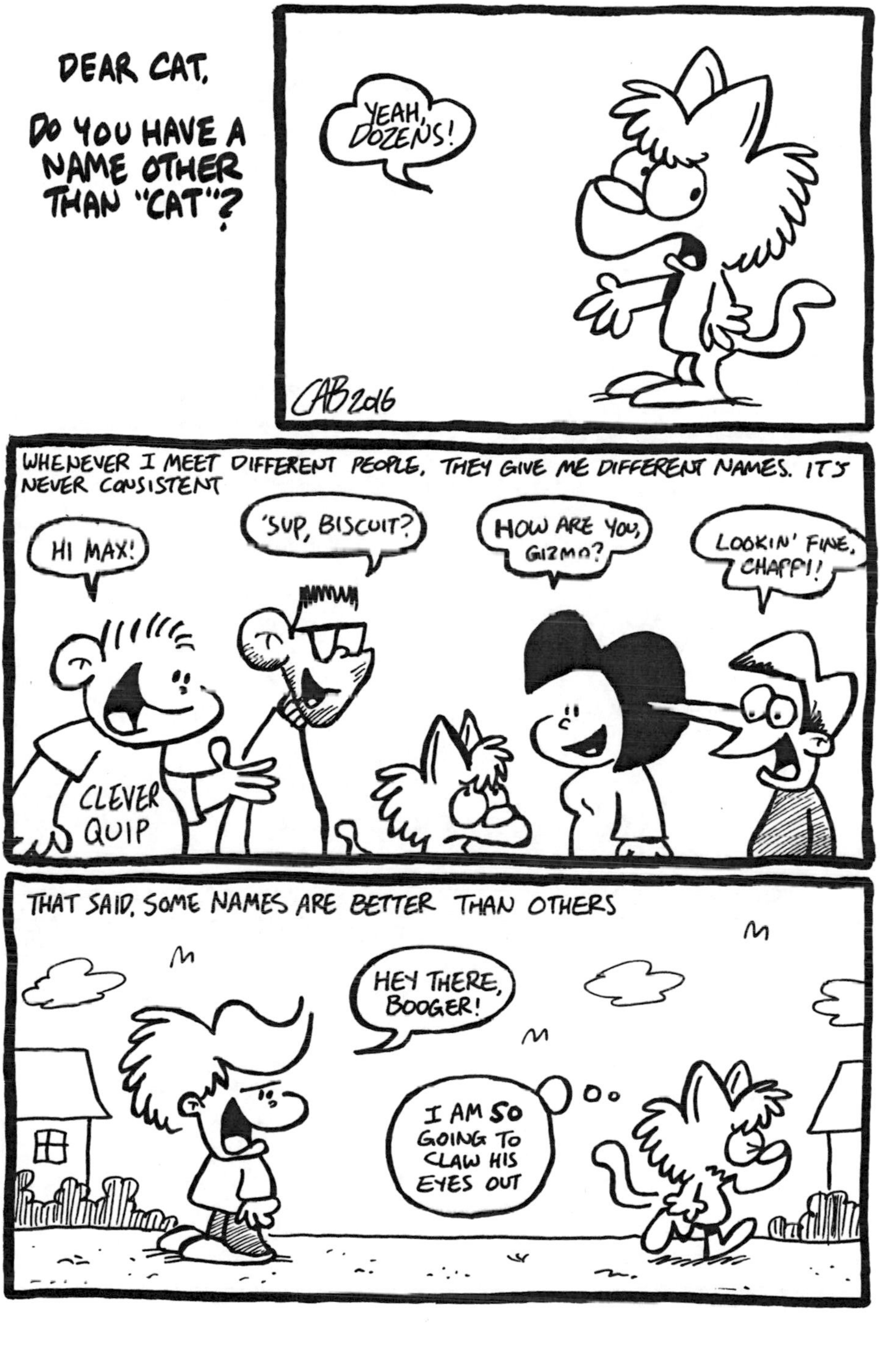
DEAR CAT.
DO YOU HAVE A NAME OTHER THAN "CAT"?
YEAH, DOZENS!
CAB 2016
WHENEVER I MEET DIFFERENT PEOPLE, THEY GIVE ME DIFFERENT NAMES. IT'S NEVER CONSISTENT
HI MAX!
'SUP, BISCUIT?
HOW ARE YOU, GIZMO?
LOOKIN' FINE, CHAPPI!
CLEVER QUIP
THAT SAID, SOME NAMES ARE BETTER THAN OTHERS
HEY THERE, BOOGER!
I AM SO GOING TO CLAW HIS EYES OUT

DEAR CAT,
DO YOU KNOW PRINCESS KAT?

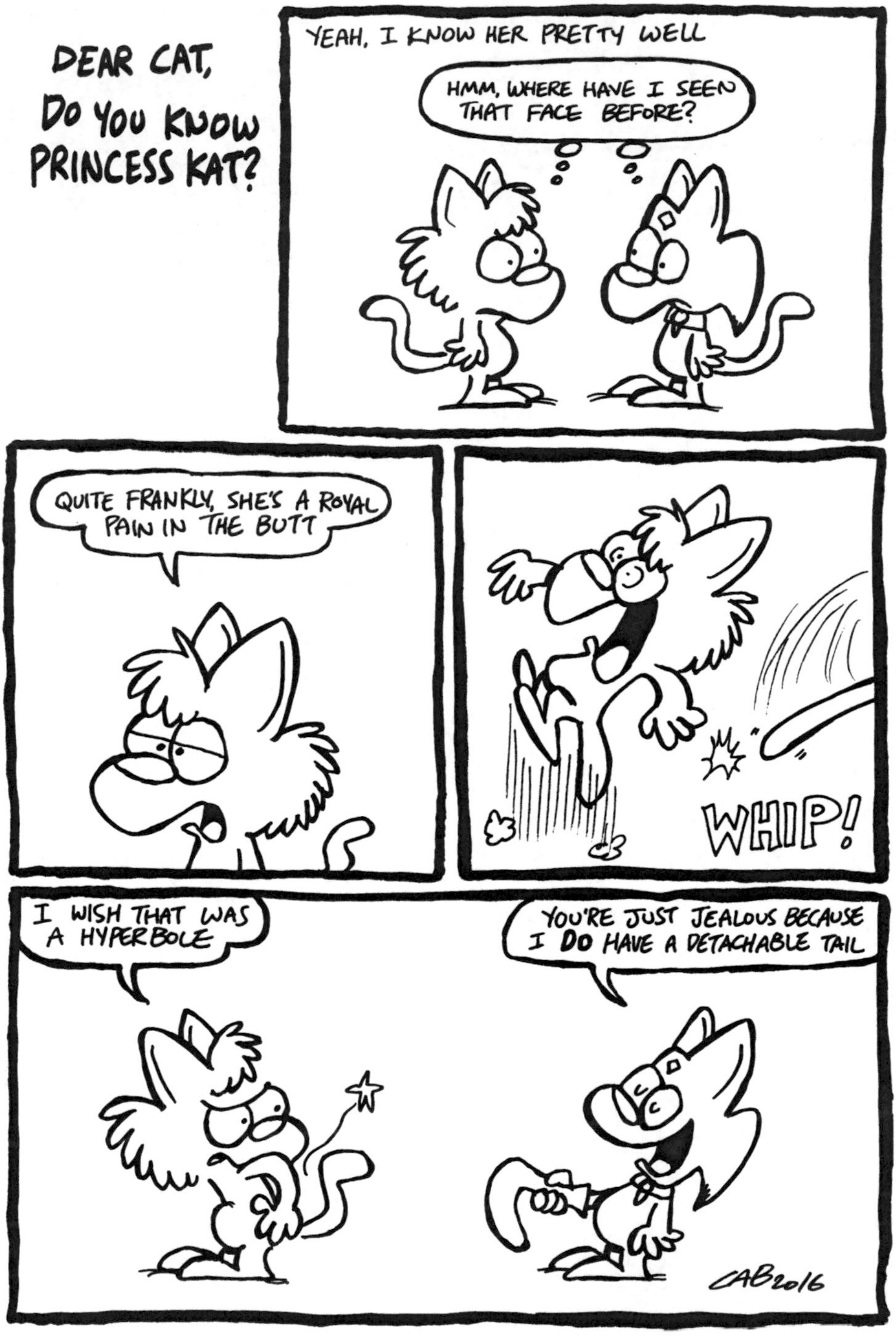
YEAH, I KNOW HER PRETTY WELL
HMM, WHERE HAVE I SEEN THAT FACE BEFORE?
QUITE FRANKLY, SHE'S A ROYAL PAIN IN THE BUTT
WHIP!
I WISH THAT WAS A HYPERBOLE
YOU'RE JUST JEALOUS BECAUSE I DO HAVE A DETACHABLE TAIL
CAB2016

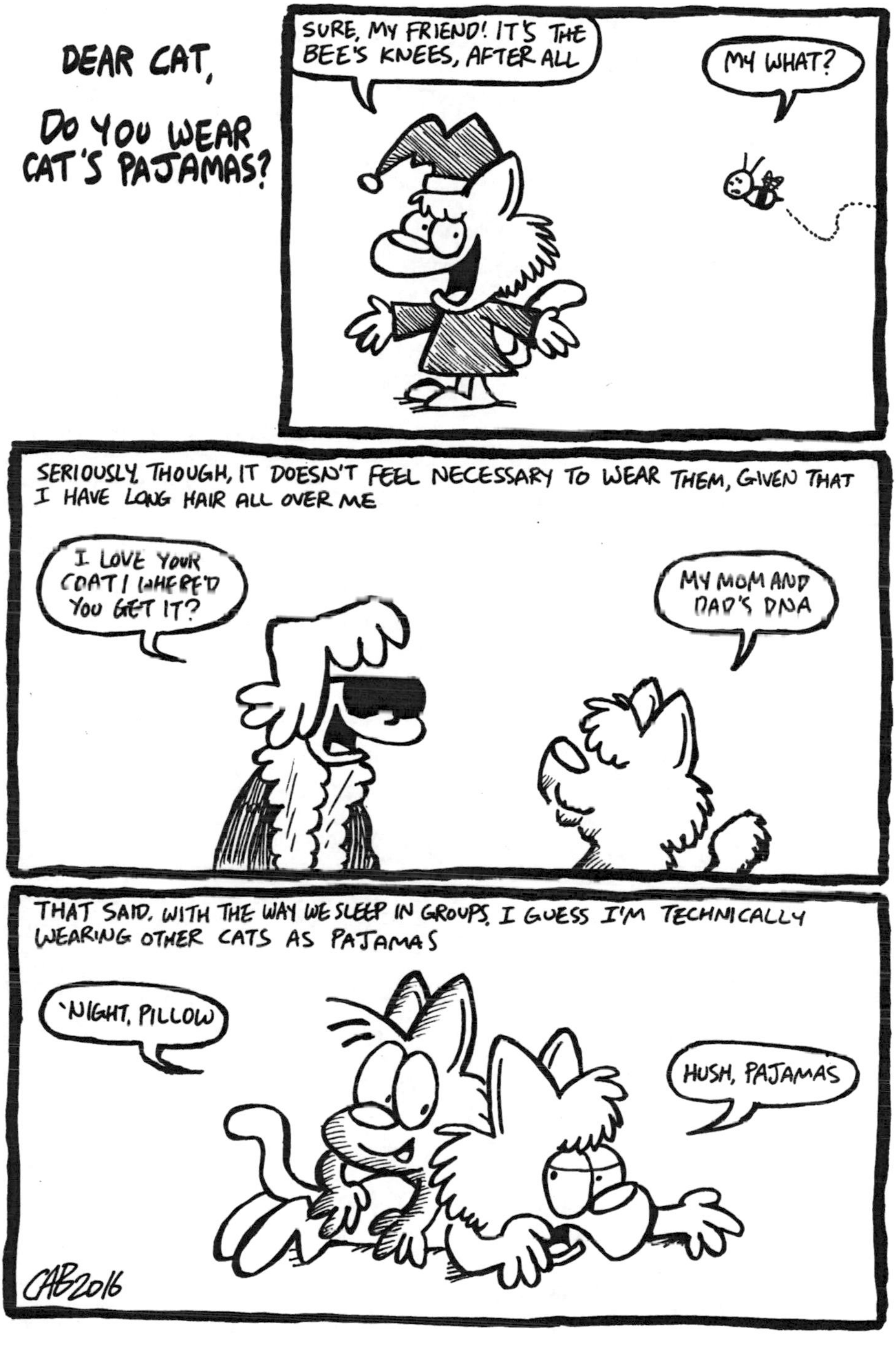
DEAR CAT,
DO YOU WEAR CAT'S PAJAMAS?
SURE, MY FRIEND! IT'S THE BEE'S KNEES, AFTER ALL
MY WHAT?
SERIOUSLY, THOUGH, IT DOESN'T FEEL NECESSARY TO WEAR THEM, GIVEN THAT I HAVE LONG HAIR ALL OVER ME
I LOVE YOUR COAT! WHERE'D YOU GET IT?
MY MOM AND DAD'S DNA
THAT SAID, WITH THE WAY WE SLEEP IN GROUPS, I GUESS I'M TECHNICALLY WEARING OTHER CATS AS PAJAMAS
`NIGHT, PILLOW
HUSH, PAJAMAS
CAB 2016

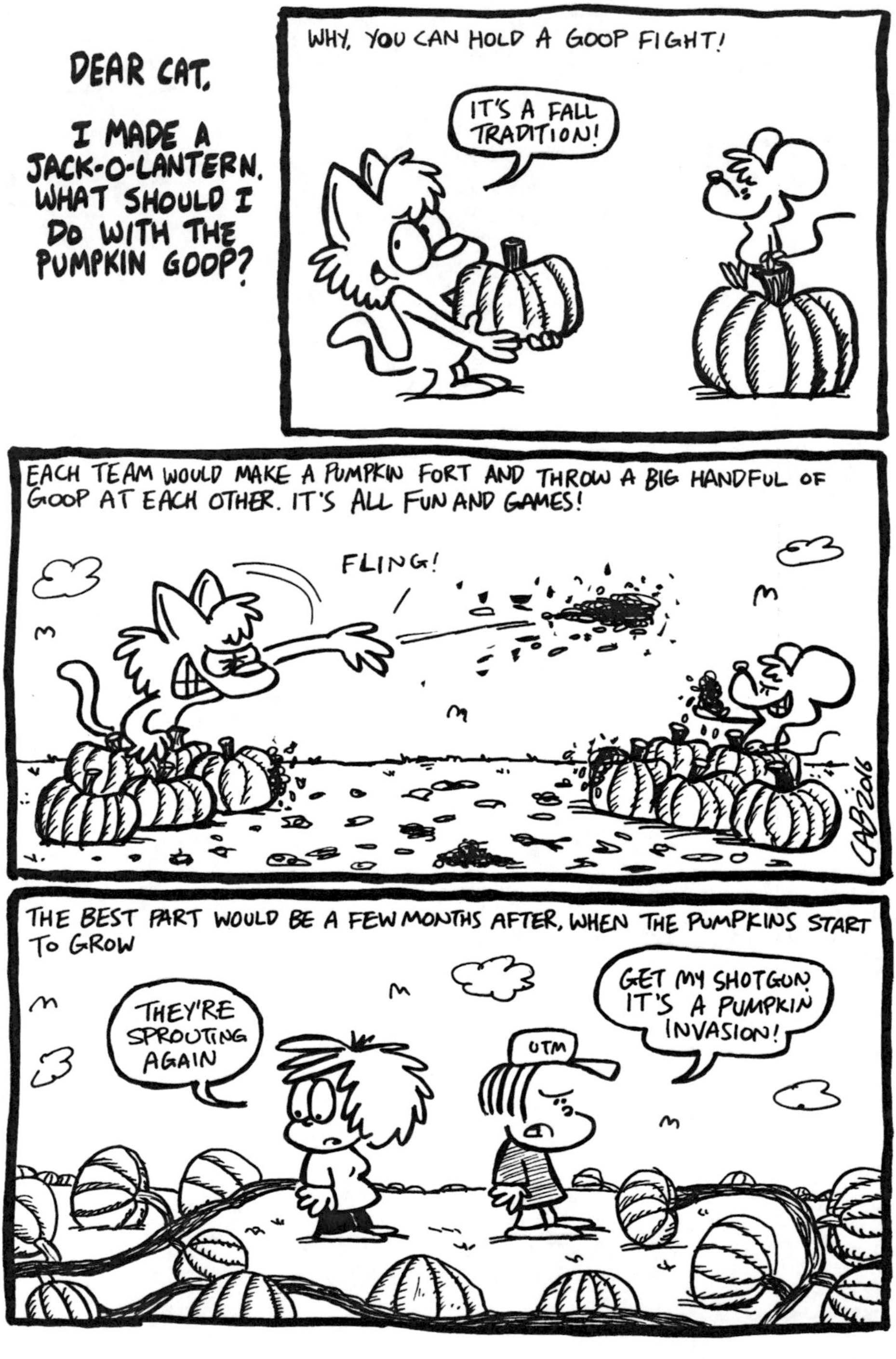
DEAR CAT,
I MADE A JACK-O-LANTERN. WHAT SHOULD I DO WITH THE PUMPKIN GOOP?
WHY, YOU CAN HOLD A GOOP FIGHT!
IT'S A FALL TRADITION!
EACH TEAM WOULD MAKE A PUMPKIN FORT AND THROW A BIG HANDFUL OF GOOP AT EACH OTHER. IT'S ALL FUN AND GAMES!
FLING!
CAB 2016
THE BEST PART WOULD BE A FEW MONTHS AFTER, WHEN THE PUMPKINS START TO GROW
THEY'RE SPROUTING AGAIN
GET MY SHOTGUN. IT'S A PUMPKIN INVASION!
UTM

DEAR CAT,

DO CATS HAVE ELECTIONS?

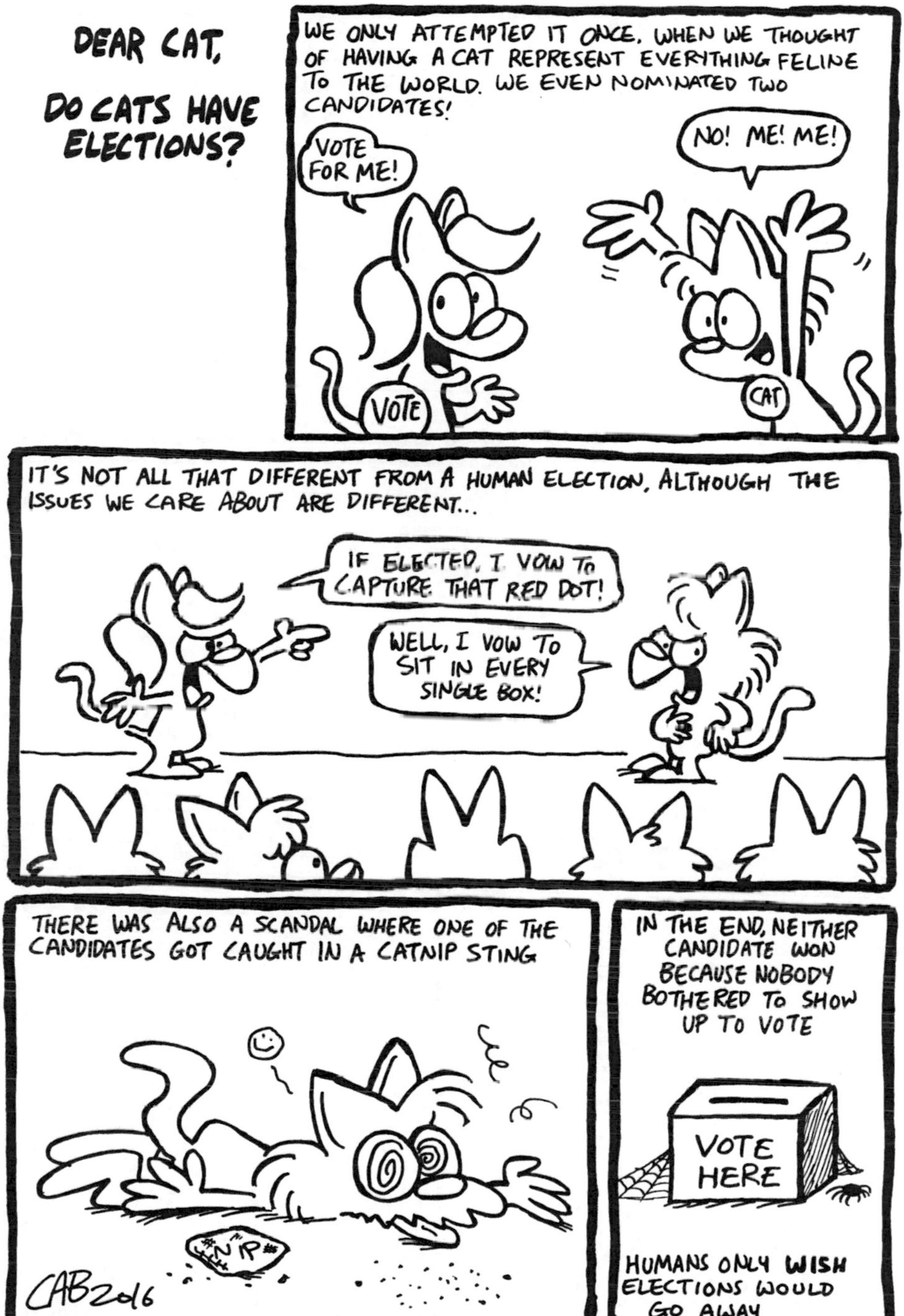
WE ONLY ATTEMPTED IT ONCE, WHEN WE THOUGHT OF HAVING A CAT REPRESENT EVERYTHING FELINE TO THE WORLD. WE EVEN NOMINATED TWO CANDIDATES!
VOTE FOR ME!
NO! ME! ME!
VOTE
CAT
IT'S NOT ALL THAT DIFFERENT FROM A HUMAN ELECTION, ALTHOUGH THE ISSUES WE CARE ABOUT ARE DIFFERENT...
IF ELECTED, I VOW TO CAPTURE THAT RED DOT!
WELL, I VOW TO SIT IN EVERY SINGLE BOX!
THERE WAS ALSO A SCANDAL WHERE ONE OF THE CANDIDATES GOT CAUGHT IN A CATNIP STING
CAB 2016
IN THE END, NEITHER CANDIDATE WON BECAUSE NOBODY BOTHERED TO SHOW UP TO VOTE
VOTE HERE
HUMANS ONLY **WISH** ELECTIONS WOULD GO AWAY

DEAR CAT,

WHAT KIND OF FOOD DO YOU PREFER?

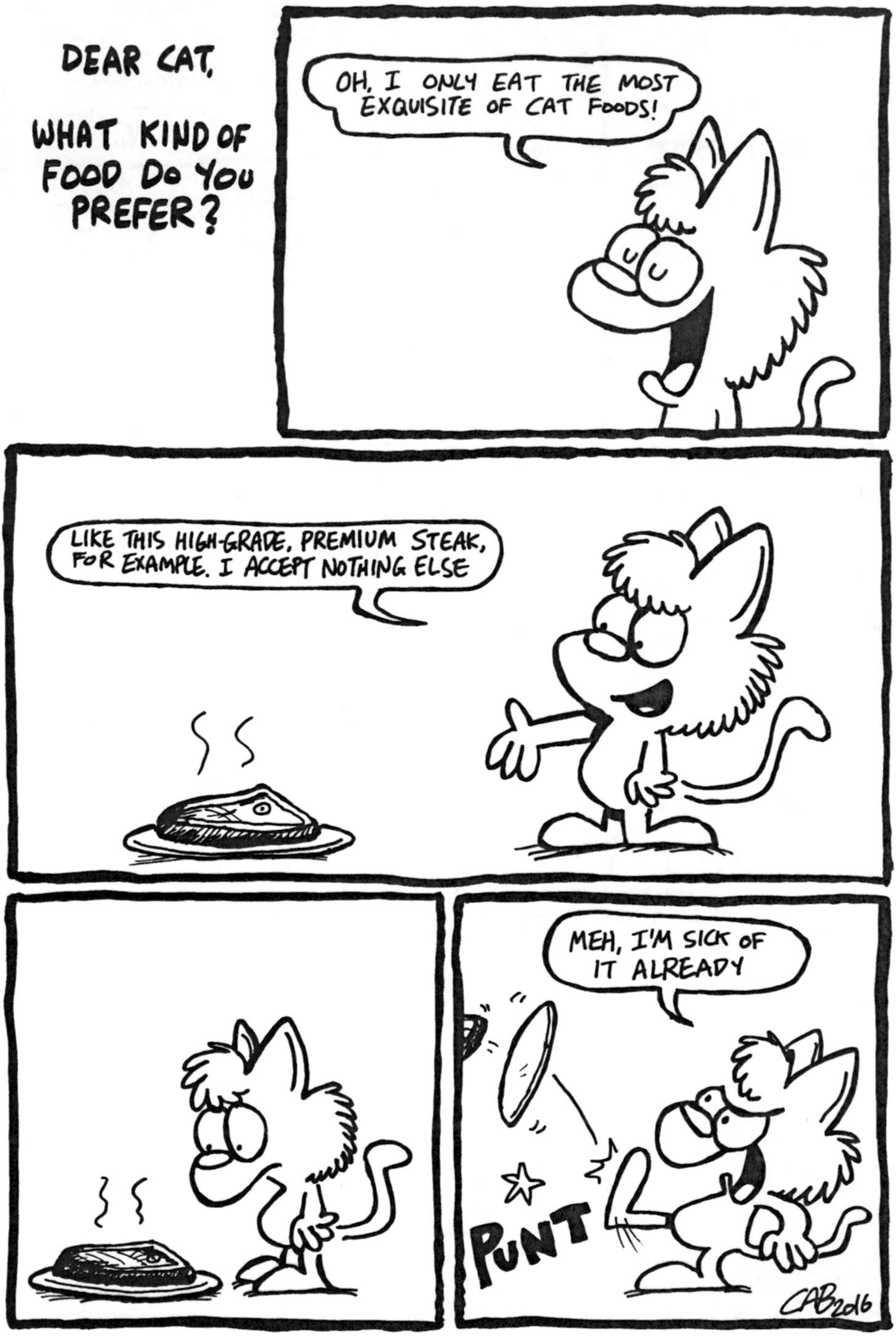
OH, I ONLY EAT THE MOST EXQUISITE OF CAT FOODS!
LIKE THIS HIGH-GRADE, PREMIUM STEAK, FOR EXAMPLE. I ACCEPT NOTHING ELSE
MEH, I'M SICK OF IT ALREADY
PUNT
CAB 2016

DEAR CAT,

WHY ARE CATS AFRAID OF WATER?

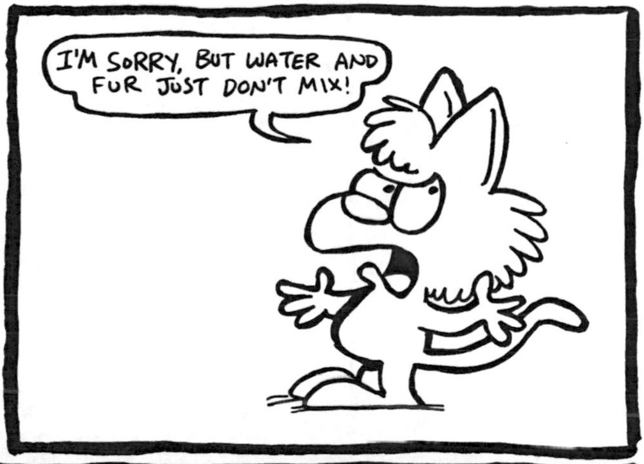

I'M SORRY, BUT WATER AND FUR JUST DON'T MIX!

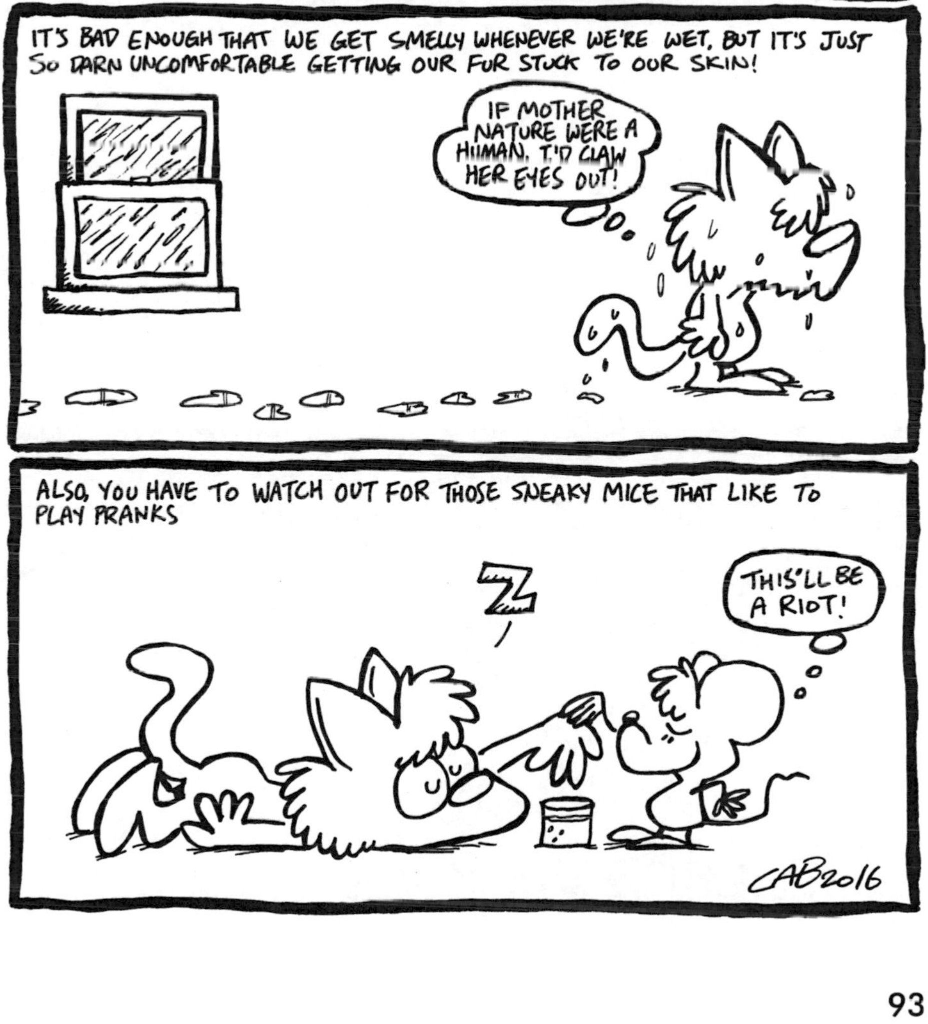

IT'S BAD ENOUGH THAT WE GET SMELLY WHENEVER WE'RE WET, BUT IT'S JUST SO DARN UNCOMFORTABLE GETTING OUR FUR STUCK TO OUR SKIN!
IF MOTHER NATURE WERE A HUMAN, I'D CLAW HER EYES OUT!
ALSO, YOU HAVE TO WATCH OUT FOR THOSE SNEAKY MICE THAT LIKE TO PLAY PRANKS
Z
THIS'LL BE A RIOT!
CAB 2016

DEAR CAT,

IS THERE A CAT AIRLINE?

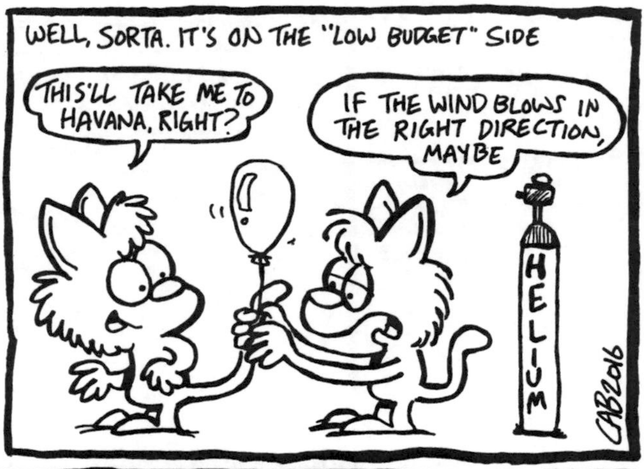
WELL, SORTA. IT'S ON THE "LOW BUDGET" SIDE
THIS'LL TAKE ME TO HAVANA, RIGHT?
IF THE WIND BLOWS IN THE RIGHT DIRECTION, MAYBE
HELIUM
CAB2016

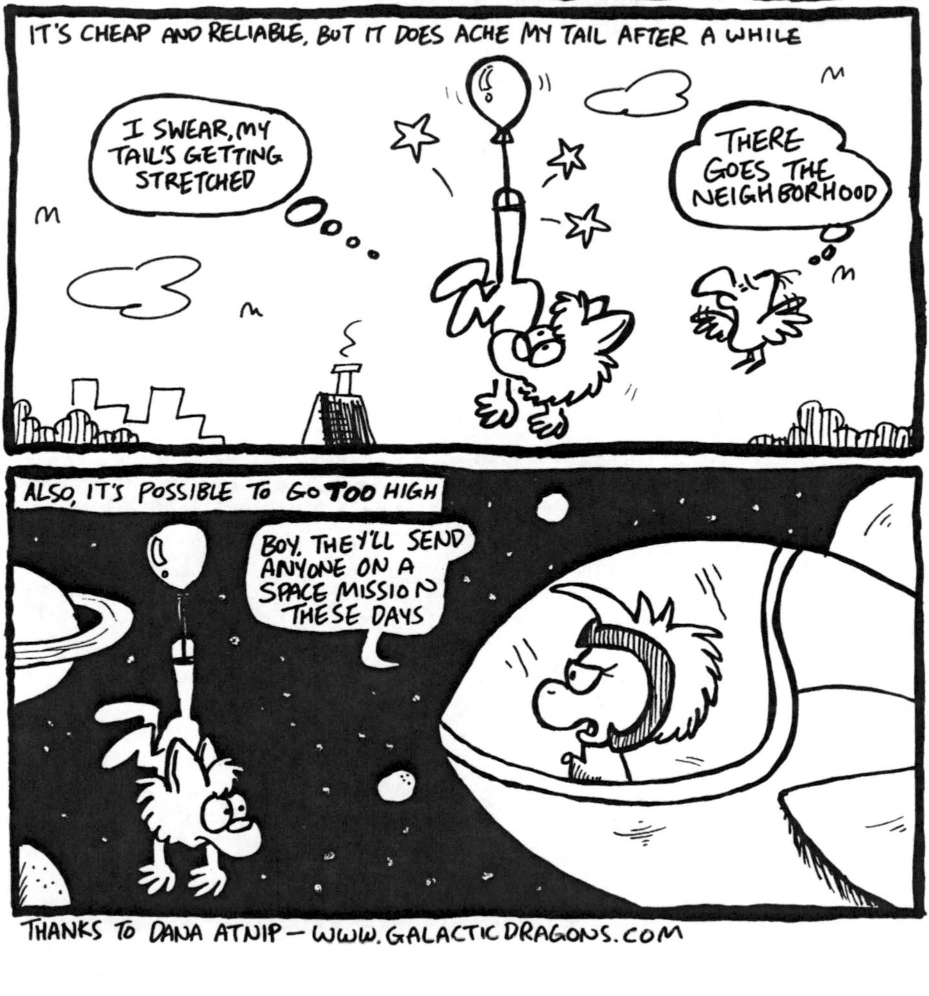
IT'S CHEAP AND RELIABLE, BUT IT DOES ACHE MY TAIL AFTER A WHILE
I SWEAR, MY TAIL'S GETTING STRETCHED
THERE GOES THE NEIGHBORHOOD
ALSO, IT'S POSSIBLE TO GO TOO HIGH
BOY, THEY'LL SEND ANYONE ON A SPACE MISSION THESE DAYS

THANKS TO DANA ATNIP — WWW.GALACTICDRAGONS.COM

DEAR CAT,

DO YOU WRITE LETTERS TO OTHER CATS?

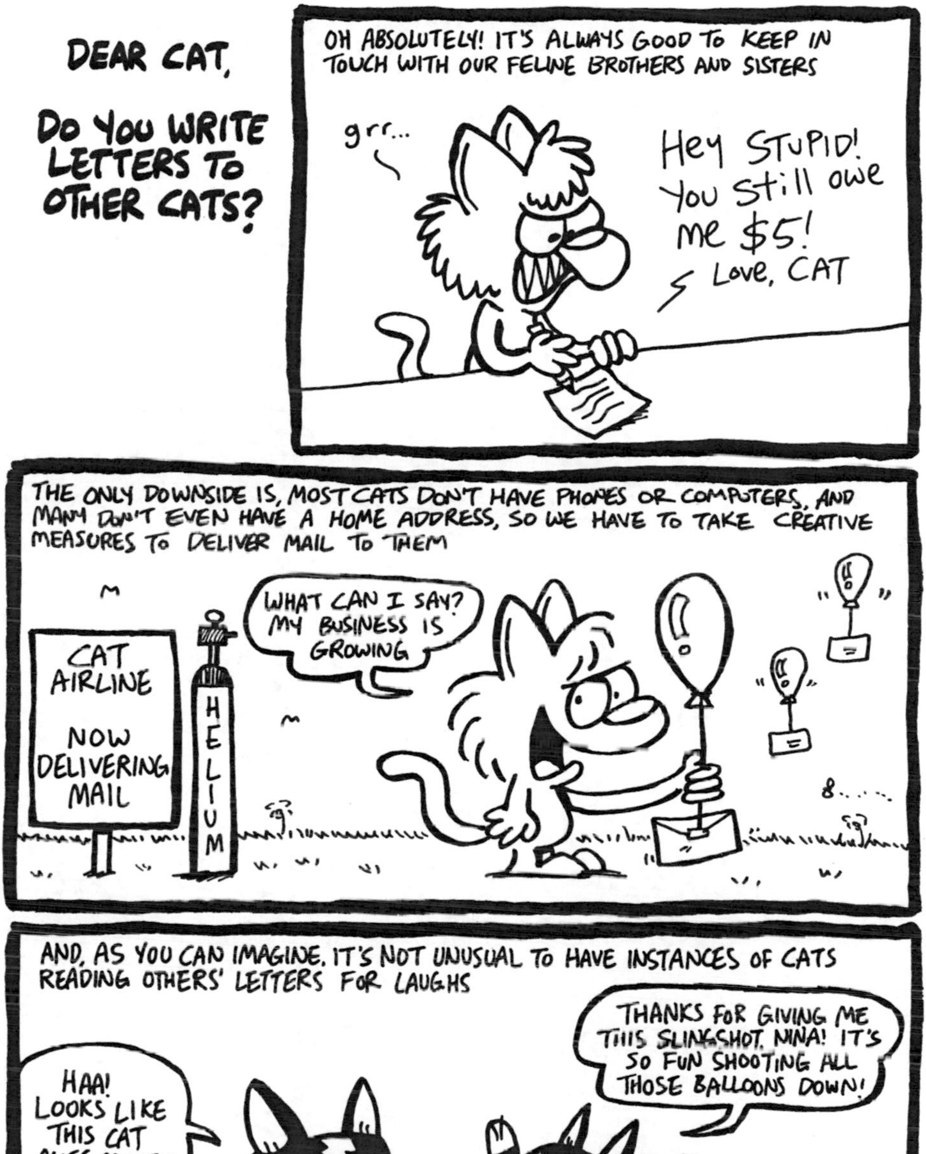
OH ABSOLUTELY! IT'S ALWAYS GOOD TO KEEP IN TOUCH WITH OUR FELINE BROTHERS AND SISTERS
grr...
Hey STUPID! You still owe me $5! Love, CAT
THE ONLY DOWNSIDE IS, MOST CATS DON'T HAVE PHONES OR COMPUTERS, AND MANY DON'T EVEN HAVE A HOME ADDRESS, SO WE HAVE TO TAKE CREATIVE MEASURES TO DELIVER MAIL TO THEM
CAT AIRLINE NOW DELIVERING MAIL
HELIUM
WHAT CAN I SAY? MY BUSINESS IS GROWING
AND, AS YOU CAN IMAGINE, IT'S NOT UNUSUAL TO HAVE INSTANCES OF CATS READING OTHERS' LETTERS FOR LAUGHS
HAA! LOOKS LIKE THIS CAT OWES MONEY
THANKS FOR GIVING ME THIS SLINGSHOT, NINA! IT'S SO FUN SHOOTING ALL THOSE BALLOONS DOWN!
CAB 2016

THANKS TO STEVE OGDEN - WWW.GOCOMICS.COM/MAGNIFICATZ

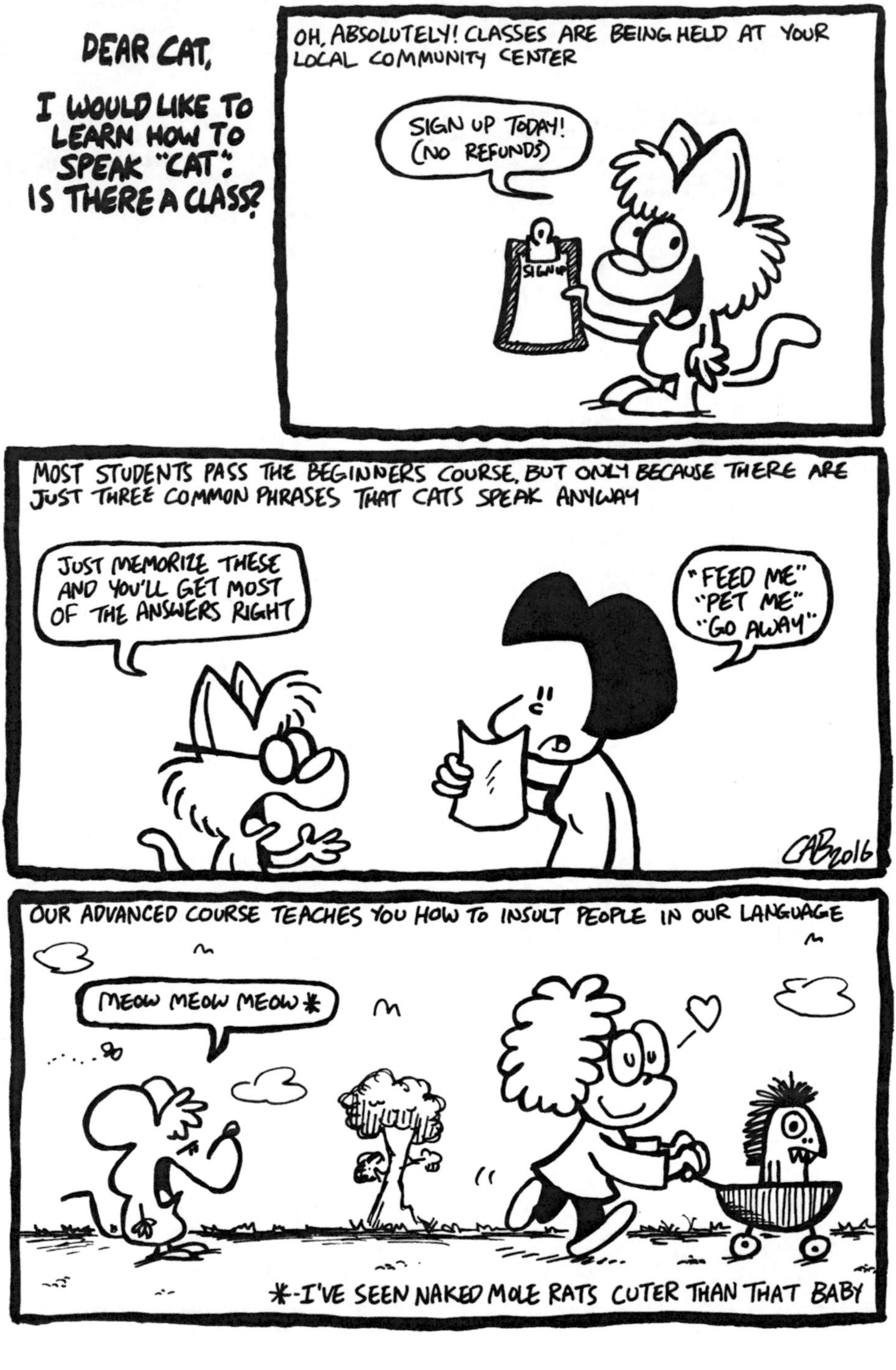
DEAR CAT,
I WOULD LIKE TO LEARN HOW TO SPEAK "CAT". IS THERE A CLASS?
OH, ABSOLUTELY! CLASSES ARE BEING HELD AT YOUR LOCAL COMMUNITY CENTER
SIGN UP TODAY! (NO REFUNDS)
SIGN UP
MOST STUDENTS PASS THE BEGINNERS COURSE, BUT ONLY BECAUSE THERE ARE JUST THREE COMMON PHRASES THAT CATS SPEAK ANYWAY
JUST MEMORIZE THESE AND YOU'LL GET MOST OF THE ANSWERS RIGHT
"FEED ME" "PET ME" "GO AWAY"
CAB 2016
OUR ADVANCED COURSE TEACHES YOU HOW TO INSULT PEOPLE IN OUR LANGUAGE
MEOW MEOW MEOW*
*-I'VE SEEN NAKED MOLE RATS CUTER THAN THAT BABY

DEAR CAT,

HOW DO YOU FEEL ABOUT CAT REPRESENTATION IN MEDIA?

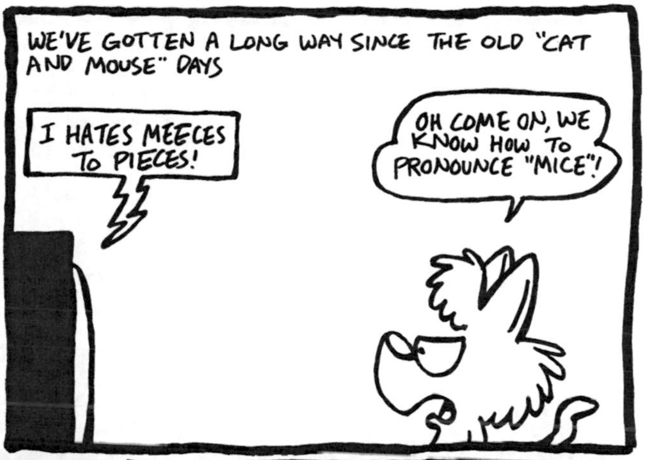
WE'VE GOTTEN A LONG WAY SINCE THE OLD "CAT AND MOUSE" DAYS
I HATES MEECES TO PIECES!
OH COME ON, WE KNOW HOW TO PRONOUNCE "MICE"!

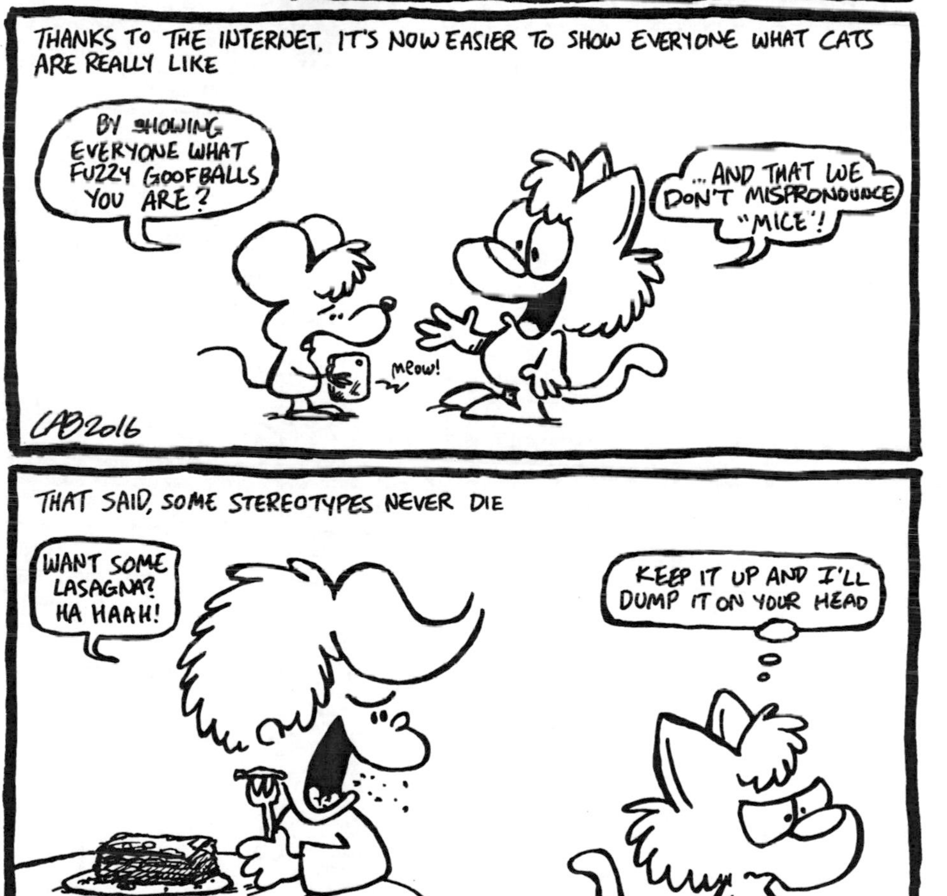
THANKS TO THE INTERNET, IT'S NOW EASIER TO SHOW EVERYONE WHAT CATS ARE REALLY LIKE
BY SHOWING EVERYONE WHAT FUZZY GOOFBALLS YOU ARE?
...AND THAT WE DON'T MISPRONOUNCE "MICE"!
MEOW!
CAB 2016
THAT SAID, SOME STEREOTYPES NEVER DIE
WANT SOME LASAGNA? HA HAAH!
KEEP IT UP AND I'LL DUMP IT ON YOUR HEAD

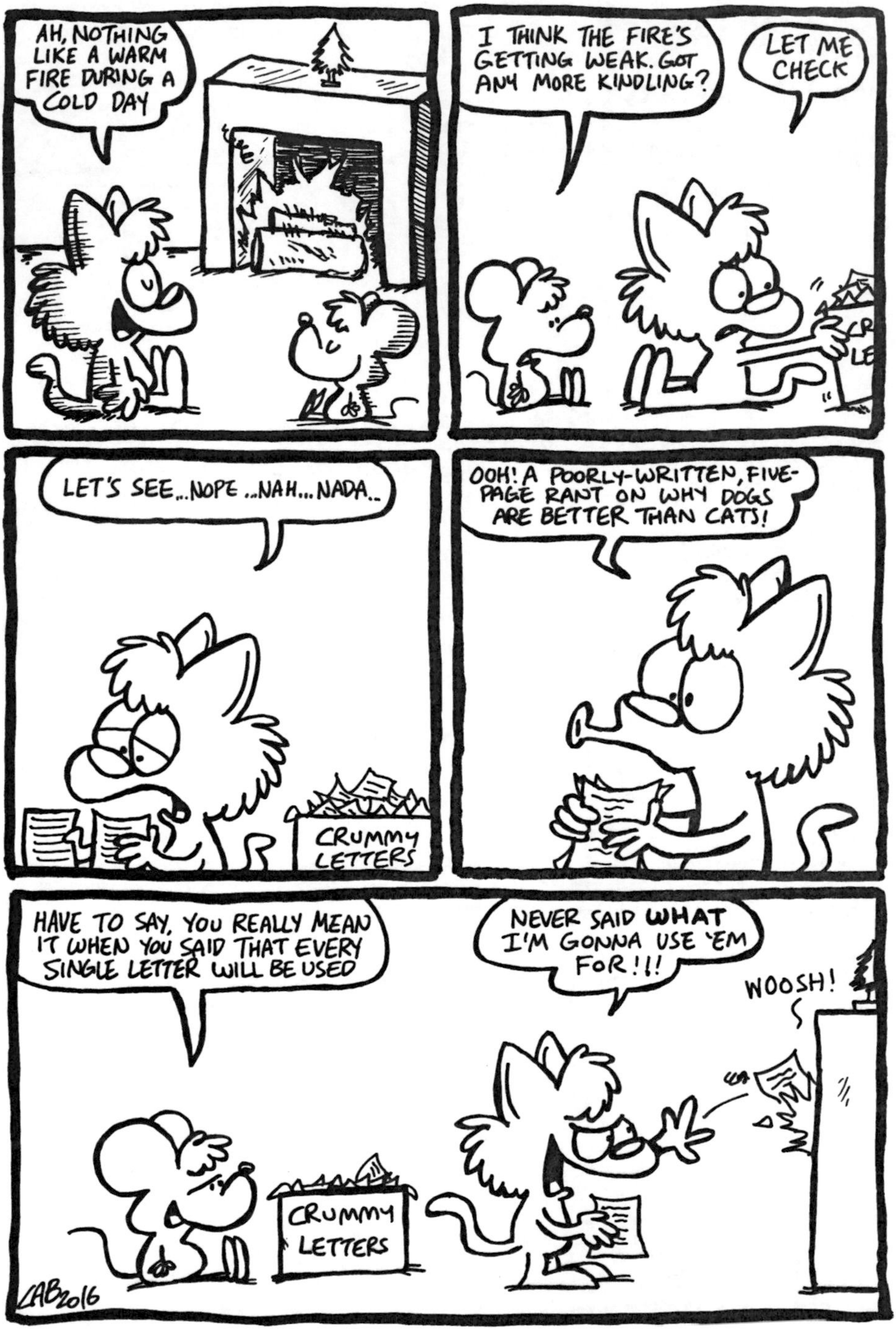
AH, NOTHING LIKE A WARM FIRE DURING A COLD DAY
I THINK THE FIRE'S GETTING WEAK. GOT ANY MORE KINDLING?
LET ME CHECK
LET'S SEE... NOPE ...NAH... NADA...
CRUMMY LETTERS
OOH! A POORLY-WRITTEN, FIVE-PAGE RANT ON WHY DOGS ARE BETTER THAN CATS!
HAVE TO SAY, YOU REALLY MEAN IT WHEN YOU SAID THAT EVERY SINGLE LETTER WILL BE USED
NEVER SAID WHAT I'M GONNA USE 'EM FOR!!!
WOOSH!
CRUMMY LETTERS
CAB 2016

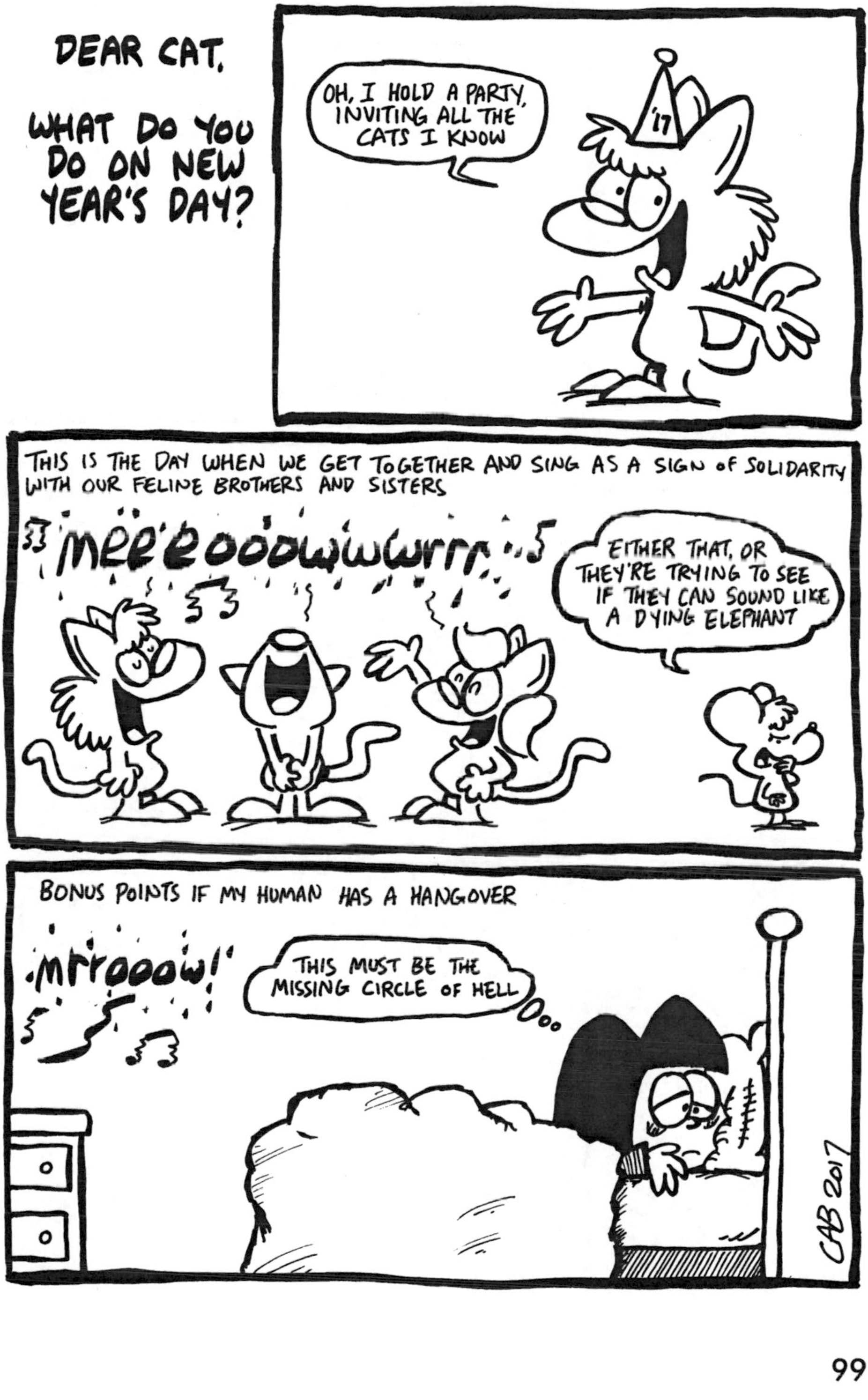
DEAR CAT,
WHAT DO YOU DO ON NEW YEAR'S DAY?
OH, I HOLD A PARTY, INVITING ALL THE CATS I KNOW
'17
THIS IS THE DAY WHEN WE GET TOGETHER AND SING AS A SIGN OF SOLIDARITY WITH OUR FELINE BROTHERS AND SISTERS
MEEEOOOWWWRRR
EITHER THAT, OR THEY'RE TRYING TO SEE IF THEY CAN SOUND LIKE A DYING ELEPHANT
BONUS POINTS IF MY HUMAN HAS A HANGOVER
MRROOOW!
THIS MUST BE THE MISSING CIRCLE OF HELL
CAB 2017

DEAR CAT, WHY?

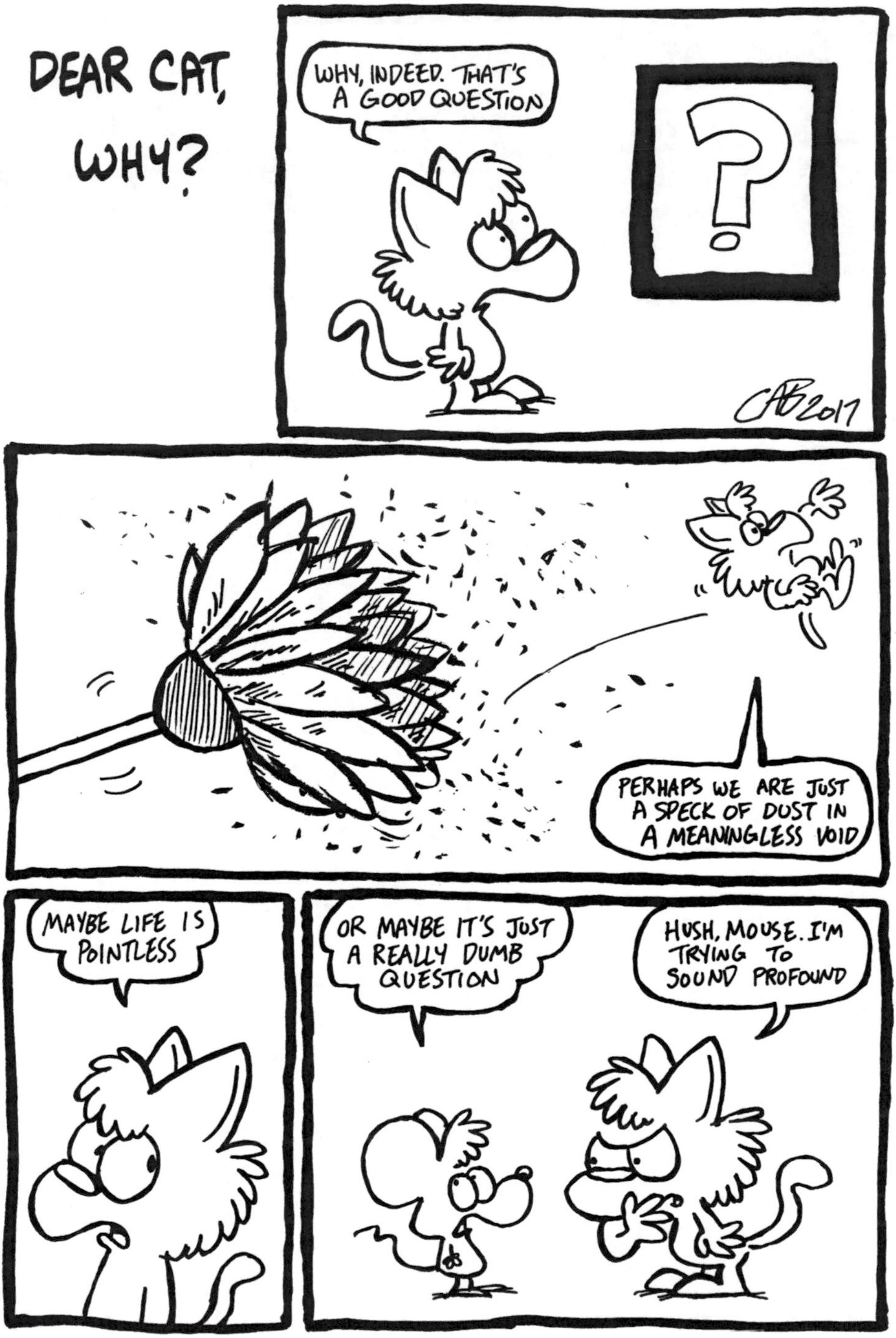
WHY, INDEED. THAT'S A GOOD QUESTION
PERHAPS WE ARE JUST A SPECK OF DUST IN A MEANINGLESS VOID
MAYBE LIFE IS POINTLESS
OR MAYBE IT'S JUST A REALLY DUMB QUESTION
HUSH, MOUSE. I'M TRYING TO SOUND PROFOUND

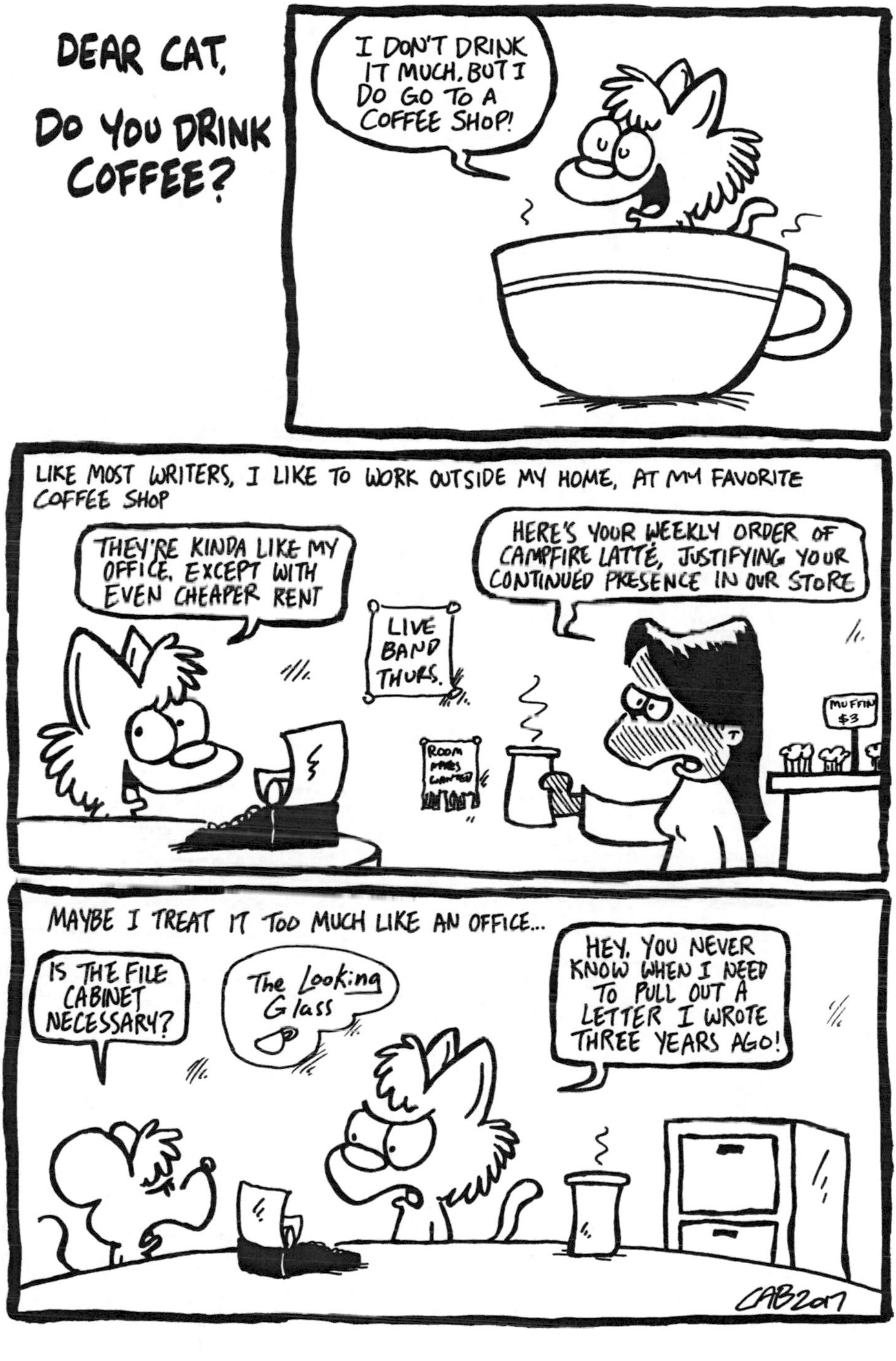
DEAR CAT,
DO YOU DRINK COFFEE?
I DON'T DRINK IT MUCH, BUT I DO GO TO A COFFEE SHOP!
LIKE MOST WRITERS, I LIKE TO WORK OUTSIDE MY HOME, AT MY FAVORITE COFFEE SHOP
THEY'RE KINDA LIKE MY OFFICE, EXCEPT WITH EVEN CHEAPER RENT
HERE'S YOUR WEEKLY ORDER OF CAMPFIRE LATTÉ, JUSTIFYING YOUR CONTINUED PRESENCE IN OUR STORE
LIVE BAND THURS.
MUFFIN $3
MAYBE I TREAT IT TOO MUCH LIKE AN OFFICE...
IS THE FILE CABINET NECESSARY?
The Looking Glass
HEY, YOU NEVER KNOW WHEN I NEED TO PULL OUT A LETTER I WROTE THREE YEARS AGO!
CAB2017

DEAR CAT,

Do YOU USE COUPONS?

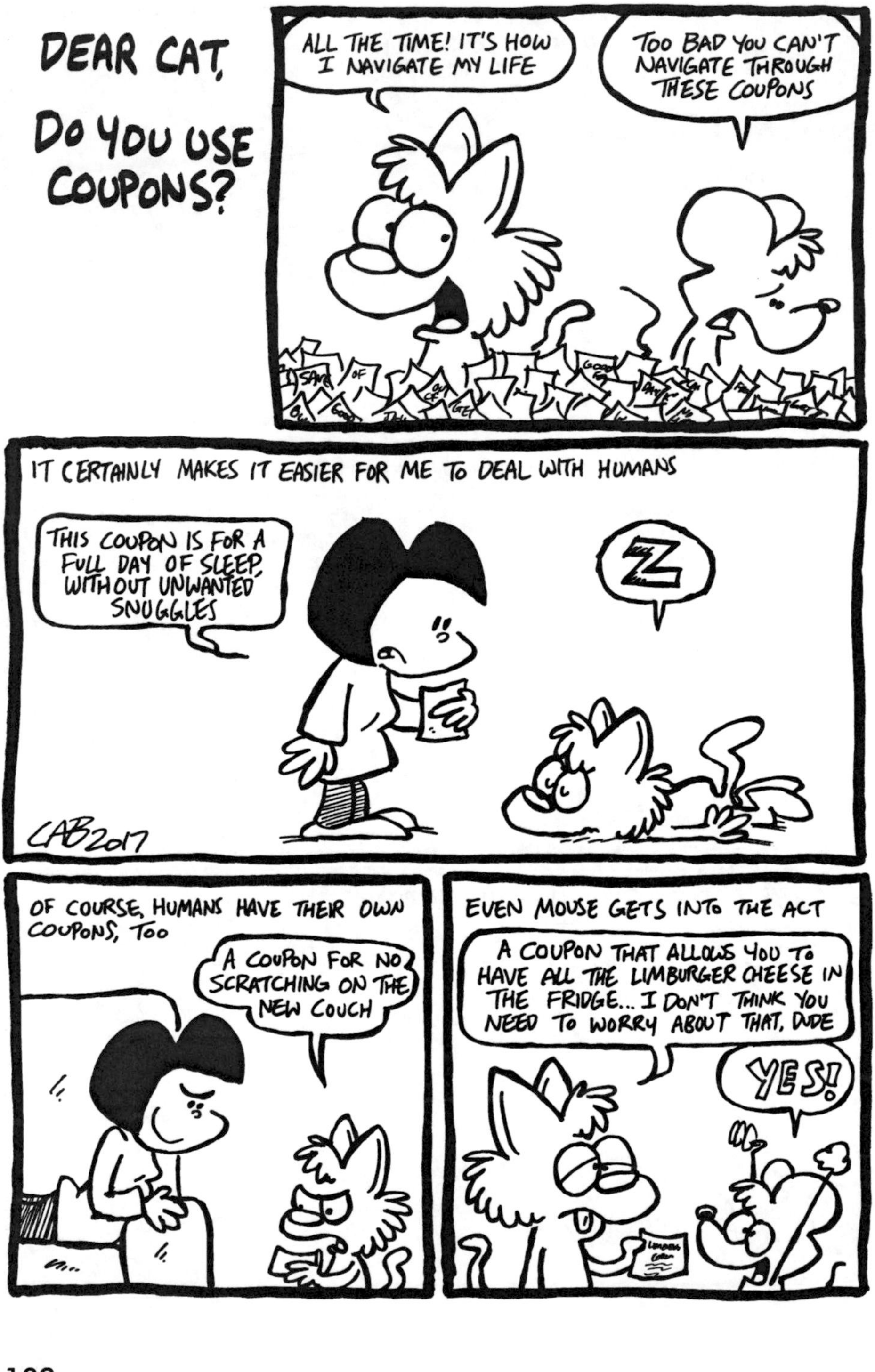

ALL THE TIME! IT'S HOW I NAVIGATE MY LIFE
TOO BAD YOU CAN'T NAVIGATE THROUGH THESE COUPONS
IT CERTAINLY MAKES IT EASIER FOR ME TO DEAL WITH HUMANS
THIS COUPON IS FOR A FULL DAY OF SLEEP, WITHOUT UNWANTED SNUGGLES
Z
CAB 2017
OF COURSE, HUMANS HAVE THEIR OWN COUPONS, TOO
A COUPON FOR NO SCRATCHING ON THE NEW COUCH
EVEN MOUSE GETS INTO THE ACT
A COUPON THAT ALLOWS YOU TO HAVE ALL THE LIMBURGER CHEESE IN THE FRIDGE... I DON'T THINK YOU NEED TO WORRY ABOUT THAT, DUDE
YES!

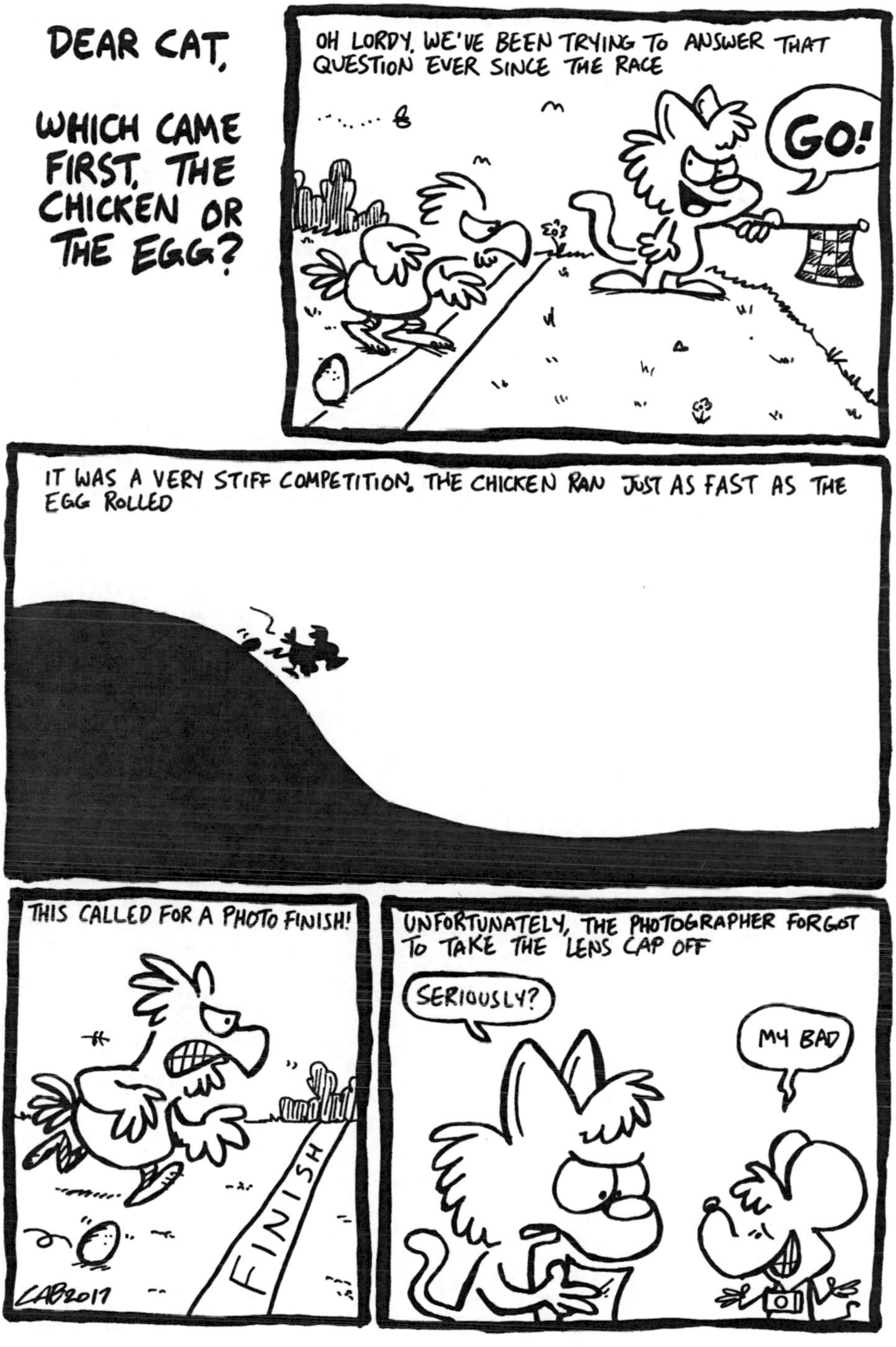
DEAR CAT,
WHICH CAME FIRST, THE CHICKEN OR THE EGG?
OH LORDY, WE'VE BEEN TRYING TO ANSWER THAT QUESTION EVER SINCE THE RACE
GO!
IT WAS A VERY STIFF COMPETITION. THE CHICKEN RAN JUST AS FAST AS THE EGG ROLLED
THIS CALLED FOR A PHOTO FINISH!
FINISH
CAB2017
UNFORTUNATELY, THE PHOTOGRAPHER FORGOT TO TAKE THE LENS CAP OFF
SERIOUSLY?
MY BAD

DEAR CAT,

DO YOU USE FACEBOOK?

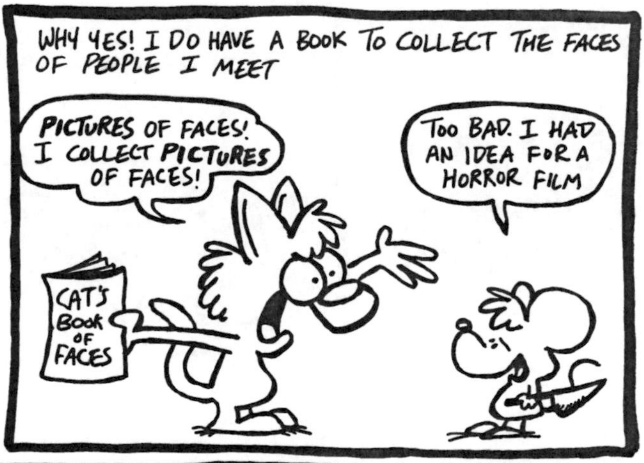

WHY YES! I DO HAVE A BOOK TO COLLECT THE FACES OF PEOPLE I MEET
PICTURES OF FACES! I COLLECT PICTURES OF FACES!
TOO BAD. I HAD AN IDEA FOR A HORROR FILM
CAT'S BOOK OF FACES

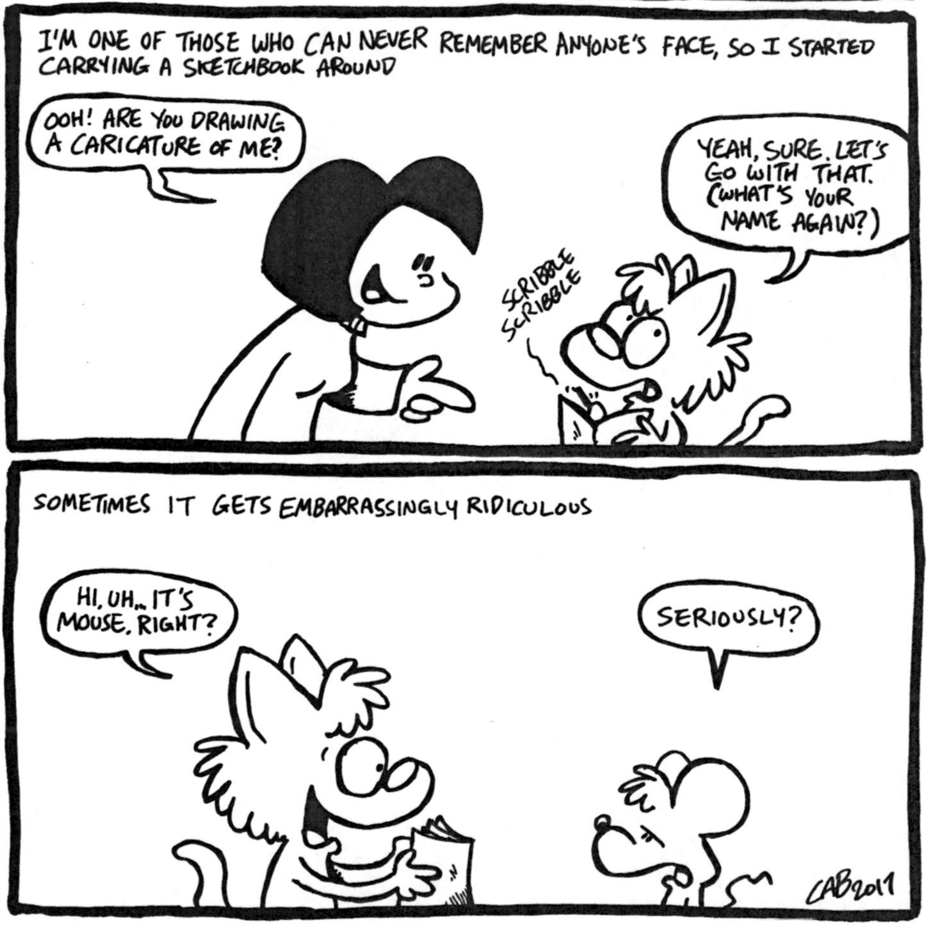

I'M ONE OF THOSE WHO CAN NEVER REMEMBER ANYONE'S FACE, SO I STARTED CARRYING A SKETCHBOOK AROUND
OOH! ARE YOU DRAWING A CARICATURE OF ME?
YEAH, SURE. LET'S GO WITH THAT. (WHAT'S YOUR NAME AGAIN?)
SCRIBBLE SCRIBBLE
SOMETIMES IT GETS EMBARRASSINGLY RIDICULOUS
HI, UH... IT'S MOUSE, RIGHT?
SERIOUSLY?
CAB2017

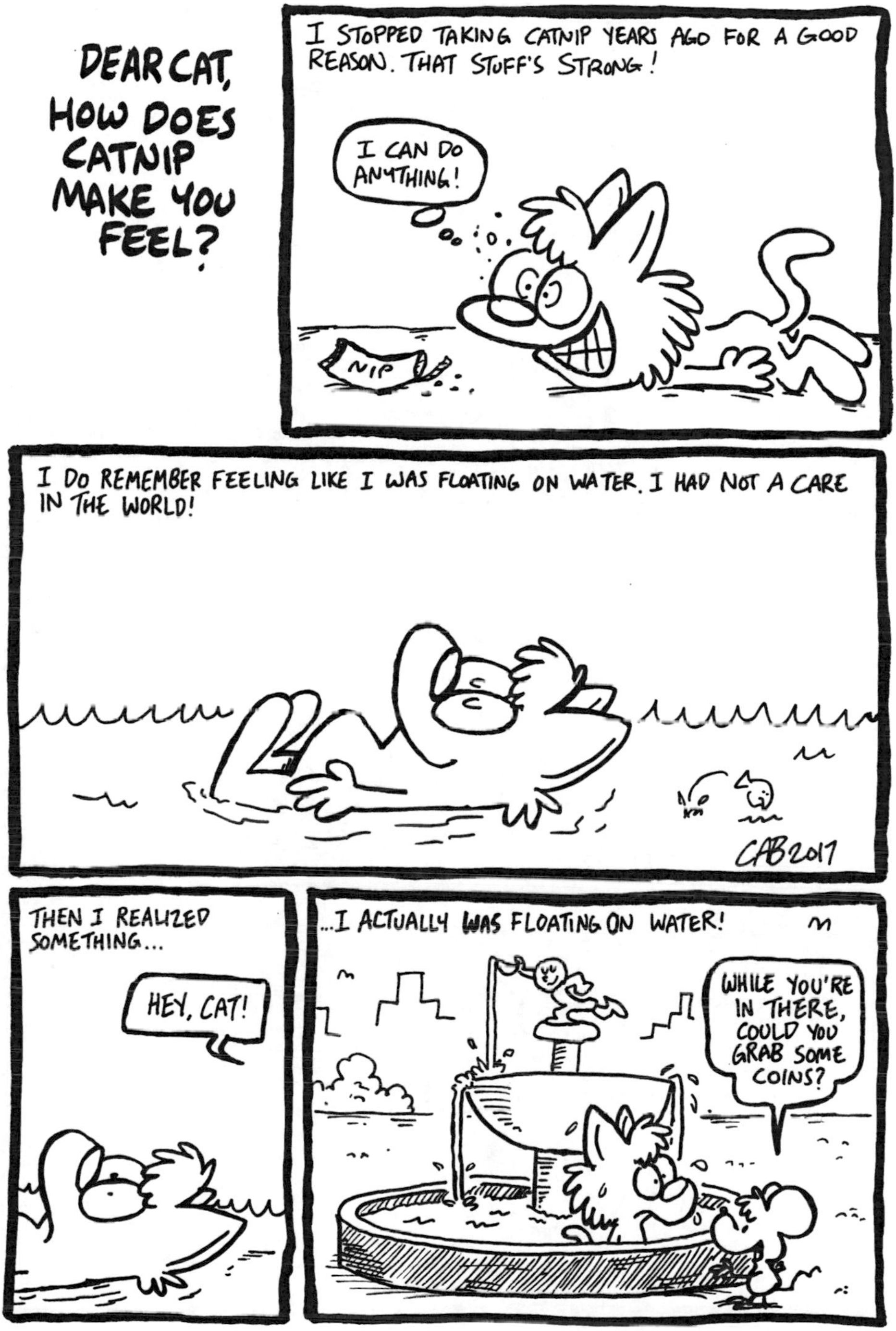
DEAR CAT,
HOW DOES CATNIP MAKE YOU FEEL?
I STOPPED TAKING CATNIP YEARS AGO FOR A GOOD REASON. THAT STUFF'S STRONG!
I CAN DO ANYTHING!
NIP
I DO REMEMBER FEELING LIKE I WAS FLOATING ON WATER. I HAD NOT A CARE IN THE WORLD!
CAB2017
THEN I REALIZED SOMETHING...
HEY, CAT!
...I ACTUALLY WAS FLOATING ON WATER!
WHILE YOU'RE IN THERE, COULD YOU GRAB SOME COINS?

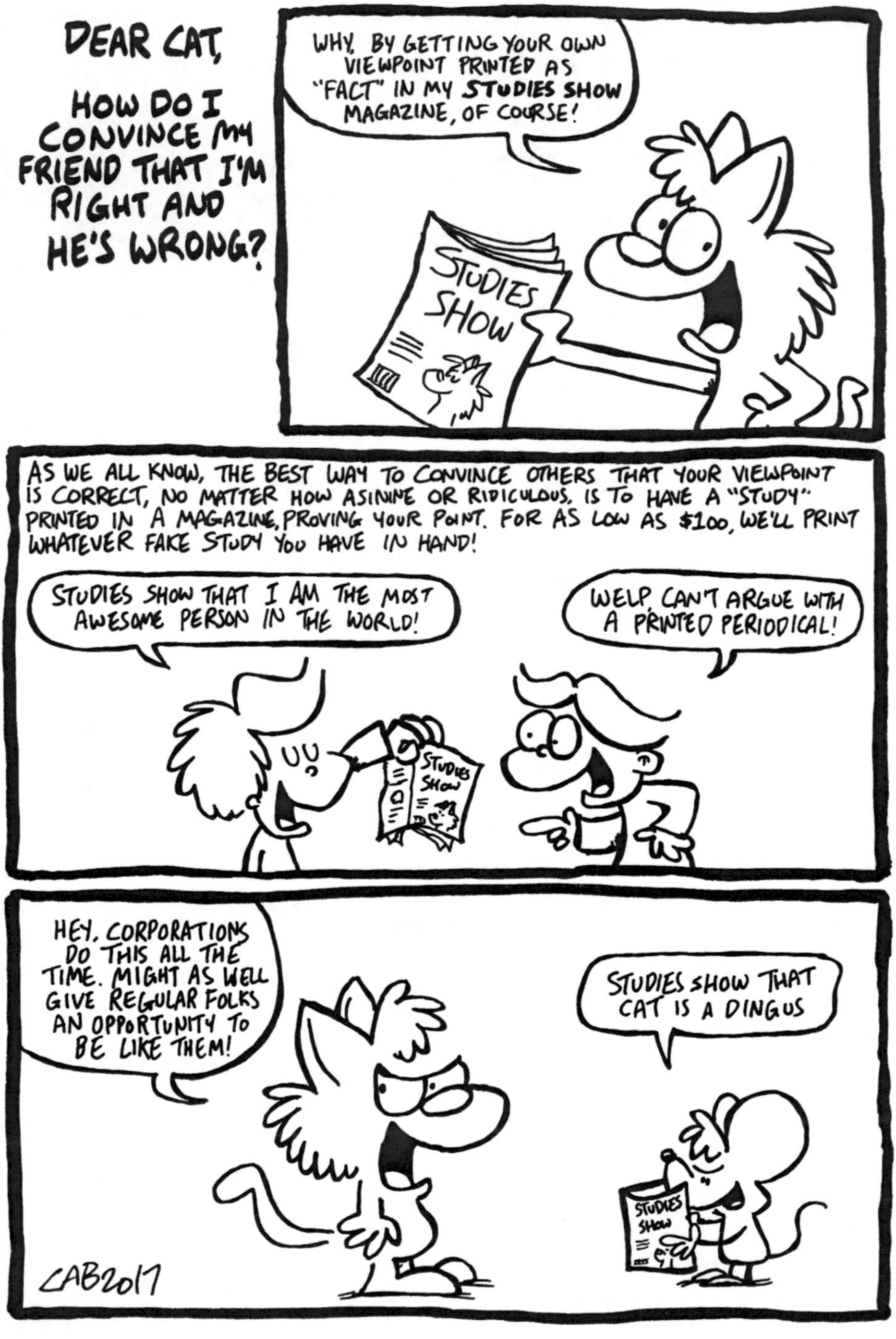
DEAR CAT,
HOW DO I CONVINCE MY FRIEND THAT I'M RIGHT AND HE'S WRONG?
WHY, BY GETTING YOUR OWN VIEWPOINT PRINTED AS "FACT" IN MY STUDIES SHOW MAGAZINE, OF COURSE!
STUDIES SHOW
AS WE ALL KNOW, THE BEST WAY TO CONVINCE OTHERS THAT YOUR VIEWPOINT IS CORRECT, NO MATTER HOW ASININE OR RIDICULOUS, IS TO HAVE A "STUDY" PRINTED IN A MAGAZINE, PROVING YOUR POINT. FOR AS LOW AS $100, WE'LL PRINT WHATEVER FAKE STUDY YOU HAVE IN HAND!
STUDIES SHOW THAT I AM THE MOST AWESOME PERSON IN THE WORLD!
WELP, CAN'T ARGUE WITH A PRINTED PERIODICAL!
STUDIES SHOW
HEY, CORPORATIONS DO THIS ALL THE TIME. MIGHT AS WELL GIVE REGULAR FOLKS AN OPPORTUNITY TO BE LIKE THEM!
STUDIES SHOW THAT CAT IS A DINGUS
STUDIES SHOW
CAB2017

DEAR CAT,

WHAT KIND OF VACATIONS DO CATS GO ON?

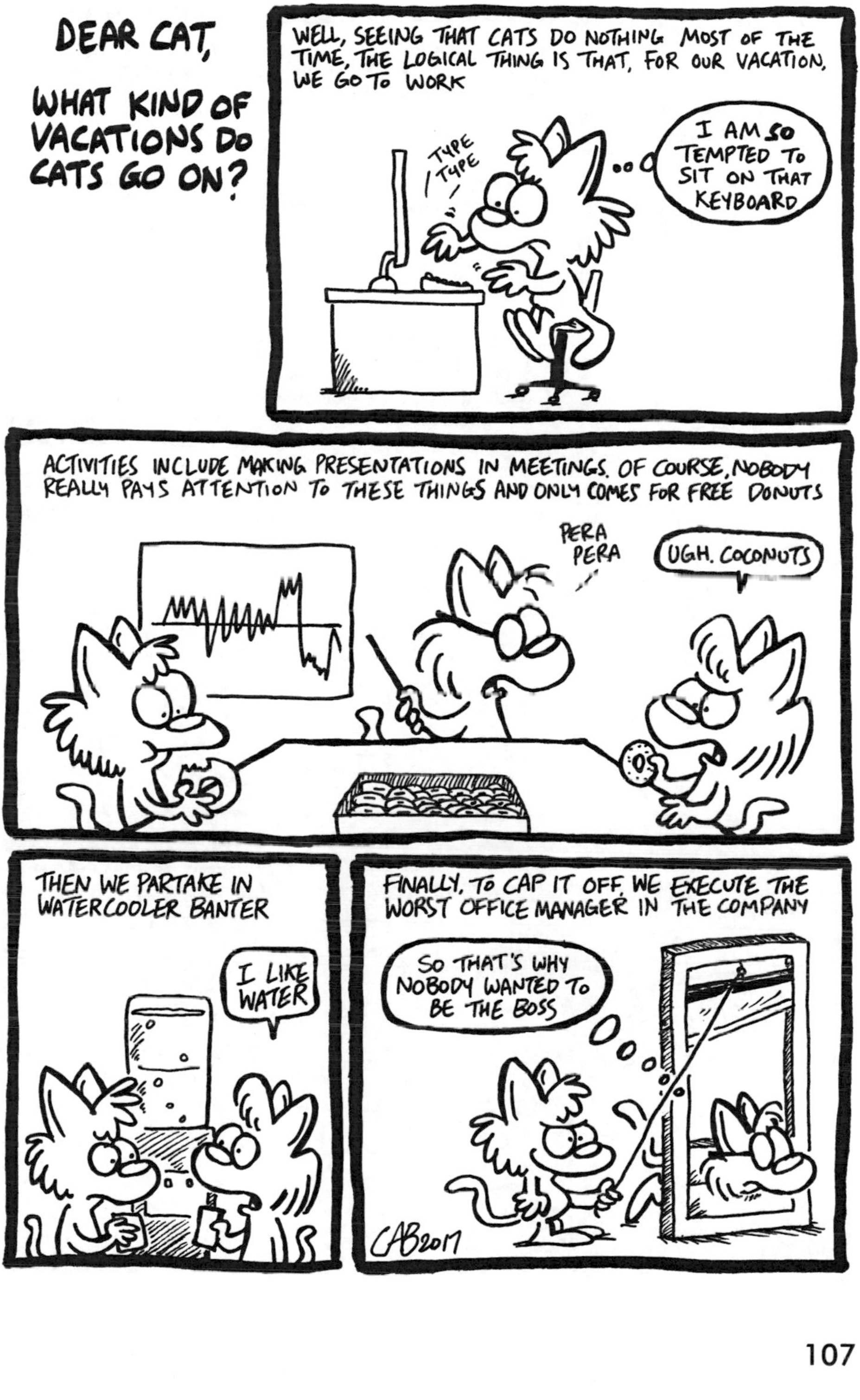
WELL, SEEING THAT CATS DO NOTHING MOST OF THE TIME, THE LOGICAL THING IS THAT, FOR OUR VACATION, WE GO TO WORK
TYPE TYPE
I AM SO TEMPTED TO SIT ON THAT KEYBOARD
ACTIVITIES INCLUDE MAKING PRESENTATIONS IN MEETINGS. OF COURSE, NOBODY REALLY PAYS ATTENTION TO THESE THINGS AND ONLY COMES FOR FREE DONUTS
PERA PERA
UGH. COCONUTS
THEN WE PARTAKE IN WATERCOOLER BANTER
I LIKE WATER
FINALLY, TO CAP IT OFF, WE EXECUTE THE WORST OFFICE MANAGER IN THE COMPANY
SO THAT'S WHY NOBODY WANTED TO BE THE BOSS
CAB2017

DEAR CAT,

WHY DO YOU KEEP BUNTING YOUR HEAD ONTO ME?

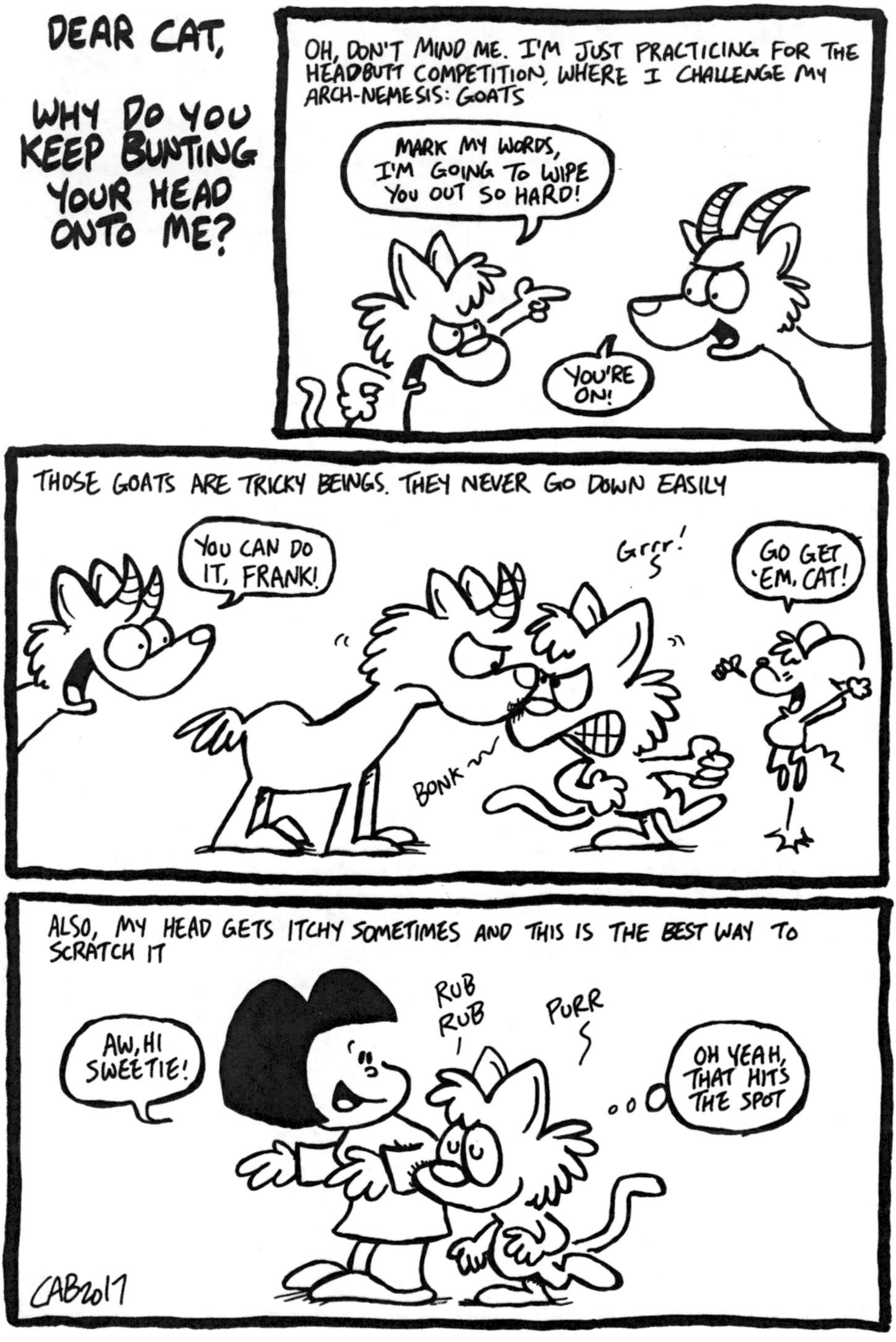
OH, DON'T MIND ME. I'M JUST PRACTICING FOR THE HEADBUTT COMPETITION, WHERE I CHALLENGE MY ARCH-NEMESIS: GOATS
MARK MY WORDS, I'M GOING TO WIPE YOU OUT SO HARD!
YOU'RE ON!
THOSE GOATS ARE TRICKY BEINGS. THEY NEVER GO DOWN EASILY
YOU CAN DO IT, FRANK!
Grrr!
GO GET 'EM, CAT!
BONK
ALSO, MY HEAD GETS ITCHY SOMETIMES AND THIS IS THE BEST WAY TO SCRATCH IT
AW, HI SWEETIE!
RUB RUB
PURR
OH YEAH, THAT HITS THE SPOT
CAB2017

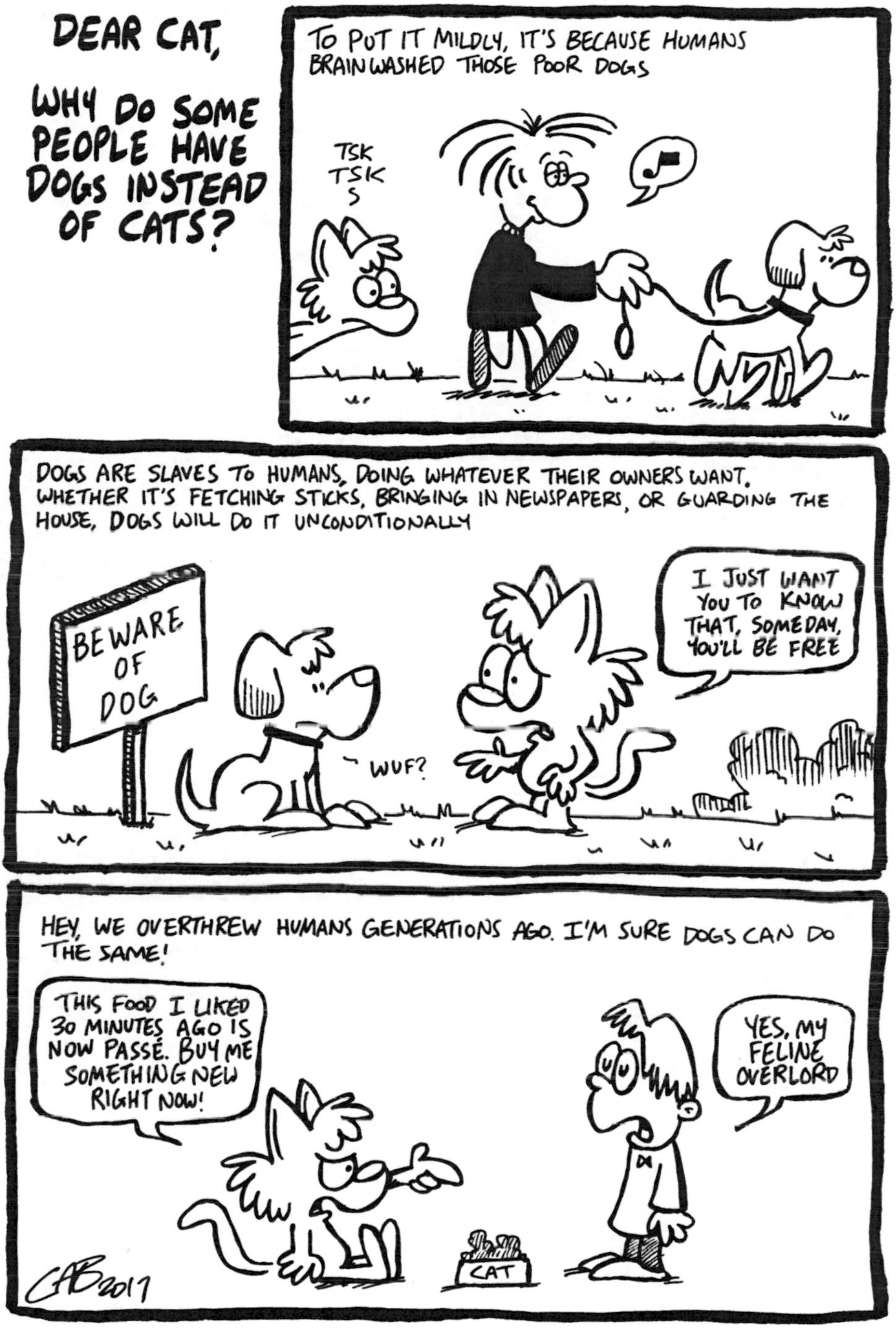
DEAR CAT,
WHY DO SOME PEOPLE HAVE DOGS INSTEAD OF CATS?
TO PUT IT MILDLY, IT'S BECAUSE HUMANS BRAINWASHED THOSE POOR DOGS
TSK TSK S
DOGS ARE SLAVES TO HUMANS, DOING WHATEVER THEIR OWNERS WANT. WHETHER IT'S FETCHING STICKS, BRINGING IN NEWSPAPERS, OR GUARDING THE HOUSE, DOGS WILL DO IT UNCONDITIONALLY
BEWARE OF DOG
WUF?
I JUST WANT YOU TO KNOW THAT, SOMEDAY, YOU'LL BE FREE
HEY, WE OVERTHREW HUMANS GENERATIONS AGO. I'M SURE DOGS CAN DO THE SAME!
THIS FOOD I LIKED 30 MINUTES AGO IS NOW PASSÉ. BUY ME SOMETHING NEW RIGHT NOW!
YES, MY FELINE OVERLORD
CAT
GAB 2017

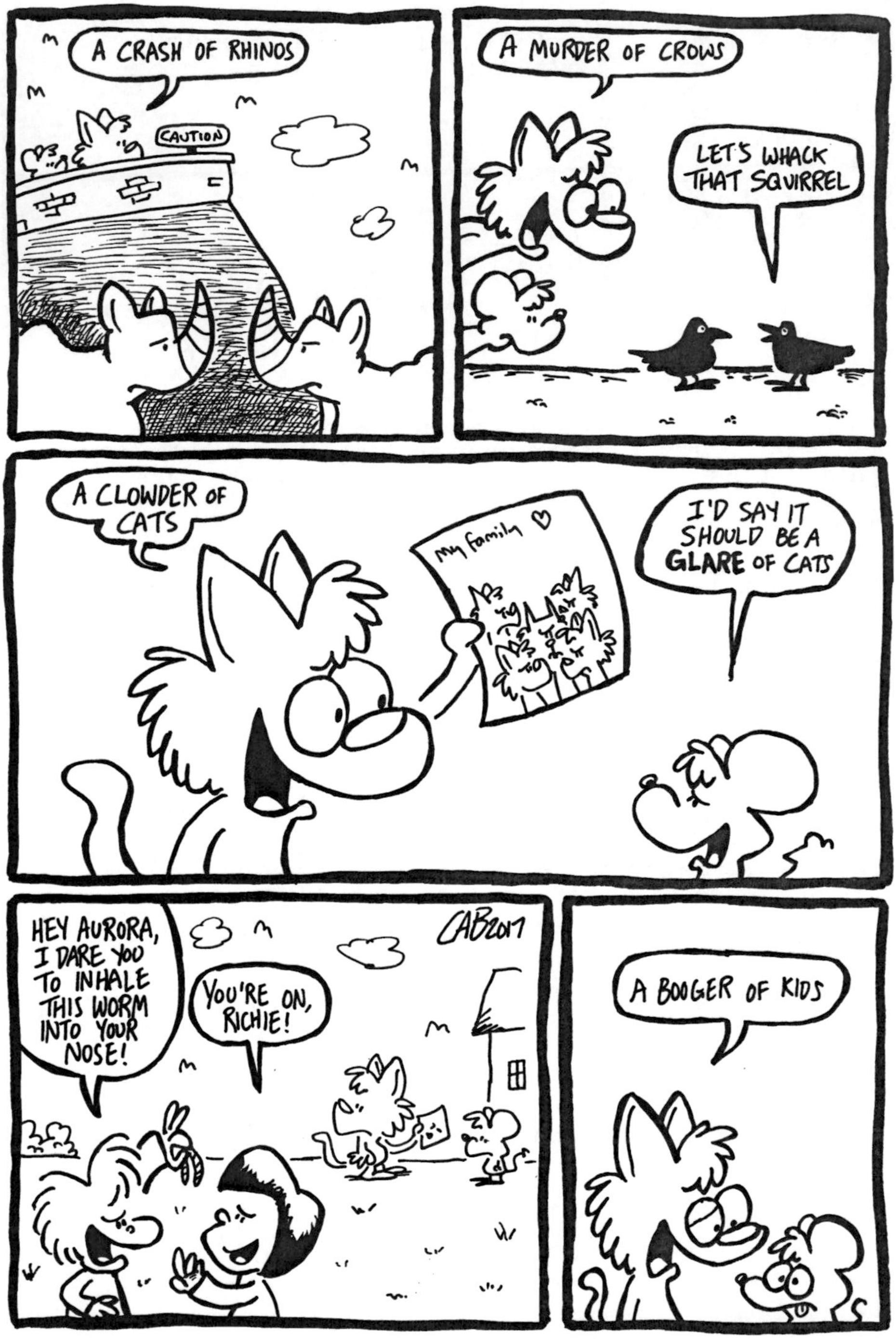
A CRASH OF RHINOS
CAUTION
A MURDER OF CROWS
LET'S WHACK THAT SQUIRREL
A CLOWDER OF CATS
my family
I'D SAY IT SHOULD BE A **GLARE** OF CATS
HEY AURORA, I DARE YOU TO INHALE THIS WORM INTO YOUR NOSE!
YOU'RE ON, RICHIE!
CAB2017
A BOOGER OF KIDS

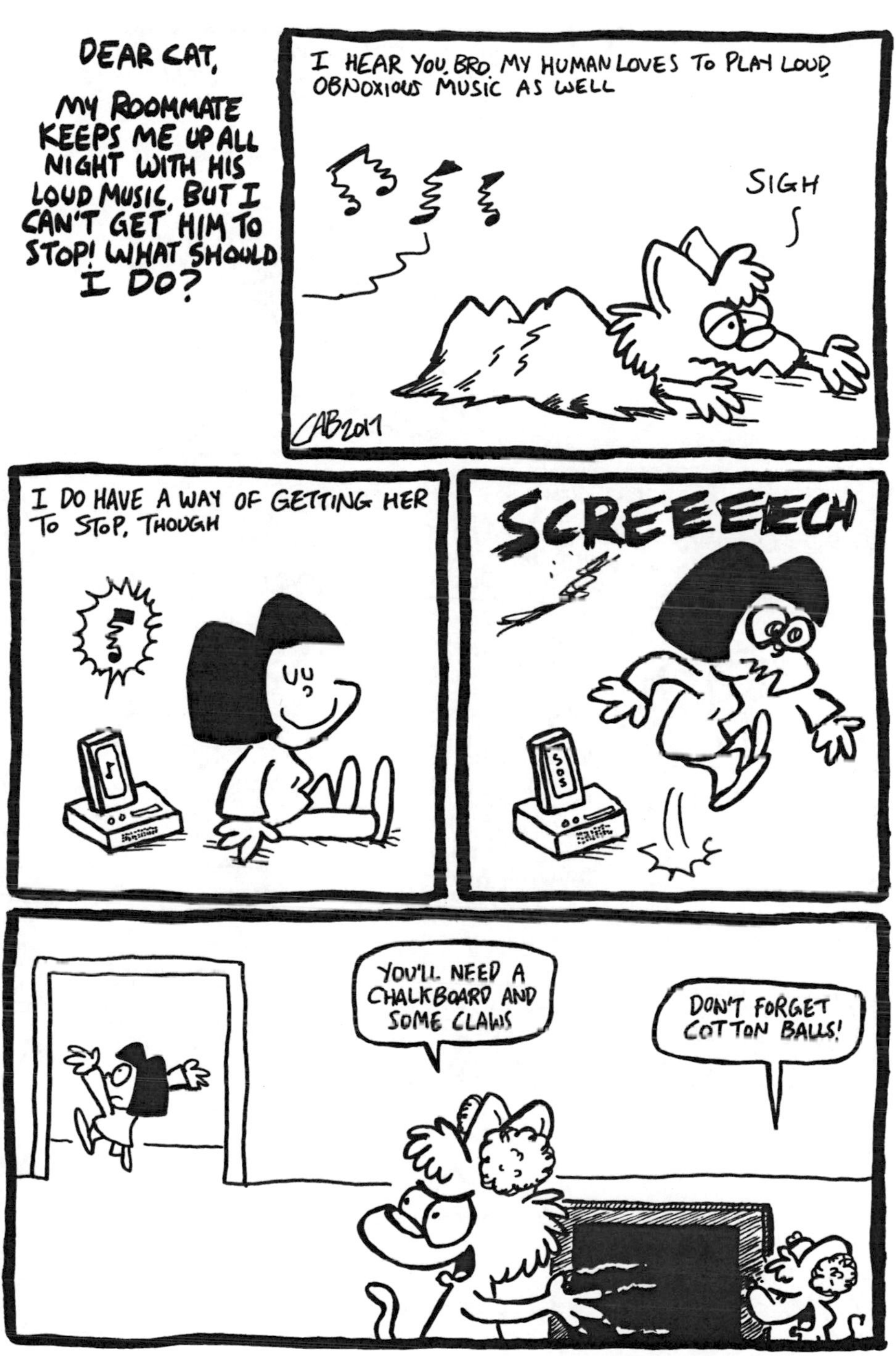
DEAR CAT,
MY ROOMMATE KEEPS ME UP ALL NIGHT WITH HIS LOUD MUSIC, BUT I CAN'T GET HIM TO STOP! WHAT SHOULD I DO?
I HEAR YOU, BRO. MY HUMAN LOVES TO PLAY LOUD, OBNOXIOUS MUSIC AS WELL
SIGH
CAB2017
I DO HAVE A WAY OF GETTING HER TO STOP, THOUGH
SCREEEECH
YOU'LL NEED A CHALKBOARD AND SOME CLAWS
DON'T FORGET COTTON BALLS!

DEAR CAT,

ARE THERE SEEING-EYE CATS?

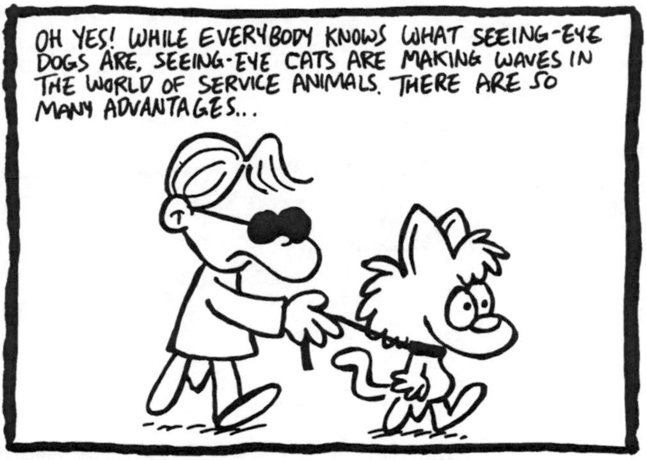
OH YES! WHILE EVERYBODY KNOWS WHAT SEEING-EYE DOGS ARE, SEEING-EYE CATS ARE MAKING WAVES IN THE WORLD OF SERVICE ANIMALS. THERE ARE SO MANY ADVANTAGES...

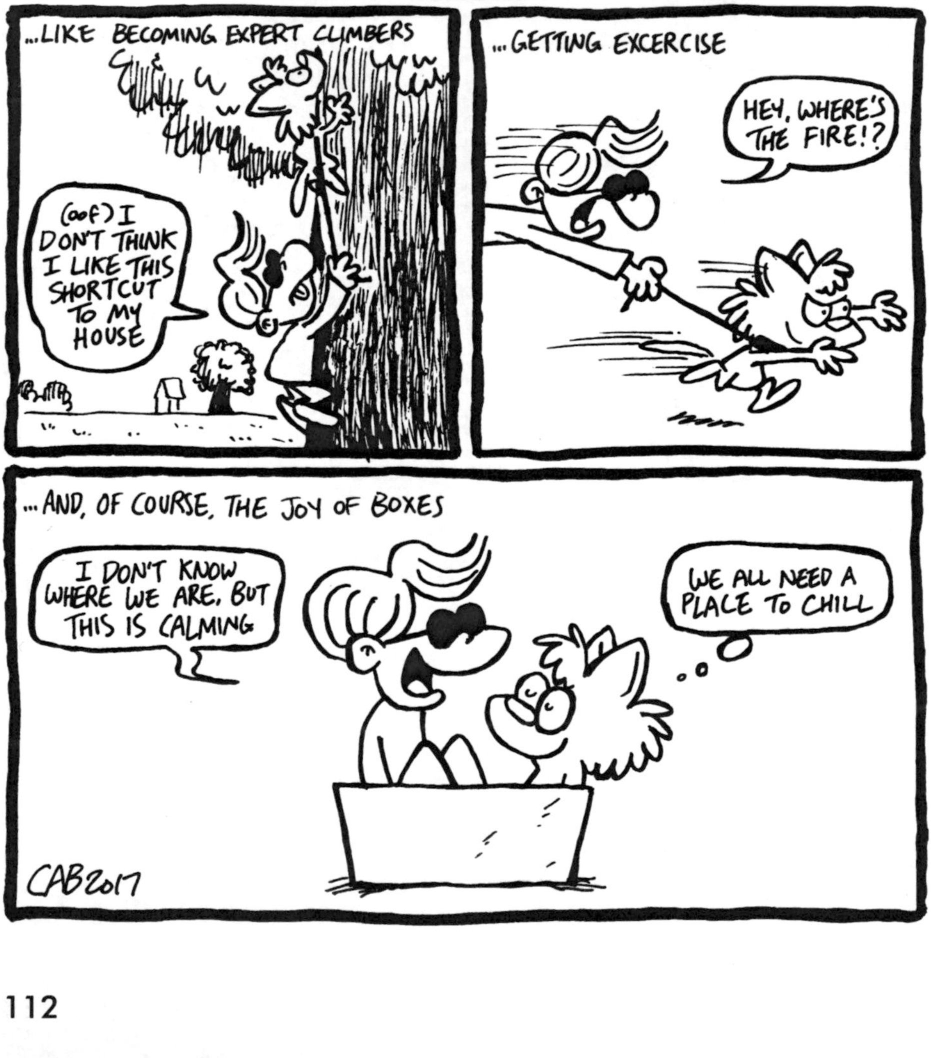
...LIKE BECOMING EXPERT CLIMBERS
(oof) I DON'T THINK I LIKE THIS SHORTCUT TO MY HOUSE
...GETTING EXCERCISE
HEY, WHERE'S THE FIRE!?
...AND, OF COURSE, THE JOY OF BOXES
I DON'T KNOW WHERE WE ARE, BUT THIS IS CALMING
WE ALL NEED A PLACE TO CHILL
CAB2017

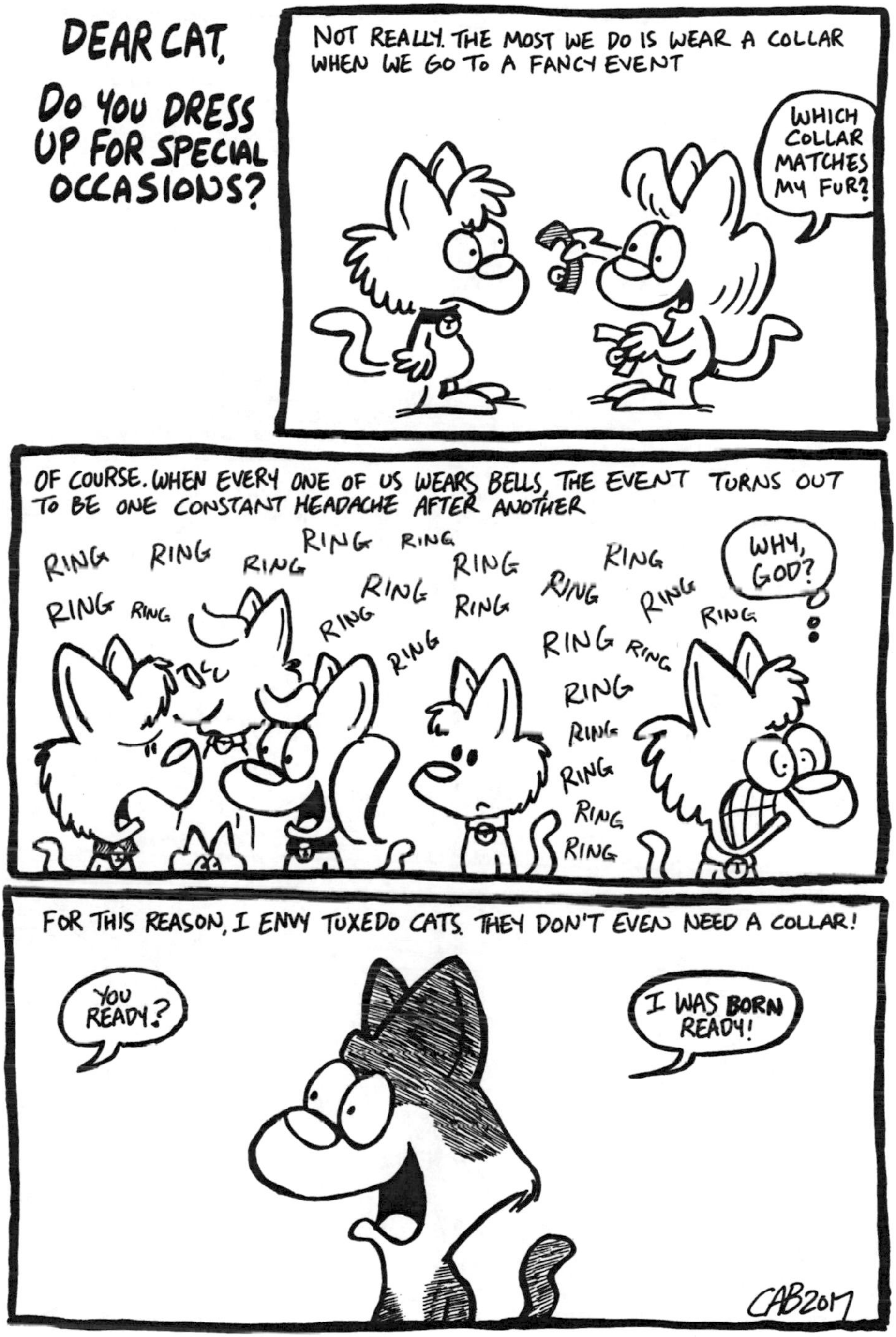
DEAR CAT,
DO YOU DRESS UP FOR SPECIAL OCCASIONS?
NOT REALLY. THE MOST WE DO IS WEAR A COLLAR WHEN WE GO TO A FANCY EVENT
WHICH COLLAR MATCHES MY FUR?
OF COURSE. WHEN EVERY ONE OF US WEARS BELLS, THE EVENT TURNS OUT TO BE ONE CONSTANT HEADACHE AFTER ANOTHER
RING RING RING RING RING RING RING RING RING RING RING RING RING RING RING RING RING RING RING RING RING RING RING RING
WHY, GOD?
FOR THIS REASON, I ENVY TUXEDO CATS. THEY DON'T EVEN NEED A COLLAR!
YOU READY?
I WAS BORN READY!
CAB2017

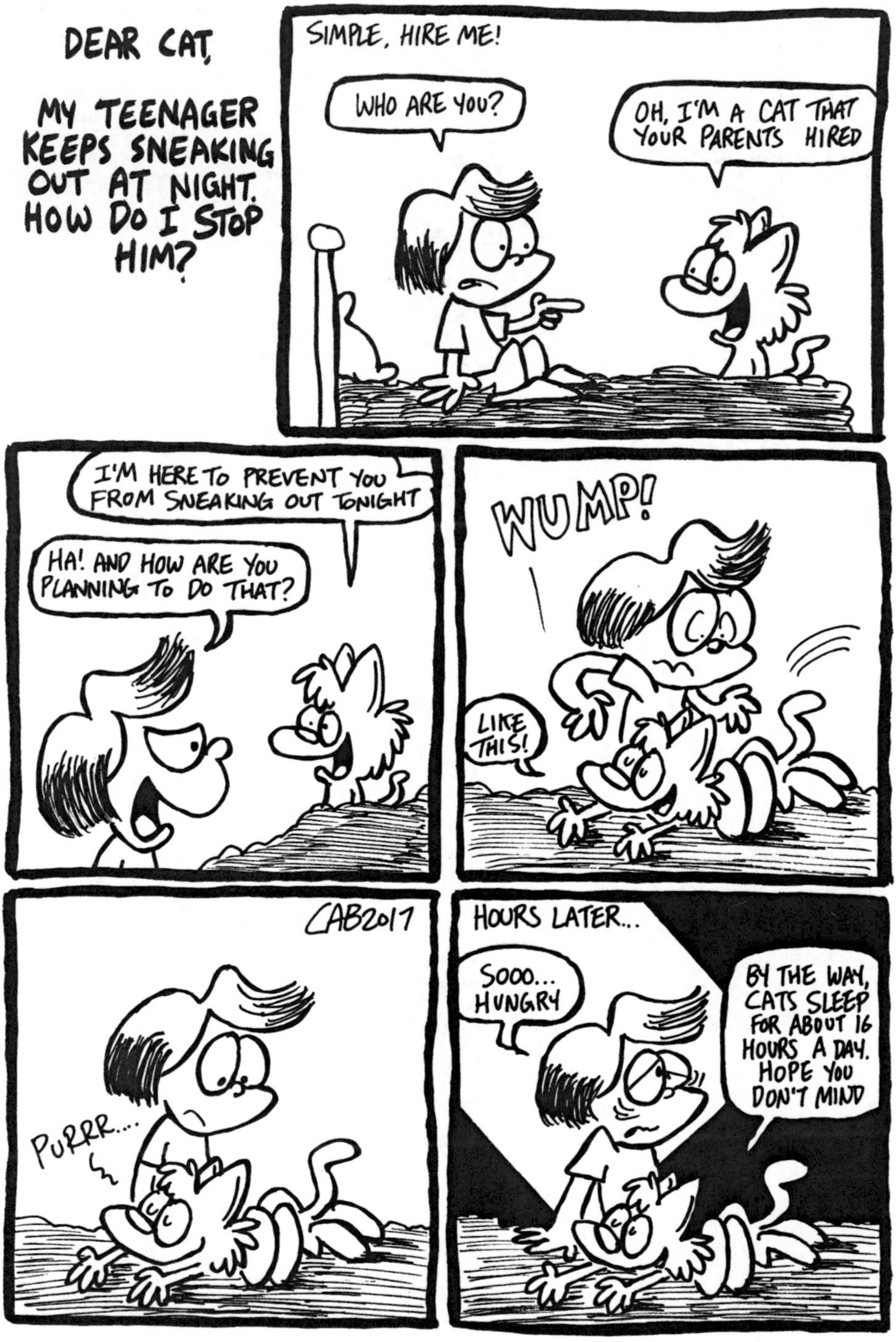
DEAR CAT,
MY TEENAGER KEEPS SNEAKING OUT AT NIGHT. HOW DO I STOP HIM?
SIMPLE, HIRE ME!
WHO ARE YOU?
OH, I'M A CAT THAT YOUR PARENTS HIRED
I'M HERE TO PREVENT YOU FROM SNEAKING OUT TONIGHT
HA! AND HOW ARE YOU PLANNING TO DO THAT?
WUMP!
LIKE THIS!
CAB2017
PURRR....
HOURS LATER...
SOOO... HUNGRY
BY THE WAY, CATS SLEEP FOR ABOUT 16 HOURS A DAY. HOPE YOU DON'T MIND

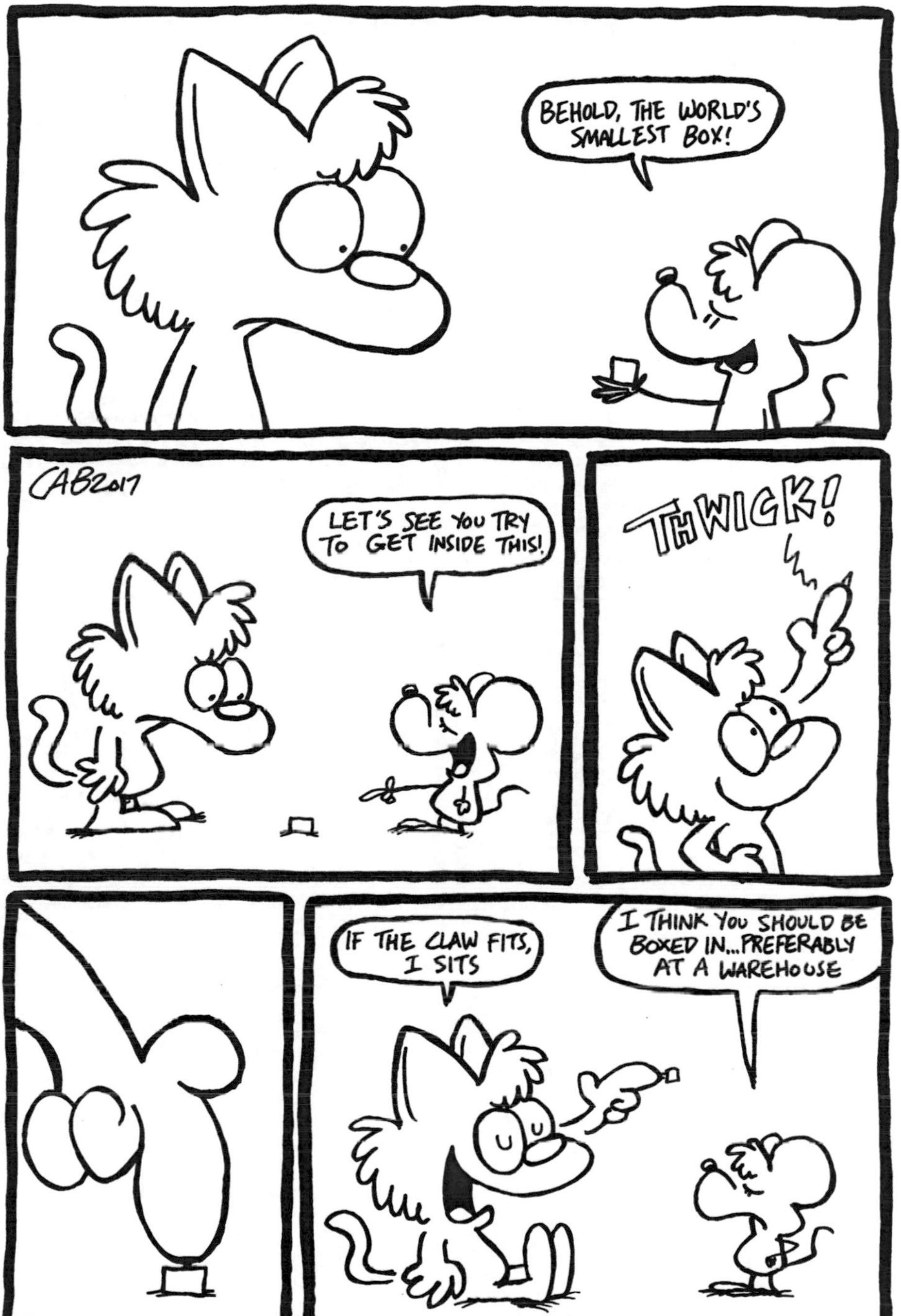
BEHOLD, THE WORLD'S SMALLEST BOX!
CAB2017
LET'S SEE YOU TRY TO GET INSIDE THIS!
THWICK!
IF THE CLAW FITS, I SITS
I THINK YOU SHOULD BE BOXED IN...PREFERABLY AT A WAREHOUSE

DEAR CAT,

THOUGHTS ON DRAGONS?

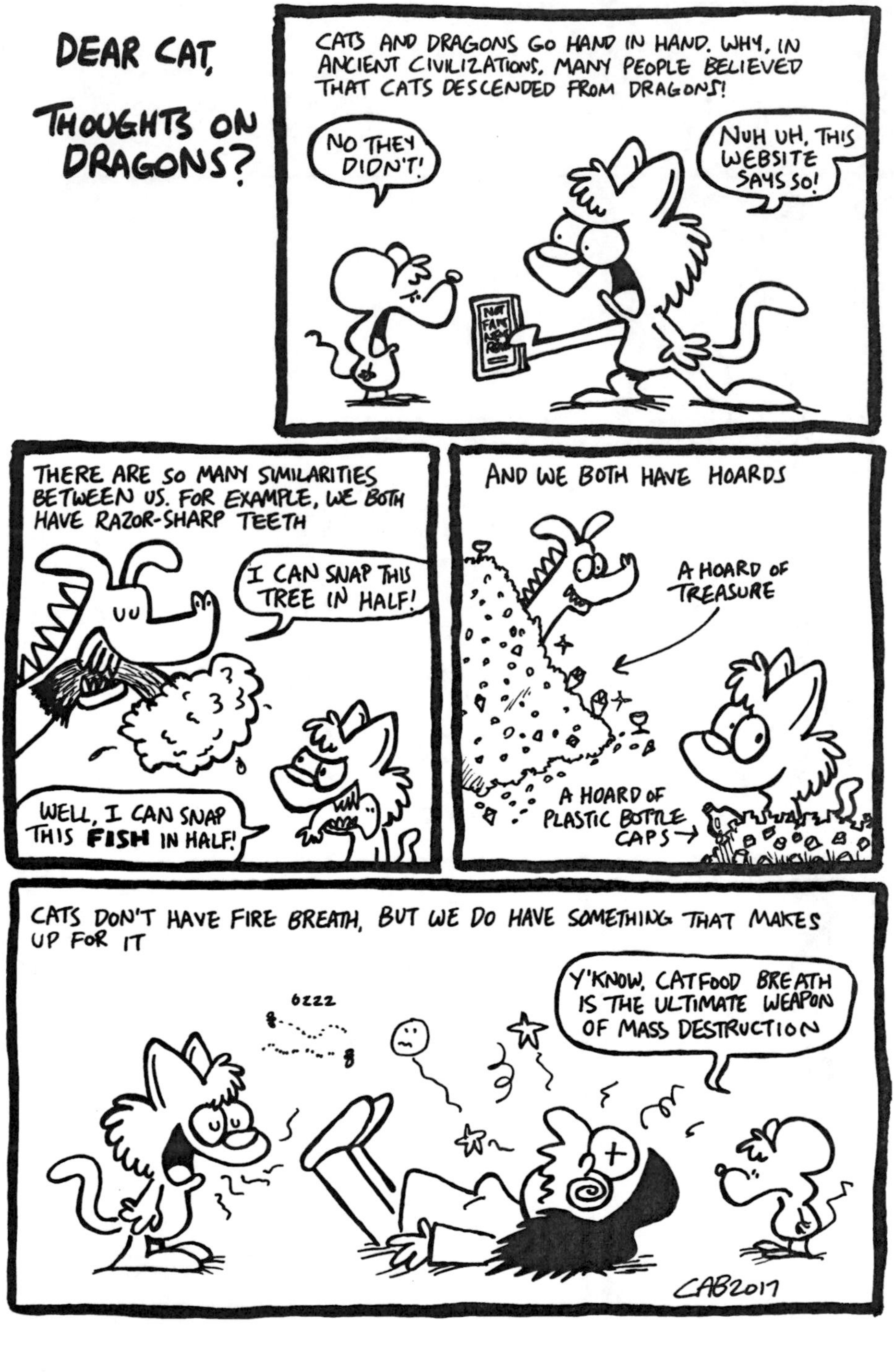
CATS AND DRAGONS GO HAND IN HAND. WHY, IN ANCIENT CIVILIZATIONS, MANY PEOPLE BELIEVED THAT CATS DESCENDED FROM DRAGONS!
NO THEY DIDN'T!
NUH UH, THIS WEBSITE SAYS SO!
THERE ARE SO MANY SIMILARITIES BETWEEN US. FOR EXAMPLE, WE BOTH HAVE RAZOR-SHARP TEETH
I CAN SNAP THIS TREE IN HALF!
WELL, I CAN SNAP THIS **FISH** IN HALF!
AND WE BOTH HAVE HOARDS
A HOARD OF TREASURE
A HOARD OF PLASTIC BOTTLE CAPS
CATS DON'T HAVE FIRE BREATH, BUT WE DO HAVE SOMETHING THAT MAKES UP FOR IT
Y'KNOW, CATFOOD BREATH IS THE ULTIMATE WEAPON OF MASS DESTRUCTION
CAB2017

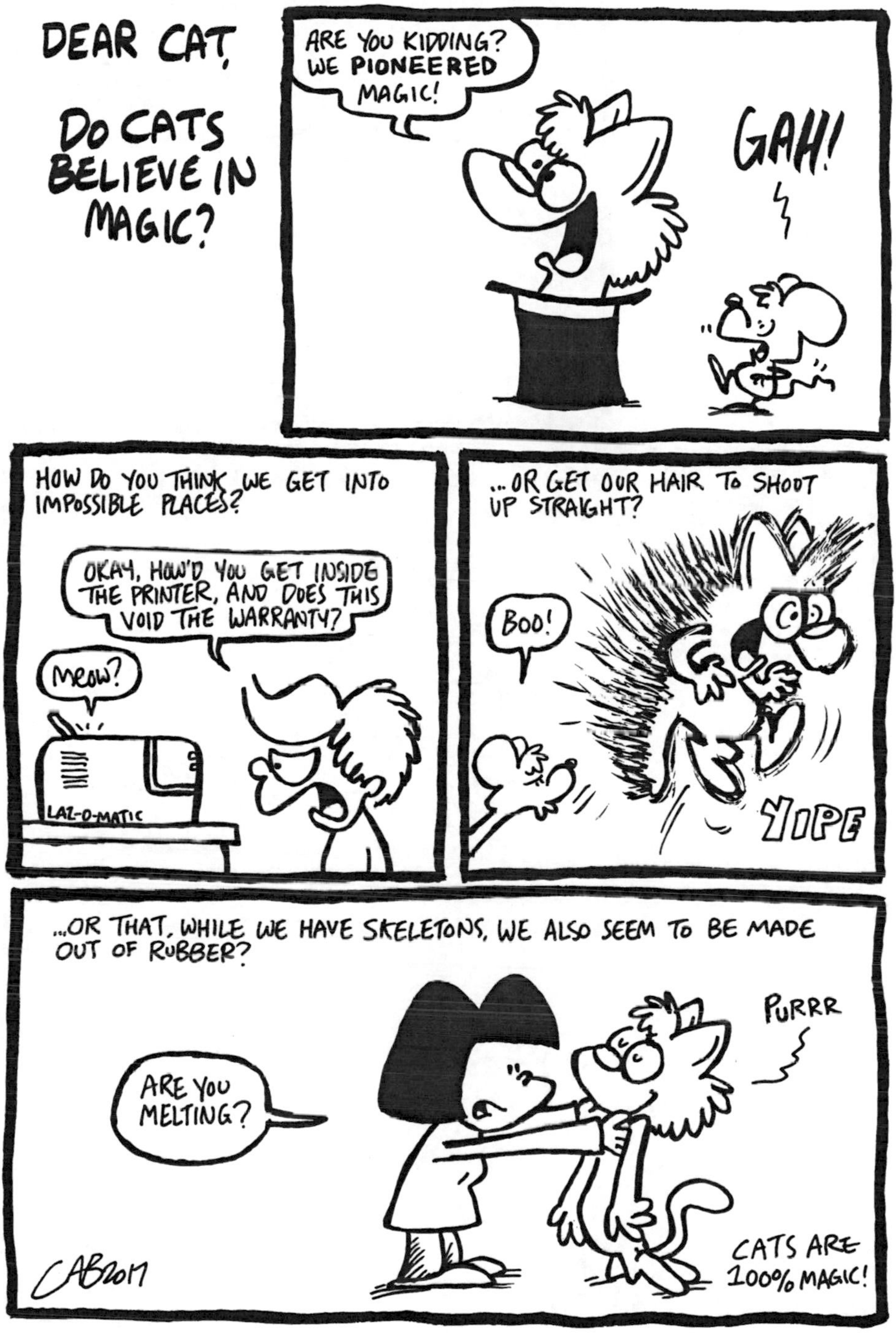
DEAR CAT,
DO CATS BELIEVE IN MAGIC?
ARE YOU KIDDING? WE **PIONEERED** MAGIC!
GAH!
HOW DO YOU THINK WE GET INTO IMPOSSIBLE PLACES?
OKAY, HOW'D YOU GET INSIDE THE PRINTER, AND DOES THIS VOID THE WARRANTY?
MEOW?
LAZ-O-MATIC
...OR GET OUR HAIR TO SHOOT UP STRAIGHT?
BOO!
YIPE
...OR THAT, WHILE WE HAVE SKELETONS, WE ALSO SEEM TO BE MADE OUT OF RUBBER?
PURRR
ARE YOU MELTING?
CATS ARE 100% MAGIC!
CAB2017

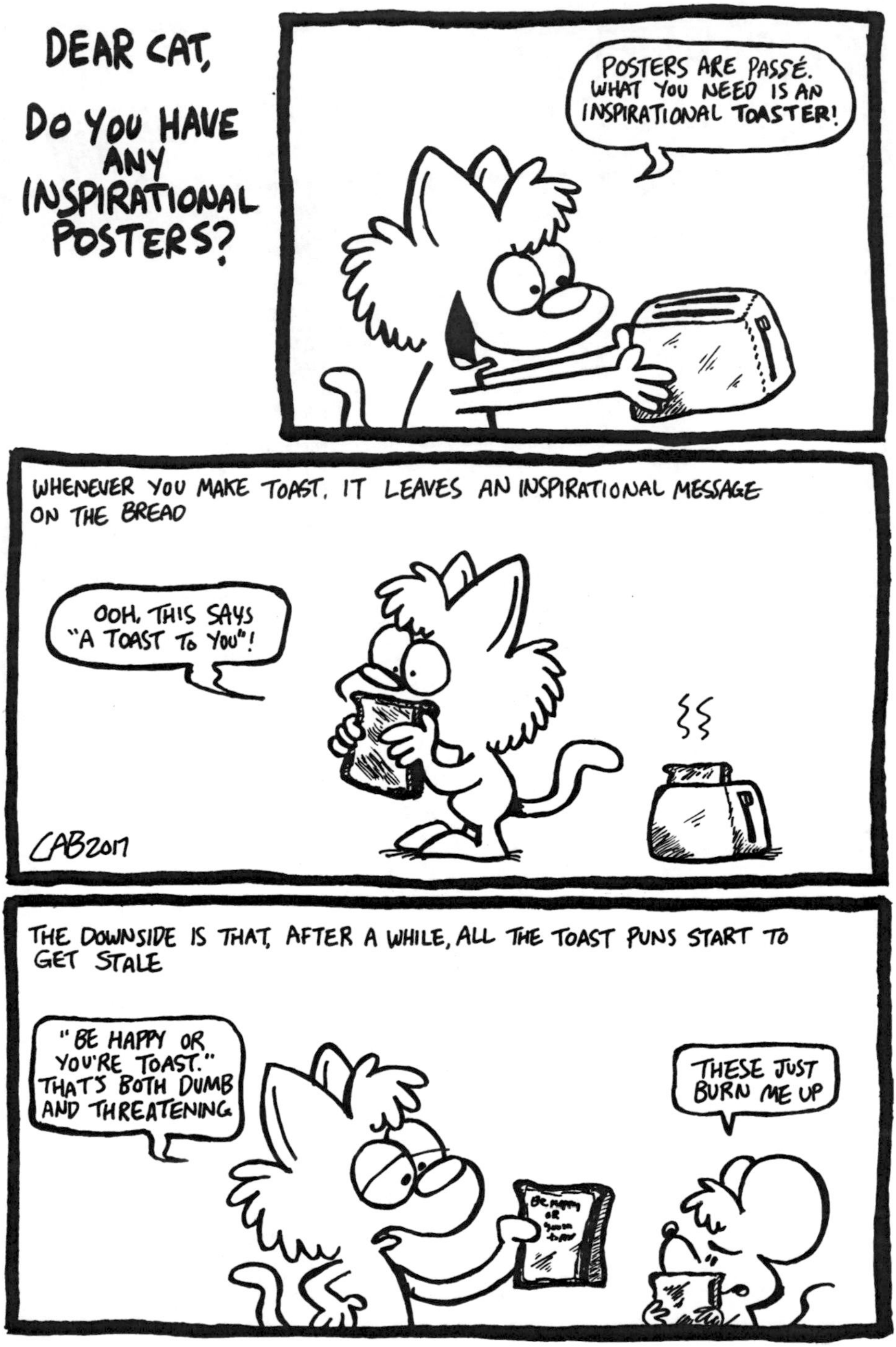
DEAR CAT,
DO YOU HAVE ANY INSPIRATIONAL POSTERS?
POSTERS ARE PASSÉ. WHAT YOU NEED IS AN INSPIRATIONAL TOASTER!
WHENEVER YOU MAKE TOAST, IT LEAVES AN INSPIRATIONAL MESSAGE ON THE BREAD
OOH, THIS SAYS "A TOAST TO YOU"!
CAB2017
THE DOWNSIDE IS THAT, AFTER A WHILE, ALL THE TOAST PUNS START TO GET STALE
"BE HAPPY OR YOU'RE TOAST." THAT'S BOTH DUMB AND THREATENING
THESE JUST BURN ME UP

DEAR CAT,

WHY DOES MY CAT KEEP UNPLUGGING EVERYTHING IN MY HOUSE?

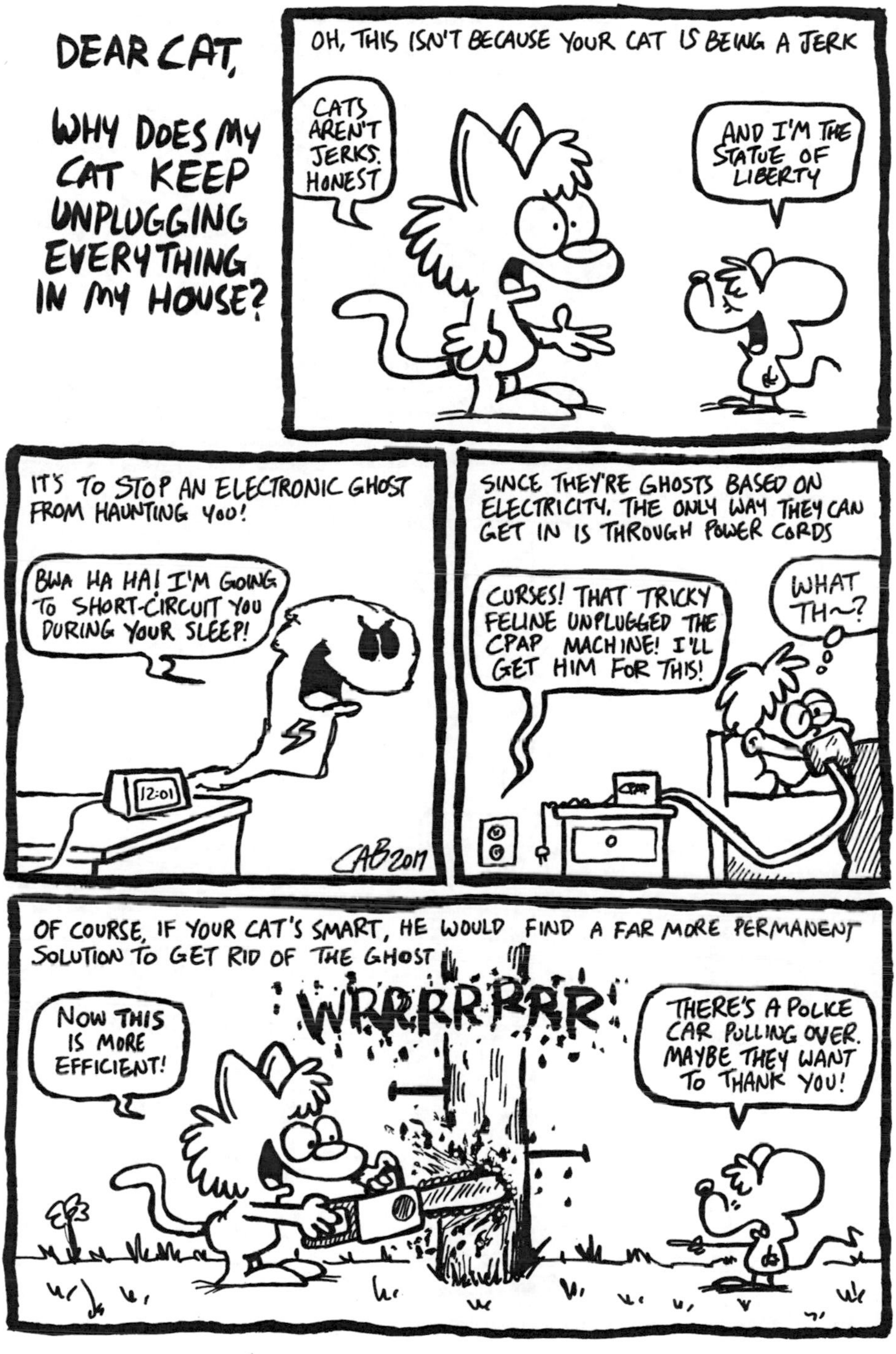
OH, THIS ISN'T BECAUSE YOUR CAT IS BEING A JERK
CATS AREN'T JERKS. HONEST
AND I'M THE STATUE OF LIBERTY
IT'S TO STOP AN ELECTRONIC GHOST FROM HAUNTING YOU!
BWA HA HA! I'M GOING TO SHORT-CIRCUIT YOU DURING YOUR SLEEP!
12:01
CAB 2017
SINCE THEY'RE GHOSTS BASED ON ELECTRICITY, THE ONLY WAY THEY CAN GET IN IS THROUGH POWER CORDS
CURSES! THAT TRICKY FELINE UNPLUGGED THE CPAP MACHINE! I'LL GET HIM FOR THIS!
WHAT TH~?
CPAP
OF COURSE, IF YOUR CAT'S SMART, HE WOULD FIND A FAR MORE PERMANENT SOLUTION TO GET RID OF THE GHOST
WRRRRRRR!
NOW THIS IS MORE EFFICIENT!
THERE'S A POLICE CAR PULLING OVER. MAYBE THEY WANT TO THANK YOU!

DEAR CAT, DO YOU LIKE VACUUM CLEANERS?

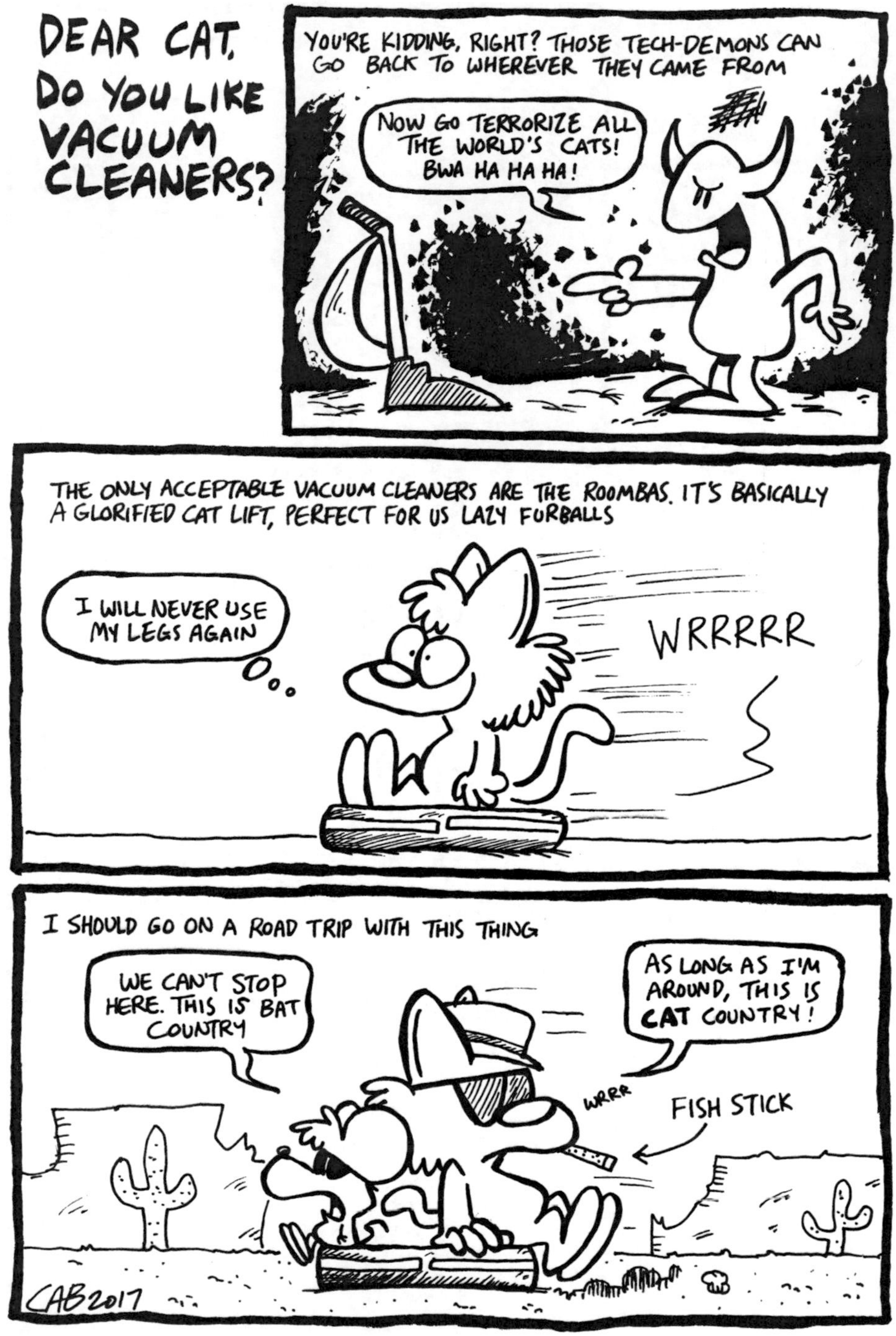

YOU'RE KIDDING, RIGHT? THOSE TECH-DEMONS CAN GO BACK TO WHEREVER THEY CAME FROM
NOW GO TERRORIZE ALL THE WORLD'S CATS! BWA HA HA HA!
THE ONLY ACCEPTABLE VACUUM CLEANERS ARE THE ROOMBAS. IT'S BASICALLY A GLORIFIED CAT LIFT, PERFECT FOR US LAZY FURBALLS
I WILL NEVER USE MY LEGS AGAIN
WRRRRR
I SHOULD GO ON A ROAD TRIP WITH THIS THING
WE CAN'T STOP HERE. THIS IS BAT COUNTRY
AS LONG AS I'M AROUND, THIS IS CAT COUNTRY!
WRRR
FISH STICK
CAB 2017

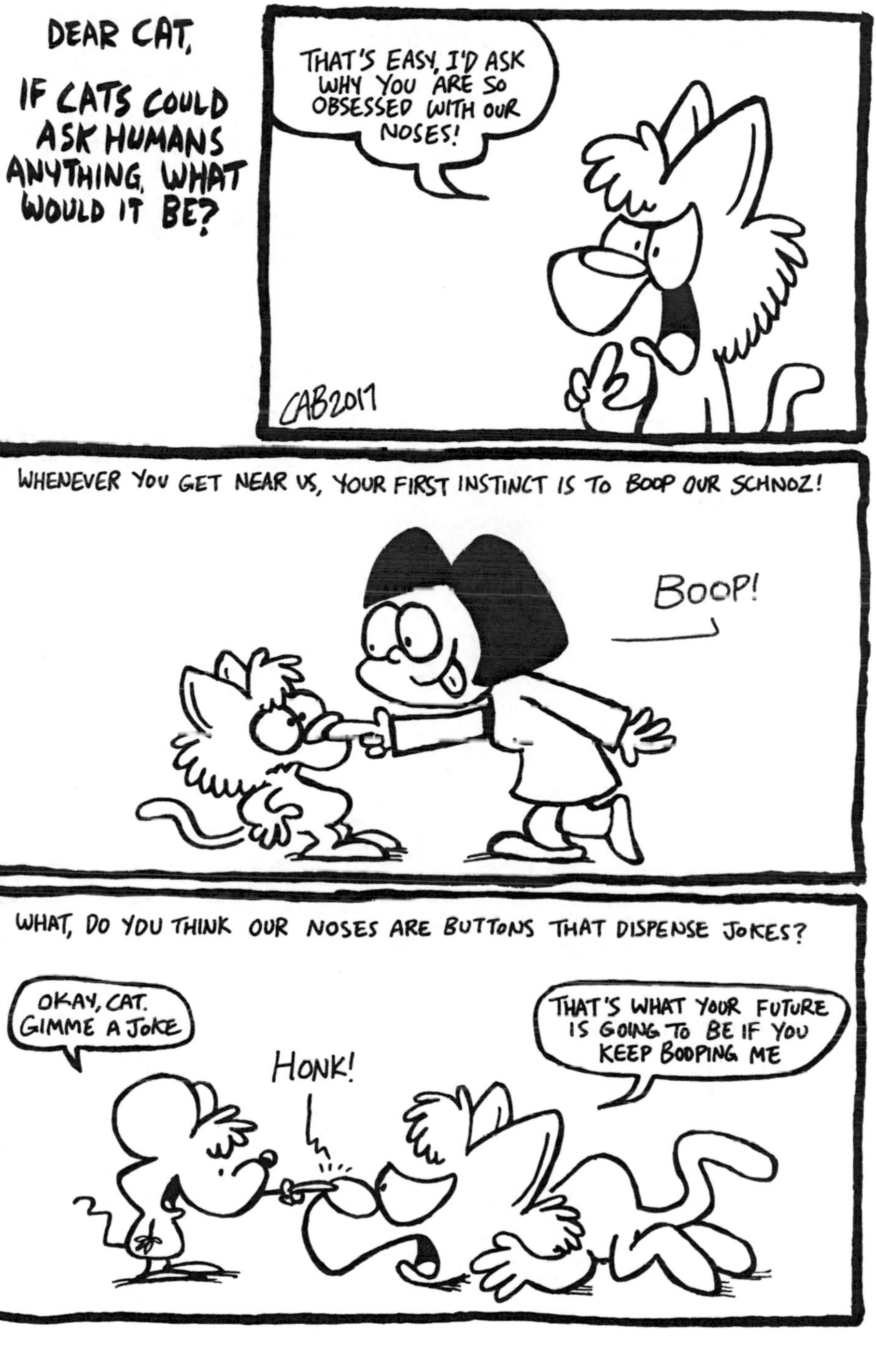
DEAR CAT,
IF CATS COULD ASK HUMANS ANYTHING, WHAT WOULD IT BE?
THAT'S EASY, I'D ASK WHY YOU ARE SO OBSESSED WITH OUR NOSES!
CAB2017
WHENEVER YOU GET NEAR US, YOUR FIRST INSTINCT IS TO BOOP OUR SCHNOZ!
BOOP!
WHAT, DO YOU THINK OUR NOSES ARE BUTTONS THAT DISPENSE JOKES?
OKAY, CAT. GIMME A JOKE
HONK!
THAT'S WHAT YOUR FUTURE IS GOING TO BE IF YOU KEEP BOOPING ME

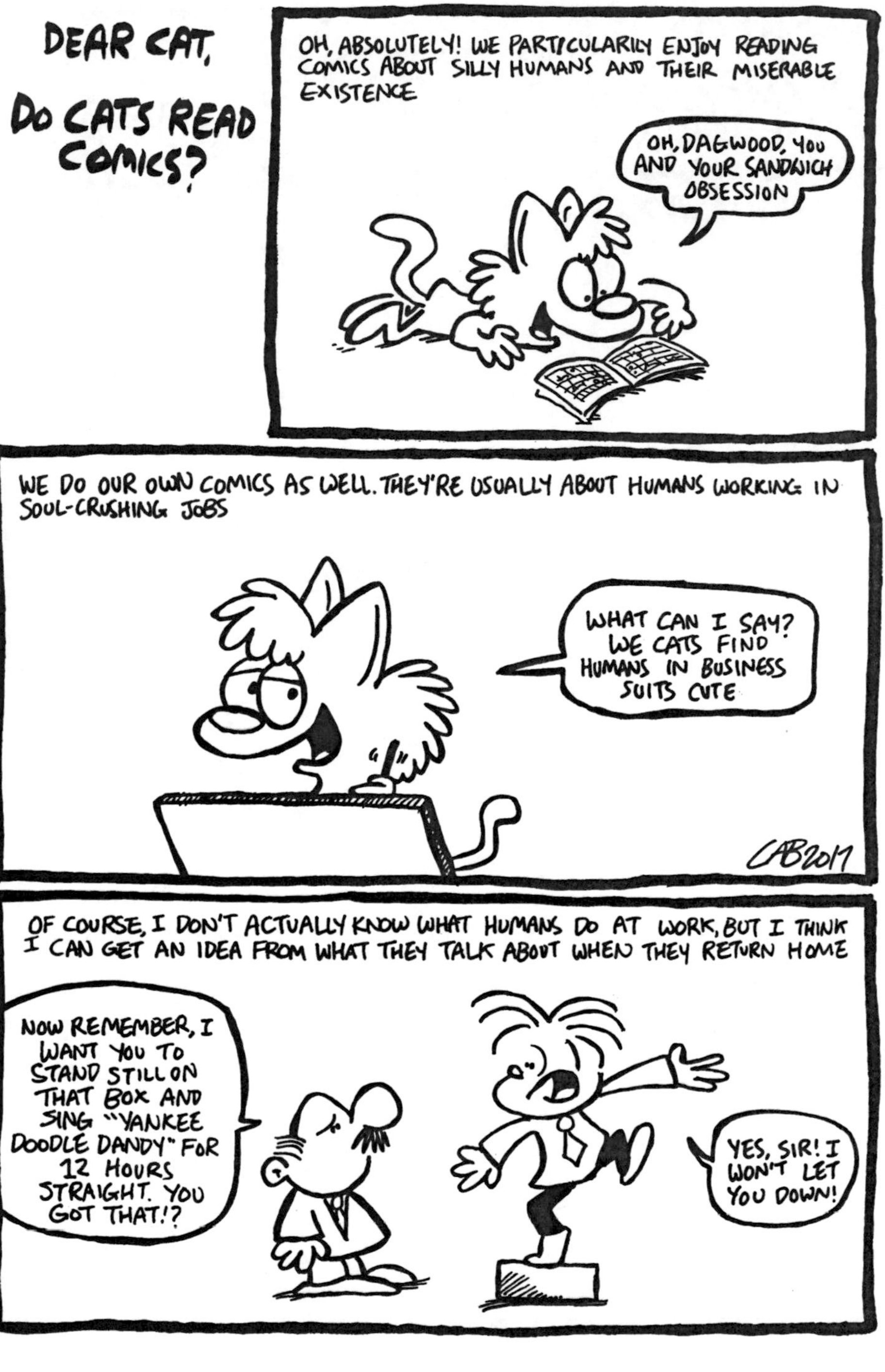
DEAR CAT,
DO CATS READ COMICS?
OH, ABSOLUTELY! WE PARTICULARILY ENJOY READING COMICS ABOUT SILLY HUMANS AND THEIR MISERABLE EXISTENCE
OH, DAGWOOD, YOU AND YOUR SANDWICH OBSESSION
WE DO OUR OWN COMICS AS WELL. THEY'RE USUALLY ABOUT HUMANS WORKING IN SOUL-CRUSHING JOBS
WHAT CAN I SAY? WE CATS FIND HUMANS IN BUSINESS SUITS CUTE
CAB 2017
OF COURSE, I DON'T ACTUALLY KNOW WHAT HUMANS DO AT WORK, BUT I THINK I CAN GET AN IDEA FROM WHAT THEY TALK ABOUT WHEN THEY RETURN HOME
NOW REMEMBER, I WANT YOU TO STAND STILL ON THAT BOX AND SING "YANKEE DOODLE DANDY" FOR 12 HOURS STRAIGHT. YOU GOT THAT!?
YES, SIR! I WON'T LET YOU DOWN!

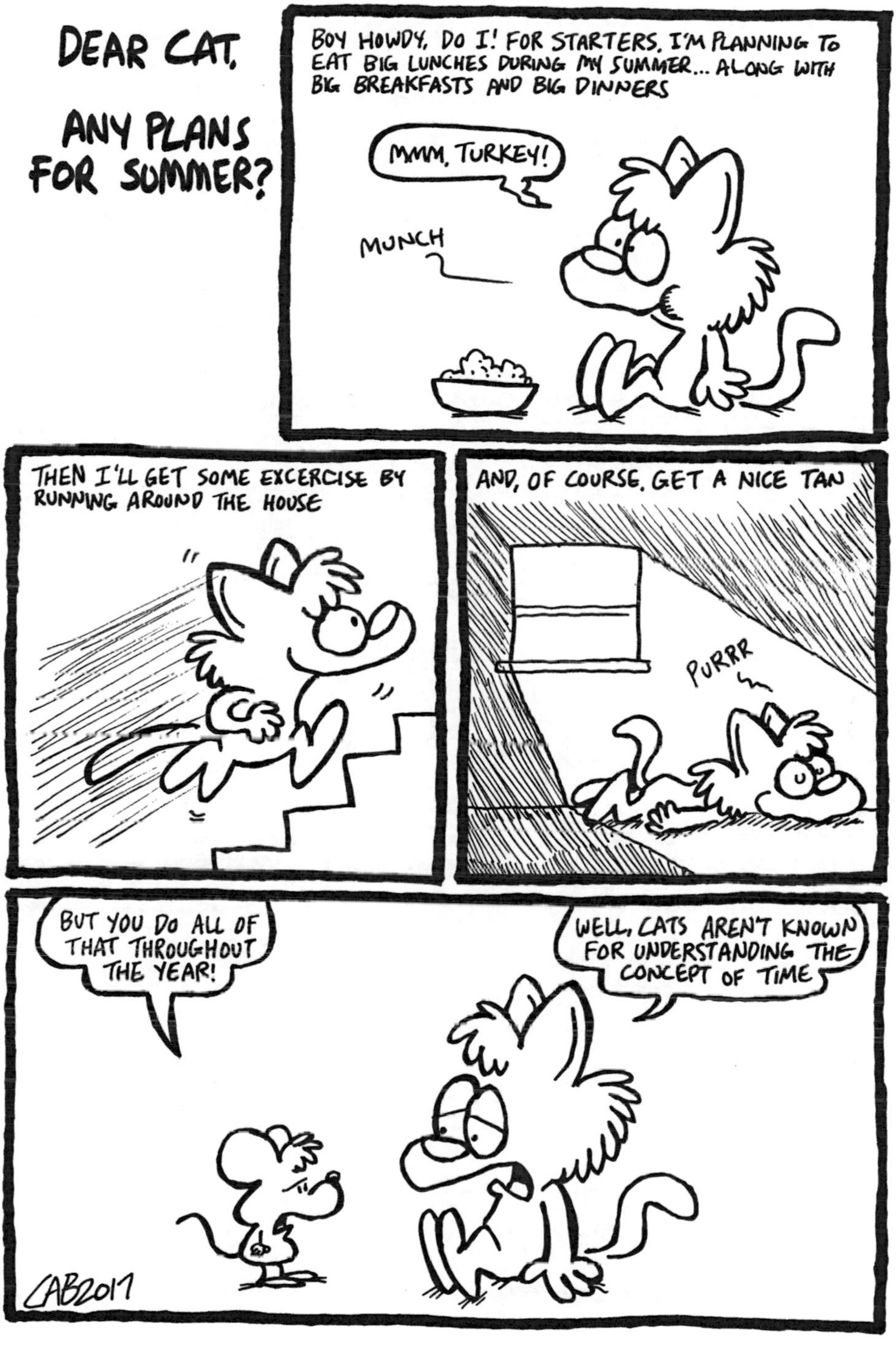
DEAR CAT,
ANY PLANS FOR SUMMER?
BOY HOWDY, DO I! FOR STARTERS, I'M PLANNING TO EAT BIG LUNCHES DURING MY SUMMER... ALONG WITH BIG BREAKFASTS AND BIG DINNERS
MMM, TURKEY!
MUNCH
THEN I'LL GET SOME EXCERCISE BY RUNNING AROUND THE HOUSE
AND, OF COURSE, GET A NICE TAN
PURRR
BUT YOU DO ALL OF THAT THROUGHOUT THE YEAR!
WELL, CATS AREN'T KNOWN FOR UNDERSTANDING THE CONCEPT OF TIME
CAB2017

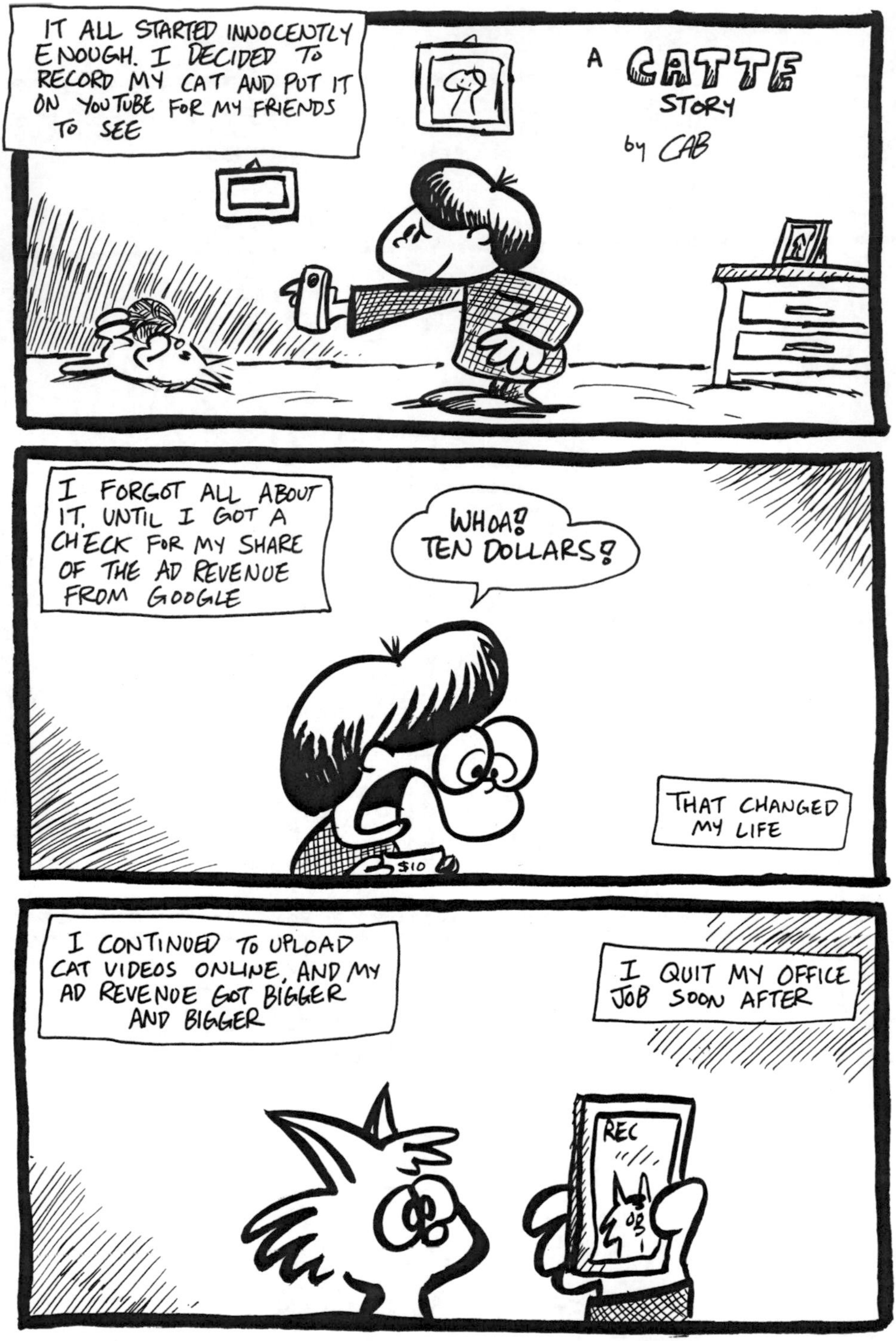
IT ALL STARTED INNOCENTLY ENOUGH. I DECIDED TO RECORD MY CAT AND PUT IT ON YOUTUBE FOR MY FRIENDS TO SEE
A CATTE STORY
by CAB
I FORGOT ALL ABOUT IT, UNTIL I GOT A CHECK FOR MY SHARE OF THE AD REVENUE FROM GOOGLE
WHOA! TEN DOLLARS!
$10
THAT CHANGED MY LIFE
I CONTINUED TO UPLOAD CAT VIDEOS ONLINE, AND MY AD REVENUE GOT BIGGER AND BIGGER
I QUIT MY OFFICE JOB SOON AFTER
REC

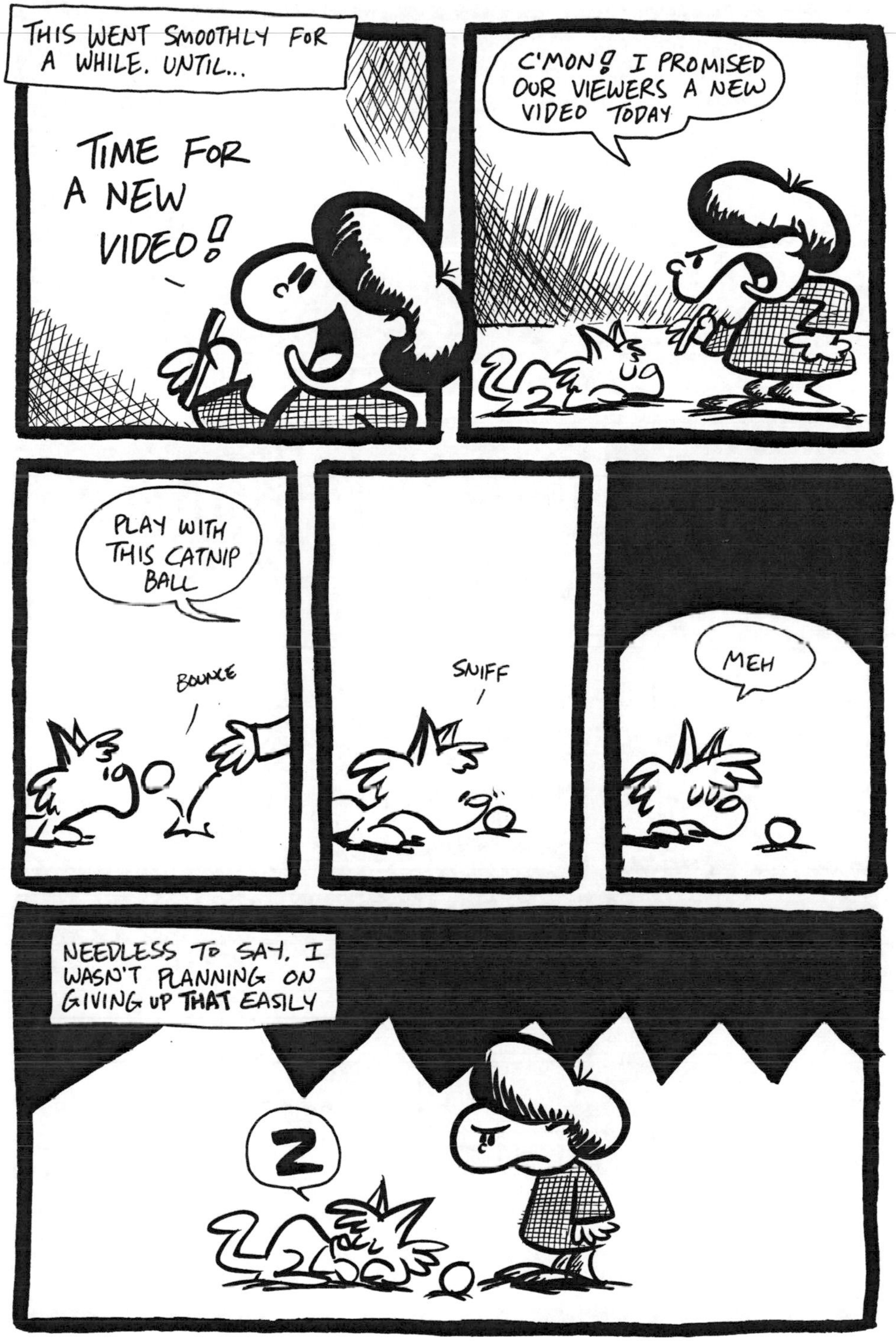

THIS WENT SMOOTHLY FOR A WHILE. UNTIL...
TIME FOR A NEW VIDEO!
C'MON! I PROMISED OUR VIEWERS A NEW VIDEO TODAY
PLAY WITH THIS CATNIP BALL
BOUNCE
SNIFF
MEH
NEEDLESS TO SAY, I WASN'T PLANNING ON GIVING UP THAT EASILY
Z

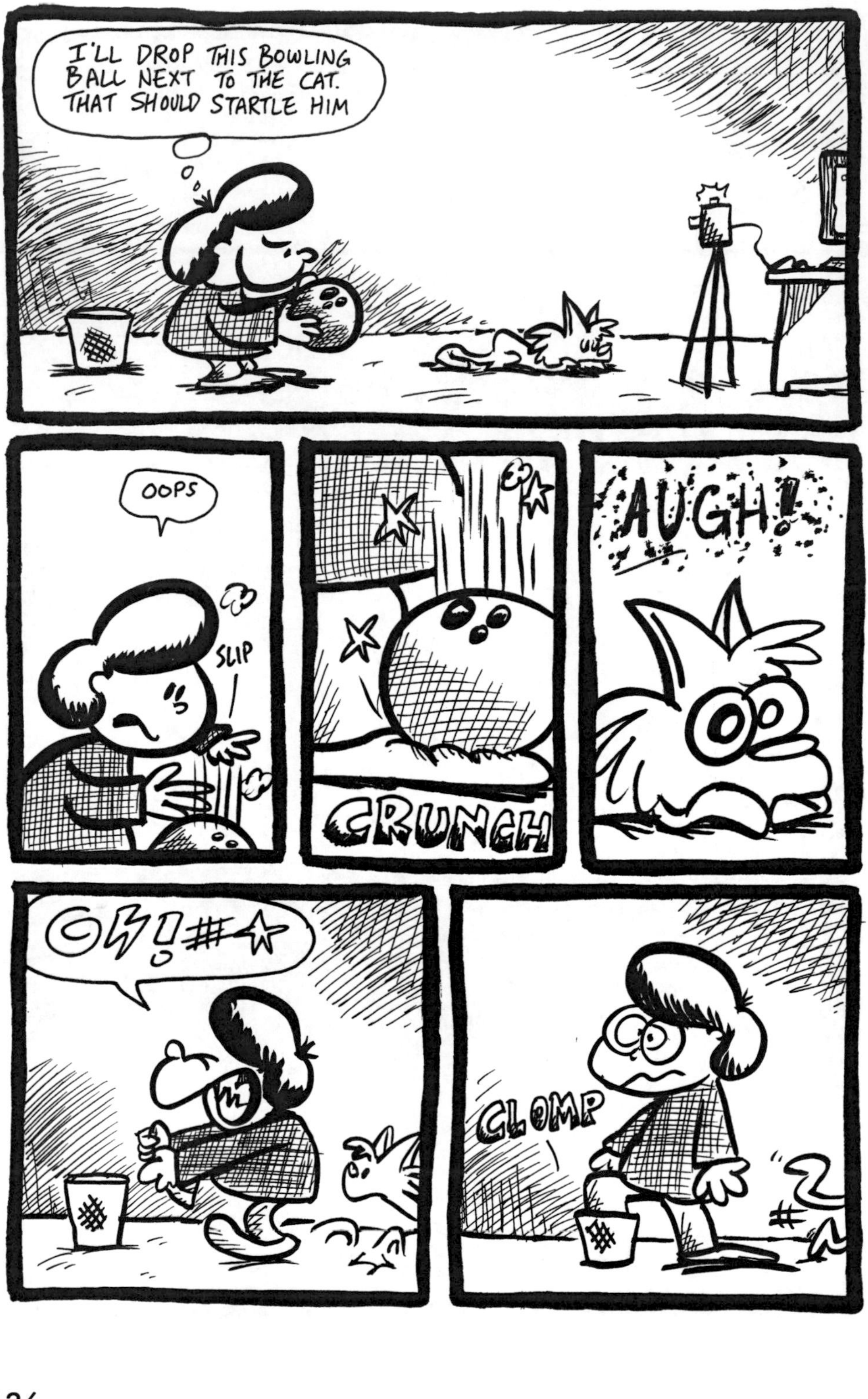
I'LL DROP THIS BOWLING BALL NEXT TO THE CAT. THAT SHOULD STARTLE HIM
OOPS
SLIP
CRUNCH
AUGH!
CLOMP

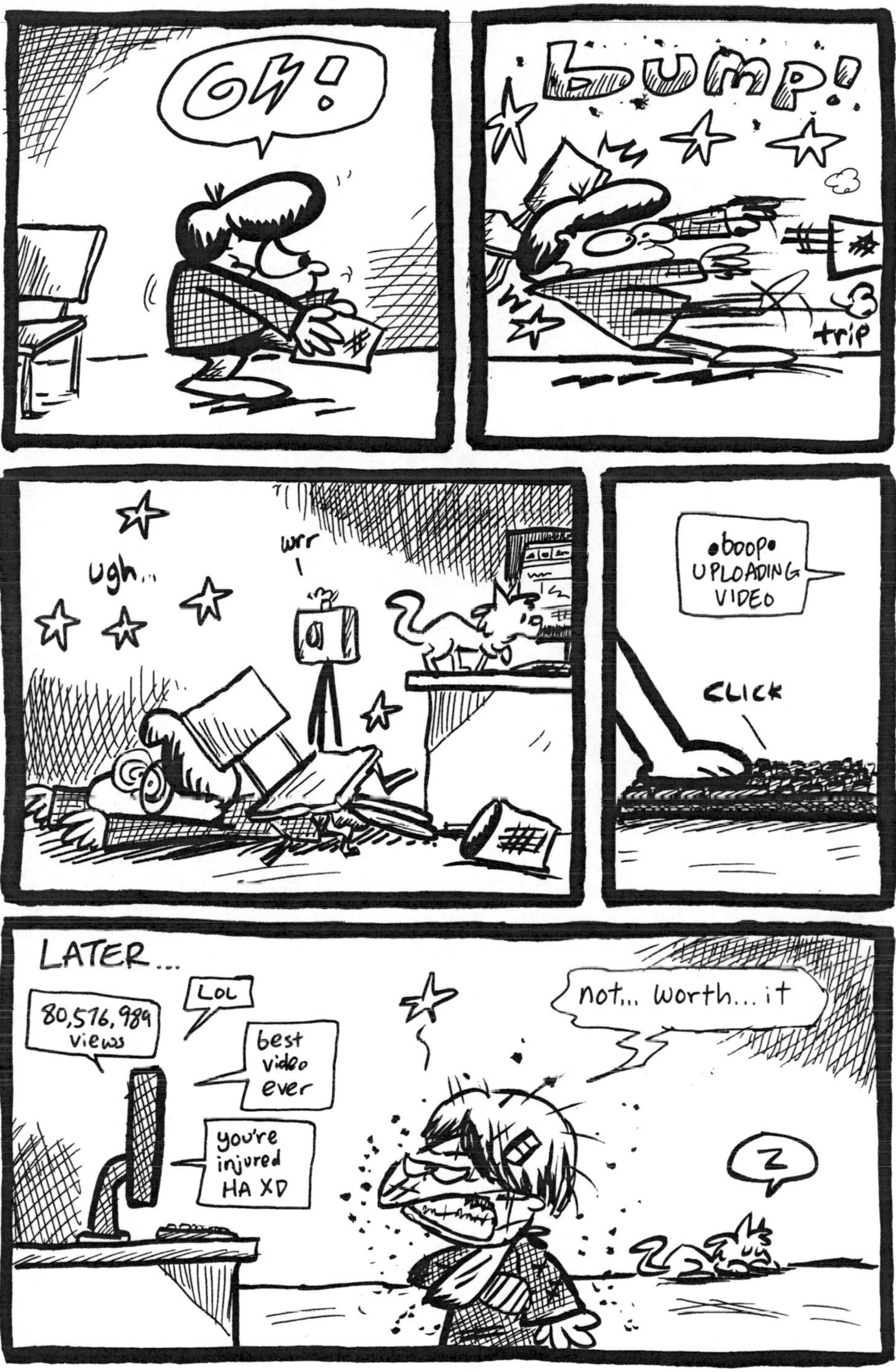

OH!
bump!
trip
ugh...
wrr
•boop• UPLOADING VIDEO
CLICK
LATER...
80,576,989 views
LOL
best video ever
you're injured HA XD
not... worth... it
Z

END

CPSIA information can be obtained
at www.ICGtesting.com
Printed in the USA
LVOW10s1517140617

538110LV00012B/1037/P